MY
SOUL
PURPOSE®

MY
SOUL
PURPOSE®

You don't have a soul.

You are a Soul.

You have a body.

C. S. LEWIS[1]

RICHARD LESLIE PARROTT, PH.D.

MY SOUL PURPOSE
PUBLISHED BY THE WOODLAND PRESS
NASHVILLE, TENNESSEE

All Scripture quotations, unless otherwise indicated, are taken from The Holy Bible, New International Version ®. NIV®. Copyright © 1973, 1978, 1984 by International Bible Society. Used by permission of Zondervan Publishing House. All rights reserved.

ISBN 978-1-61658-532-7

Printed in the United States of America
2010 — First Edition

10 9 8 7 6 5 4 3 2 1

Dedicated to the memory of my father,
Alonzo Leslie Parrott
1922 – 2007

Deep within us there is an amazing inner sanctuary of the soul,
a holy place, a Divine Center, a speaking Voice,
to which we may continuously return.
Eternity is at our hearts,
pressing upon our time-torn lives,
warming us with intimations of an astounding destiny,
calling us home unto Itself.

THOMAS KELLY[2]

When I look back upon the seventy years of my own life,
I see quite clearly that I owe my present inner happiness,
my peace, my confidence and my joy essentially to one fact:
I am certain that I am infinitely loved by God.

DOUGLAS V. STEERE[3]

TABLE OF CONTENTS

PART 1 – SOUL PURPOSE

PART 2 – SOUL CRISIS

PART 3 – SOUL JOURNEY

MY SOUL PURPOSE

Foreword

As we enter the second decade of the New Millennium, the economic and national security interests of the United States have become threatened in ways we scarcely could have imagined as "Y2K" approached. The seismic events of 9/11, engagement of full-scale war on terrorism on two fronts, a world wide economic meltdown and recession resulting in massive multi-trillion dollar deficits, have together shaken the confidence of Americans in our self-determination to the core.

Many of the premises of a decade ago which provided the underpinnings of our self-reliance have since been shattered: 1) the two great oceans would serve as a natural barrier from attack upon our native soil, 2) our homes would serve as our primary investment by building equity and increasing in value every year, 3) the stock market would provide us with double-digit annual returns on our ownership of shares in public companies, 4) our 401(K) Plan assets (supplemented by Social Security payments) would allow us to retire early to begin our dream retirement, 5) gasoline would remain plentiful and affordable to power our SUV's, minivans and pickup trucks, 6) and the U.S. of A. would continue to reign as the lone economic and military superpower for generations to come.

In short, as citizens of the most powerful and prosperous nation in the history of the world, we came to believe that we could trust completely in our inherent resources and capabilities; and the concept of a Sovereign God who was essential to our well-being was not something we allowed for in our public consciousness nor embraced in our personal lives.

In his timely and important new book, *My Soul Purpose*, Richard Parrott stands atop the scrap heap of our fractured autonomy and sounds the clarion call of a foundational and singular truth—that we are each one an Eternal Soul in search of our unique meaning and destiny, which will only be revealed through oneness and personal relationship with our Creator.

Dr. Parrott confronts us to defy conventional wisdom by stripping away our counterfeit sense of self-sufficiency and challenges us to risk a deep dive into an exploration of who and what we are at this point in our lives…and how and why we got there.

He serves as our mentor, by providing the analytical framework that allows us to tear down the false assumptions we have used to buttress our faulty belief system—that what we yearn for out of life may be found externally through career, possessions, or position.

My Soul Purpose is not a self-help book. It is not the latest addition to the positive thinking lineage. It is not the sparse book you grab at the airport sundries store to devour on your 90-minute flight. Whether you are the wealthy corporate CEO or the school teacher struggling to make ends meet, no matter how you define yourself or who you believe you are in the eyes of other people, this book demands that you roll up sleeves and do some heavy lifting work on yourself.

Richard Parrott speaks to all of us who are brave enough to acknowledge that somehow on our journey we have lost touch with that God-given internal compass that kept us pointed at our true and best self. He enables us to lay aside our accumulated baggage and discover the revelation that informs and supersedes all of our other cherished precepts about ourselves:

That what my Soul needs and what the World needs
is *me*—real, authentic, in harmony with God, and
fully alive!

MARK T. MAISH, ESQ.
Senior Vice President (Retired)
J.P. Morgan Wealth Management

CHAPTER 1

WHAT'S YOUR QUESTION?

Soul: The principle of life;
the principle of thought and action;
the spiritual part in contrast to the physical;
the seat of the emotions, feelings or sentiment.
ADAPTED FROM THE OXFORD ENGLISH DICTIONARY

I took out an ad in the local newspaper, posting this question with a hotline for responses.

"If you could ask God any question—
And you knew you would receive a clear answer—
What would you ask?"

In addition, hundreds of copies of the question were mailed across the city. I printed the question on small cards and gave them out in the café where I had lunch, to people I met in the grocery store, to church members as well as people who rarely attend church. I gave them to adults, teens, and children. In short, I put the question in the hands of as many people as possible in the college community where I served as pastor.

It didn't take long. People wrote, phoned, mailed, and passed along their responses, their deeply personal questions. A few weeks later, I drove a thousand miles to the Florida coast for a week of research and writing. I chose one day at the beginning of the week to visit Manatee Springs State Park located in the swamps on the gulf coast. I went there to prepare a series of messages responding to the questions people had submitted.

Armed with pencil and paper, sandwiches and soda pop, and hundreds of questions, I took over a sheltered picnic table that protected me from the sweltering sun. There, I spread out the questions in neat little piles and topics. I read them again and again—trying to make order of what people wanted to ask God. However, the more I studied the questions, the more I wondered whether I was looking at the questions or they were looking at me.

Nothing happened.

My mind wandered through the emotions and thoughts I imagined people had as they wrote their questions on the little cards before me. Surely, God would speak to me in this moment. Surely, inspiration would come. I was confident insight would strike and I'd see patterns and categories in these questions. God would reveal something clever and brilliant, but nothing happened. No grand thought, no deep insight.

Nothing.

It was disappointing. I had worked diligently and at some expense to collect all these heart-felt questions. The idea of gathering them seemed quite clever to me. Surely, God would respond with great thoughts of weighty wisdom. I sat quietly and waited. I did all I knew to open my soul and mind, to offer the words of my heart in prayer, but I didn't receive a thought higher than the oppressive heat that, by now, sent the first drop of perspiration rolling down my temple and into the collar of my shirt.

Waiting in the sweltering heat was, well, boring. Apparently, my spiritual attention span was about as long as a hummingbird's concentration on a flower devoid of nectar. I couldn't stay focused. The place was like an adventure ride at Disneyland. The sounds of the insects, the breeze that blew in the tops of the trees but never at ground level, and the sun reflecting off the water kidnapped my attention. I discovered a little trick. If I'd flip peanut butter on the ground and remain very still, squirrels would come and eat it. It was entertaining to watch, but, there was no word from God.

I went for a walk, and an armadillo startled me. I'd never seen an armadillo except in books. He didn't seem to be troubled at my presence. I gazed at a great crane standing like a statue in the swamp. Lizards would scoot about on the trail.

Again, nothing.

At the edge of a swampy lake, I focused on a great log floating in the water. Then I realized it was staring back at me. A moment later, the alligator dove under the surface. On the shore an old man with a pole and line pulled in a catfish. He was proud.

> *Beneath my educated, professional, competent, and genuine concern for others, the facts, failures, and falsehood of my own life rose up to face me.*

I still sensed nothing.

I crawled up in the crook of a tree and sat like a wounded osprey waiting for inspiration to come. Waiting, waiting, waiting, and still nothing. I backed down the tree and followed the trail to the picnic shelter where I had started. The little white cards were exactly as I had left them. It had been a wasted day.

It was almost evening. Hundreds of turkey vultures had gathered in the trees above me. A deep sigh heaved forth from my empty chest as the orange ball of sunlight disappeared. Another steamy day on the edge of a Florida swamp was about over. There was no inspiration, only weariness.

It was then, only then, that something happened, something that startled me. I felt the touch of a cool breeze brush across my face. Just as unobtrusively, a thought breathed a whisper in my heart. "Richard, what's *your* question?"

The clarity of the Inner Voice, God's silent voice, startled me. Beneath my educated, professional, competent, and genuine concern for others, the facts, failures, and falsehood of my own life rose up to face me.

I wept.

I believe God wants to relate to each of us personally. When I was growing up, my Sunday school teachers and Church camp counselors consistently told us to have a "personal relationship with God." I believe each of us wants intimacy with God, to hear His silent, inner voice. We read the Bible, and God speaks through the written Word. We listen to sermons and discuss the Christian life, and in this way God speaks. We open our hearts and offer our words to God, but do we hear from God in return? Are we supposed to hear from God? What does it mean to have a "personal relationship" with God?

I believe we can develop an authentic, meaningful, and two-way relationship with God. It is real and it is wonderful. I believe God wants to whisper His silent, personal, and living word in our souls. I believe God desires and longs to have a meaningful relationship with us.

Here is what I have learned that I never picked up in Sunday school or church camp—a living relationship with God is a matter of spiritual attention and authenticity. That is what this book is about.

Spiritual Attention. We are distracted by all that daily life heaps upon us. It is a swamp out there: a place of worries, expectations, and demands. We must learn to pay attention, spiritual attention. Heart-focused attention is essential for spiritual life.

When I was a child in those Sunday school and church camp days, I received the advice to "read your Bible and pray." It's true, but not very helpful. What I needed to know was what I should actually do? That is, how do I read the Bible and how do I pray in such a way that I actually experience God's presence?

I want you to know that you can read the Bible and experience the presence of God. You can pray and often sense the silent voice of God inside you. It is true for me, and it can be true for you.

This book will teach you what I have learned about paying attention—spiritual attention. It will teach you how to get started in a life of prayer that fits you uniquely, for you are uniquely made. We already know each person is different physically, and it stands to reason that we are all unique spiritually. God made you and knows how to relate to you. You can have a vibrant and meaningful relationship with God.

We are open to God's living word when we learn to pay attention. When we turn from the outer world with all its stress and anxiety and learn, yes, learn, to turn inward, a meaningful relationship with Him comes to life. In this book you will learn to hear from heaven and grow with God's wisdom by paying spiritual attention.

Spiritual Authenticity. To hear God's voice is a calling. It is a calling to live true to your best as God has made you. It is a calling to be shaped into the image of Christ in a way that fits exactly God's design for you. It is a calling to walk in the Spirit of God.

However, there is a hard truth about becoming spiritually authentic. I think it is something that is easily missed. At least I don't remember learning about it. However, it is a truth I have learned, and learned the hard way. It is something I want you to learn. Here it is: the only way to relate to God is through you: your fears, your failures, and your falsehood, as well as your trust, your commitment, and your potential.

> *God loves you as you are, but He loves you so much He is not content to leave you as you are.*

There is a grand moment of faith and forgiveness when God in Christ really does change you. This is the beginning, a moment of glorious freedom. It is also the moment that marks the beginning of a spiritual journey, a journey of growth, struggles, and some tough lessons. God loves you as you are, but He loves you so much He is not content to leave you as you are. God has a grand vision for you—that you live true to your best in Christ every day.

I often wish I could find the jet-stream to God that avoids facing me. Sometimes we think of the Christian life or are taught that life in Christ is a way of steering clear of ourselves, of dodging the difficult questions, or of stepping around the mud and the mire in our lives. After all, we declare "God loves me and forgives me." Yes, but there is more. God has designs on you. He is transforming you from the inside out. God is God, and He designs how the spiritual life, your spiritual life, works. In essence, God says, "If you are going to live in me, we are going to deal with you."

> *God says, "If you are going to live in me, we are going to deal with you."*

I want to tell you what I have learned about "coming clean" with God, about facing the truth about my life and living toward my hope in God. When you know, really know, God loves you, you can face yourself and become open to the deep change God plans for your life. You can be real from the inside out.

I wish I could tell you that my day in the swamp in Florida, more than fifteen years ago, was the moment of complete and perfect renewal. It was not.

However, it was the moment I confessed that I was not on my true path. It was the beginning of a journey and a crisis of transformation. Things got worse before I improved. Twenty months later I found myself living in a basement apartment at the edge of a university, alone and divorced, estranged from my family and unsure of my friends.

Life was scattered in pieces: broken relationships, fading dreams, lost inspiration, bad choices, cowardly reactions, and projects never completed. What had happened to me? What had happened to living true to my best in Christ?

I was born into and raised by a wonderful family. I had accepted and fulfilled the roles assigned to me: student, husband, minister, father, administrator, and professor. I also had earned two master's degrees and a Ph.D. I had served several congregations as minister, had directed a doctoral program at a seminary (D.Min.), had taught as a professor, and was the founding Executive Director of a leadership center.

Across the years, there were times when I experienced a deep sense of authenticity and spiritual vitality. There were other times, dark times, when the challenges, struggles, expectations, and demands pushed aside authenticity for falsehood and brokenness. I hit bottom. In a basement apartment, I found myself utterly alone.

In the years since those lonely, broken days, I have learned to walk the path of renewal. The journey is a process of commitment to my soul's purpose, of facing the crisis of my inner life, and of giving priority to living true to my best in Christ. It is a journey that is energized, sustained, and guided by God's love. It is a journey of hearing, trusting, and following His inner wisdom.

THE SOUL'S PURPOSE

God has created us to hear, trust, and follow His voice. This is the highest purpose of the soul. You can think of it this way: The soul is heaven's echo chamber on earth.

We are created to live in allegiance to God, but the daily challenges of life make us prisoners of worries, expectations, and demands that are heaped upon us in a world that doesn't allow a time or place for God.

You are created to live with God now and forever. God sends His presence, His Spirit of perfect love, into your soul to shape the image of Christ in you. This is the great gift of God for you and the work of God in you.

Energized by the presence of God, *the soul's purpose is to bring your true and best in Christ to life every day.* The soul tirelessly toils to make sense of life and find meaning in it. The soul's intention in this relentless labor is spiritual authenticity, to shape the true image of God's best in you.

When I was in college, I was required to purchase and read many books. I am certain I did not read all of them. I certainly didn't read them thoroughly, but one story from one book stands out at this moment:

> Martin Buber, a Jewish theologian, tells the Hasidic tale of Rabbi
> Zusya. When he was an old man, the Rabbi mused, "In the coming
> world, they will not ask me: why were you not Moses? They will ask
> me: why were you not Zusya?"[1]

It is a fact that no surgeon can remove your soul nor can a technician digitize it for analysis. Your soul will simply not submit to scientific methods or the accountant's Excel chart. The essence of your humanity and the hope of eternity reside within the soul.[2] It is the realm of poets, mystics, theologians, and infants.

Remember what it is like to look on the face of a newborn baby? I believe that at that moment, you can almost see the human soul. For a brief moment, the first few months of life, the soul seems to make its home on the hands and in the eyes of an infant.

> *The essence of your humanity and the hope of eternity reside within the soul.*

Mother gives birth to a child. From that moment forward, the little one is constantly trying to make sense of what is happening in life. Tiny hands reach out. She takes hold, turns loose, and experiences life. Her large, bright eyes and oversized brow, common to every newborn, attract the attention of her mother. This is a survival skill for she is utterly dependent on the care of her mother.

The Hands and Eyes of the Soul

The baby's reaching hands and beckoning eyes[3] are apt images of the soul's work. The soul takes hold of life in order to make sense of it and discover God's meaning in it. It is a task echoed in the phrases "getting a grip on things" and "grasping the meaning of it."

The soul grasps at the events, perceptions, emotions, and motivations of our lives, carries them into the inner workshop, and there transforms them into our experience. Our experience is not what goes into the soul's workshop but what comes out of it. Think of it: You are your soul's partner in this delicate work.

When we take to this task as a calling from God and labor faithfully, the result is the gift of authenticity, your true and best in Christ. You discover a deeper purpose for your life and are better equipped to nurture healthy relationships. A higher quality of character matures as you respond to the voice of God's inner wisdom. In this way, God's presence in your soul shapes your life.

In addition to tiny hands, the newborn has wide eyes and an oversized forehead. The eyes are designed to recruit and sustain her mother's attention. Without a caring mother to attend to her needs, the baby will die. It is a blessing that most babies have a mother who cares. However, if your mother did not care for you, you were put in harm's way, both body and soul.

If your soul has been wounded, and all souls are wounded to some degree, there is hope for recovery. You and I know that all parents are imperfect, all people experience pain and remorse, and every soul, including yours and mine, needs healing. Your soul can recover, for your soul has another parent, God himself. God is the great parent, both father and mother. God is determined to make you whole. However, your cooperation is required. You must attend to your soul.

Pay Attention

The soul requires attention. You must pay attention to what God is saying and doing in you. I find this to be challenging. To hear God, I must slow down, examine my inner life, and submit myself to God's loving judgment, guidance, forgiveness, and empowerment. It is also frustrating because there are so many other voices in my life clamoring for attention. I sometimes chide myself, "Richard, what could you possibly do that is more important than listening for the words from your heavenly Father?"

The essential and eternal *you* needs spiritual attention which is spiritual awareness, nurture, determination, and power. These are gifts of God's lavish and attentive love in your soul. This is the activity of His Spirit within you. This is God's work in lifting you into His presence and shaping you in His image. Reflect on the words of Simone Weil, who combined social activism and Christian spirituality in her short life of 34 years:

> There are people who try to raise their souls like a man continually taking standing jumps in the hopes that, if he jumps higher every day, a time may come when he will no longer fall back but will go right up to the sky. Thus occupied he cannot look at the sky. He cannot take a single step toward heaven. It is not our power to travel in a vertical direction. If, however, we look heavenward for a long time, God comes and takes us up. He raises us easily.[4]

Once you are recruited as your soul's partner, you embark on a journey of personal insights that sharpen the image of your true self and empower the value of your best self. The soul focuses attention on what matters and what gives life significance. Your task is to attend to your soul. The process is simple to state: listen, trust, and follow the inner voice of God's wisdom. To put this into practice takes a life time. It is like parenting: the moment you figure out how to be a good parent to your eight year old, the little one turns into a teenager and you have to learn a new way to be a good parent. In the same way, you learn how to hear God's voice at one moment in life, but then life changes and you must learn a new lesson. What remains constant is to pay attention: listen, trust, and follow.

> *The soul focuses attention on what matters and what gives life significance. Your task is to attend to your soul.*

TOOLS OF THE SOUL'S WORKSHOP

The tools of the soul's workshop are not the calendar, calculator, and compass of the outer world, but the spiritual virtues of faith and hope and love. Faith aligns life with what God does for you and in you. Faith opens the spiritual life. Trust that God's voice speaks inside you and that His voice comes from beyond you. Hope is grounded in the truth, your personal truth and God's great truth. Love is the beginning and the ending of all things in the spiritual life. Carlo Carretto, who left public ministry to join a desert community of Christian brothers, has penned a prayer for the inner life:

> Our Father, give us the faith to believe that it is possible to live victoriously even in the midst of dangerous opportunity that we call crisis.
>
> Help us to see that there is something better than patient endurance or keeping a stiff upper lip, and that whistling in the dark is not really bravery.
>
> Bless us with the greatness of humility that we may feel no shame in expressing our need of a living God.
>
> Forgive the pride that causes us to strut about like knights in shining armor when we know full well we are but beggars in tattered rags.
>
> Plant a seed of faith in us today and nurture it that it may grow.
> Then, trusting in thee may we have the faith that goes singing in the rain, knowing that all things work together for good to them that love thee.

A vision of your true and best in Christ guides your soul's work. Your soul will search through light and dark, face triumph and defeat, battle enemies and opposition on your behalf in order to protect and develop your Christian authenticity. Your soul longs to open your inner life to the source of vitality and meaning, the infinite love of God.

STRONG, PASSIONATE, GREAT SOULS

Today, people need to talk about, understand, experience, and live a healthy, vital inner life, a soul life. The outward stability once found in business, government, and nations has been shaken. When stability cannot be found in the outward life, the search turns within.

Strong, passionate, great souls are needed in families, enterprise, and society. The soul's strength of authentic vitality is characterized by inner *compassion, commitment, confidence,* and *courage.* These are the potent muscles of the inner life. They are strengthened by cooperating with God, by living true to one's best in Christ. The quality of the inner life impacts all life, at home, at work, and in society.

> ➤ Happy, healthy homes and families are built with soul strength. It is strength of soul that is passed from generation to generation.

> ➤ American business can no longer ask people to "park your soul" at the door. Today's challenges beg for the creativity and determination of impassioned souls.

> ➤ Democracy itself assumes the presence and power of great souls who are willing to tackle social concerns and political negotiations for the sake of the greater good.

From bedrooms to board rooms, from small towns to Capitol Hill, from business start ups to multi-national corporations, from inner city classrooms to Ivy League graduate programs, people need the strength and authentic vitality of the human soul. Volunteer organizations, commercial enterprises, and society's deepest ills all cry out for great souls to lead them. A deep,

> *A deep, rich soul life births and matures authentic living*

rich soul life births and matures authentic living. This is your unique gift to the world. Your soul-gift is characterized by *healthy relationships, good character, meaningful purpose,* and *inner wisdom.* Indeed, it is God's gift through you.

Evelyn Underhill was a wonderful Christian teacher of the inner life. Her spiritual retreats appealed to people from all walks of life. She explains that the spiritual life is God's work in us.

Our spiritual life is his affair; because, whatever we may think to the contrary, it is really produced by his steady attraction, and our humble and self-forgetful response to it. It consists in being drawn, at his pace and in his way, to the place where he wants us to be; not the place we fancied for ourselves.[6]

THE LOSS OF SOUL WISDOM

What happens within you makes a difference around you. A mature person pays attention to what is happening in the soul. Confucius, the Chinese philosopher, said, "In the archer there is the resemblance of the mature person. When he misses the bull's eye, he turns and seeks the reason for his failure in himself."[7]

Despite the need for people to learn the ways of the inner life, lessons in soul-care and soul-work, essential to authentic living, have been relegated to society's side-lines. Through the centuries, the most common school house of soul-life was home and family. Today, however, the demands, stress, and pressures placed on contemporary young families have turned many homes into a struggle for soul survival rather than a safe place of soul-strength.

Among religious leaders and organizations charged with the care of souls are outstanding examples of individuals and groups that teach the ways of the inner life. However, many people do not grasp the connection between religious teaching and soul life due to sectarian skirmishes, religious language, or society's persistent and often empty debate over the separation of church and state. A wall segregates the inner and outer life. This wall of divide imprisons the inner life, the soul life, while the outer life is set adrift on an endless sea.[8]

RUNNING IN THE DARK

It was the most important day in history, the first Easter. In John's gospel we read the story, which begins, *"On the first day of the week, while it was still dark...."* In the darkness, Mary Magdalene runs from the empty tomb to town. Peter and John run from town to the tomb. And the paragraph ends by stating that *"they still did not understand..."* (John 20:1-9).

It is a picture of running in the dark, a picture of lost soul chasing after shadows. You know what happens when you run in the dark. You bump into things. You trip over things. You harm yourself and others. You wear yourself down.

When a human soul is void of its spiritual vitality, a human being suffers. Life becomes empty, fearful, powerless, and apathetic. The outcome is personal: heartache at home, survival motivation at work, and an endless parade of empty distractions. I know this is true, for it was true for me. I tripped and fell. I crashed into an immovable wall. I hurt myself, my family, and people who loved me. My marriage was broken, my family was divided, and I was alone and full of fear. I can tell you what happens:

> *When a human soul is void of its spiritual vitality, a human being suffers. Life becomes empty, fearful, powerless, and apathetic.*

When the soul's vitality is drained, the inner compassion that supports healthy relationships gives way to apathy and cynicism. Life withers in the soul and concern for the good of others and the greater good of all dissolves into selfish ambition, toxic interactions, and dangerous, personal isolation.

When the soul loses vitality, the strength of inner commitment which births and matures good character, gives way to pervasive emptiness. The needle on the inner compass spins, unable to find true north. Ethical breakdowns litter the highways that connect home, commerce, and government.

When the vitality of the soul recedes, inner confidence, the spring that feeds personal and meaningful purpose in life, gives way to a feeling of powerlessness. It leaves you feeling like a victim waiting for rescue. It turns the holy calling of life into a quiet, desperate search for the next means of escape from the pain and fear.

When soul vitality wanes, the inner courage that strengthens mature wisdom gives way to low-level anxiety that permeates life. The fear is masked in a multitude of defenses. Appearing incognito, anxiety puts life under its cold hand of control. Inner wisdom is silenced, and the need to control the pain is made master.

Human beings need soul vitality as they need bread on the table and shelter from a storm. This book is the result of recovering my own authentic self in Christ. It is a reflection of what I knew and then forgot and then learned again as if I had never known it before.

DO WHAT KEEPS YOU ALIVE

A strong, impassioned, great soul is authenticity embodied and personalized. Such a soul was Howard Thurman,[9] an early leader of the Civil Rights movement. He understood that to set free an oppressed people in society you must first set free the soul that is held prisoner by the oppression.

He was a great leader, minister, and teacher. Students across the years remember a saying he never put into print but wrote with indelible ink on the tablets of their minds and hearts:

> Don't do what the world needs you to do.
> Find out what keeps you alive and do that.
> For what the world needs is you, full of life!

What do we need to do to be full of life in Christ? The *first principle* of the soul's life is found in the story of the first Easter. The scripture says, *"Mary stood…"* (see John 20:10-18). *Stop running and be still.* Once she stood still, she began to see and hear God in her life. She saw angels, heard Jesus call her by name, and could report, *"I have seen the Lord."* Your spiritual life begins when you are still. It is more than physical stillness. It means to quiet your emotions, motivations, and aspirations.

Eric Liddell is the athlete who became famous in the 1924 Olympics for refusing to run on the Sabbath. His story is told in the film *Chariots of Fire.* Eric's favorite hymn was "Be still my soul, the Lord is on thy side." Imprisoned by the Chinese in World War II, he taught the hymn to others in the prison camp: "Be still my soul: thy best, thy heavenly Friend / through thorny ways leads to a joyful end."[10]

There is a *second principle* for the soul's life. Again, the scripture says, *"the* evening of that first day of the week, when the disciples were together, with the doors locked for fear…, Jesus came and stood among them…" (John 20:19). *Receive God into your fears.* Recognize Him and welcome Him. The life of the soul is not about appearing strong, but facing weakness, especially fear. The Scripture promises "…perfect love drives out fear, because fear has to do with punishment" (1 John 4:18). God's love can drive out fear if you confess the fear in your soul and receive God's love.

The *third principle* of soul-life is found in the story of Thomas, doubting Thomas, who touched the wounds of Jesus and believed. Jesus said to him, *"Because you have seen me, you have believed; blessed are those who have not seen and yet have believed"* (John 20:24-31). Here is a difficult lesson: *What is most important in life cannot be seen or touched.* The baby's hands and eyes touch and see the physical world. The soul must learn to touch and see what is spiritual. And then, you and I must learn to stake our lives on it.

AN INTRODUCTION TO SOUL-LIFE

This book is a primer on soul-life, the inner life. It outlines the movements and dynamics of the soul's shaping of perceptions, emotions, and motivations with the single intent of bringing your true and best in Christ to life every day. In part 1 of the book, *Soul Purpose,* the focus is on God's desire to give, shape, and sustain an authentic Christian life in you. You are unique and valuable. You are a spiritual being in search of spiritual meaning. Your soul is bound in eternal allegiance to God. God loves you and longs to take up residence in your soul. God, the creator, has chosen to work in you to create your life. You have the privilege of cooperating with God.

When you persistently compromise the pursuit of authenticity for the appearance of effectiveness, you are in a *Soul Crisis*, discussed in part 2. Pain-filled experience, fearful projections, poor

> *Your soul is bound in eternal allegiance to God.*

choices, and destructive inner habits imprison the inner life behind walls of self-destruction. The soul is an escape artist. It takes courage to break free. Liberation is through soul-to-soul encounters with soul friends and with God.

Part 3 follows the *Soul Journey*. Beyond the prison walls is exile. The soul set free finds itself in the wilderness. It is a new life and a new way of living. You learn to live in the desert. Build an inner room, a house of prayer. It is your home for the journey. You will learn the art of holy listening. Along the way you meet truth and hope, friends and enemies, silence and wisdom as you receive the gifts and grace of God's eternal love.

Douglas V. Steere was a great scholar of the inner life, a Quaker with a rich heritage and life experience in the ways of the soul. In his classic work, *Together in Solitude*, he provides an apt beginning to the quest for an authentic life.

> A speaker was once introduced by the perfect chairman who said simply, "Mr. Weaver, we are ready. Are you ready?"
>
> When I gather myself for prayer it is almost as if God were so addressing me, "Douglas Steere, I am ready. Are you ready?"
>
> And my answer is, "Oh Lord, you are always ready, but am I ever ready? O Lord, make me ready, or at least make me ready to be more ready."[11]

If the birth of Christ teaches us anything, it is that God is a wonderful parent. He desires to be your Heavenly Parent. He loves His children, and God loves you. Can you comprehend how much He loves you? It is His love that opens your soul to receive His gift of life. Your life has meaning and value within the love of God. You are unique in strength and weakness, in blessing and pain. Your uniqueness is the path of God's calling.

It is your *Soul Purpose* to live true to your best in Christ every day. We will look at the purpose of the soul in the first part of the book; you will learn how to find and secure life's meaning, value, and unique calling in God.

PART ONE

SOUL PURPOSE

Our Father in heaven
hallowed be your name
your kingdom come,
your will be done
on earth as it is in heaven.

MATTHEW 6:9-10

CHAPTER 2

SOUL PURPOSE

Choice of attention—to pay attention to this and ignore that—is to the inner life what choice of action is to the outer. In both cases, a person is responsible for their choice and must accept the consequences.
W. H. Auden[1]

The egg of an eagle was hatched in a chicken coop. How the egg arrived in the chicken coop is unknown and inconsequential to the story. The egg produced an odd offspring. It looked like an eagle, but lived like a chicken. Months of this disquieting life produced a strange bird, pecking and scratching on the outside, but unsettled and hollow within.

Then, one day (there is always one day in these stories) a strange sound was heard from above. It frightened the other chickens but seemed oddly familiar to the barnyard quirk. The distant, yet distinct cry of an adult eagle awakened the true identity in the misplaced eaglet. The young bird discovered personal truth. The feathered creature, enthroned on the standards of Roman Emperors and the abiding symbol of the United States, stretched its wings and moved toward the sky.

Thus ends the tale of the "eagle born in a chicken coop." However, it is certainly not the end of the story. Indeed, it is only the beginning. Knowledge of one's true self must be joined to living one's best. To be awakened to the truth but never live it may be a worse fate than never knowing the truth at all. Knowing must be wed to being. The soul's purpose is to bring the true and best in Christ to life, everyday.

God's Invitation

What am I supposed to do with my life?

What difference am I supposed to make?

What is my destiny and how can I follow it?

How should I make a living?

What am I going to be when I grow up?

There are multiple ways to probe the purpose of life. Each question above is answered with a course of action, a task to complete, an assignment to shoulder, or a choice of career. These are important questions, and the career counselors, job placement departments, caring friends, and parents are ready to give guidance.

However, there is a more important issue that must take precedence over all others. It is to hear the voice of God and respond. The highest function of the soul is to hear and respond to God's invitation, God's call. But what is God's call? As a child, I imagined the call of God as otherworldly. I distinctly remember a missionary tell of waking in the night to see a glowing map of Africa on an empty wall. Ministers told spell-binding stories of hearing God's voice call them to a lifetime of service. My child-like reason concluded that God's call is both an unusual experience and a special task. I have known such a call from time to time in my life. Perhaps you have as well. However, this type of call is a secondary matter. There is a far more basic, fundamental, and primary call of God. It is not a call to do something for God, but a call to live in God. It is a living, growing relationship He desires. Consider the insight of Albert Edward Day, a Methodist minister and extraordinary preacher:

But God is present in reality no matter what unreality our practices
and our ponderings imply. He is forever trying to establish communication; forever aware of the wrong directions we are taking and wishing to warn us; forever offering solutions for the problems that baffle
us; forever standing at the door of our loneliness, eager to bring us
such comradeship as the most intelligent living mortal could not sup-
ply; forever clinging to our indifference in the hope that someday our
needs, or at least our tragedies, will waken us to respond to his
advances. The Real Presence is just that, real and life-transforming.[2]

When you have time with the one you love, how tempting and disappointing it is to focus attention and energy on "what we will do today." The
more significant purpose and value is simply *being* together. How many honey-
moons have been marred or family vacations ruined because attention was
focused on the itinerary instead of intimacy. The same is true of your soul's
life. Some people concentrate on getting
things done for themselves, for others, or
even for God, to the neglect of answering
the invitation to live in God.

> *Some people concentrate on
> getting things done for
> themselves, for others, or
> even for God, to the neglect
> of answering the invitation
> to live in God.*

The most famous invitation of Jesus
was not a call to a task, a mission, or a ministry. It was an invitation to live with him
and in him. *"Come to me all you who labor
and are heavy laden. Take my yoke upon you and learn of me for I am gentle and
humble of heart and you shall find rest for your souls"* (Matthew 11:28).

Consider the story of creation as told in the Hebrew Bible, the Old
Testament. It opens with the familiar words, *"In the beginning…"*
Then, God does his work, *"…the first day …the second day …the
third day"* (Genesis 1:1, 5, 8, 13) for five days. Then, on the sixth
day, God creates human beings to walk with them in the cool of the
day (Genesis 1:38; 3:8). God created and designed humanity to live
with Him and in Him.

Now look at the story of the new creation in the New Testament, the writings of the Christian church. The gospel of John opens with the same words we find in Genesis, *"In the beginning…"* (John 1:1). You will find a reminder of God's creative work in the words, *"the next day …the next day …the next day"* (John 1:29, 35, 43). Jesus has come to make the world new. This profound and poetic passage of Scripture says nothing of assignments, tasks or missions delegated to His followers. That will come later, but it is not first or primary. The scripture declares clearly that His purpose was to make His *"dwelling among us"* (John 1:14).

This is the foundation of our inner life, the call of God for you and me—to live in God. It is our true calling. Everything else is built on this heavenly invitation. Yet there is an alluring spirit in the world that pulls us away from our true vocation. For some, God's invitation is drowned out by the struggle to manage life's demands and expectations, by outwardly successful examples of self-centeredness, or by a toxic dose of debilitating and degrading relationships. Abandoning God's call is apparent when someone falls into every type of evil. For others, ignoring the invitation is hidden in hollow inner lives of shallow piety. They do good, fulfill their duty, and serve others, yet they do not have an intimate relationship with God. In either case, they have lost their calling—the call to center life in God.

A moment of truth occurs for everyone. In that moment, you see your true and best in Christ waiting for you. The inner wisdom of God will find the way if you are willing to listen, trust, and follow. Will you continue begging for help to change while clinging tenaciously to your old ways? Will you ask for more voices, different voices, new voices because you dare not trust God's inner voice? Or will you descend into the inner chamber, the workshop of your soul, and put your inner hands and eyes to the art of finding spiritual meaning in life. God reveals your true calling, the call to live in God. This call, this truth will set you free to be your best in Christ.

In the prayer of our Lord, we respond to God's invitation. The prayer anchors our life in Him as our heritage, our hope, and our purpose, His will, at work in us.

Our Father in heaven,
Hallowed be your name,
Your kingdom come,
Your will be done
On earth as it is in heaven.
MATTHEW 6:9-10

The prayer realigns life with God's invitation and intention, His presence and purpose. Each petition answers the call to live life in God; to return to the source of spiritual meaning in life, our Father; to reestablish eternal value in His kingdom; and to remember our unique calling to live out the will, the way, and the wisdom of God on earth, to live true to our best in Christ.

Do you dare try your wings? Will you enter the battle and fight for your authenticity? Will you embrace the purpose of your soul? Will you answer the invitation to live in God? This is the first step toward freedom.

THE SOUL'S WORKSHOP

At its best, the soul is an echo chamber for God's voice. Jesus is God's Word for you. The soul urges you to hear, trust, and follow God's word, to live in Christ. The soul has one purpose: to bring your true and best in Christ to life every day. The soul is home-base for life in God. In your soul you anchor your life in God.

> *Deep within you is an unseen chamber. It is located between what happens to you and how you respond. In this place, the soul is at home and at work.*

Yet here is the thorn. Our days are filled with practical, confusing, frightening, and distracting alternatives. It is a continual task to sort them out and choose how to respond in ways that are true to our best in Christ. This is the work of the soul.

Deep within you is an unseen chamber. It is located between what happens to you and how you respond.[3] In this place, the soul is at home and at work. It is a cottage industry with one client—you.

The hidden chamber within you is a workshop busy with the task of making sense of life. Life does not come pre-assembled. Fragments of experience and bits of memory are knit together in ways that provide meaning or emptiness, clarity or confusion. The assorted fragments on the shop table come from

… love and work,

… success and failure,

… loss and gain,

… happiness and sorrow,

… security and anxiety,

… beginnings and endings,

… family and solitude,

… acceptance and rejection,

… marriage and divorce,

… intimacy and abandonment,

… birth and death,

… kindness and cruelty,

… confinement and freedom,

… pleasure and pain,

… sickness and healing,

… control and chaos,

… conflict and quiet,

… miracles and monsters.

I invite you to descend into the workshop. It is filled with fears and hopes, voices and longings, needs and desires. It is here you will learn to distinguish another Voice, the voice of God. God speaks in your soul. The soul is your essential and eternal self. What happens here does more than influence your life: it *is* your life. It is your life in God.

Some years ago, when I was having dinner with a pastor friend, we discussed a common theme: the difficulties of leading a church. We exchanged stories of younger days, how as young pastors we were going to change the church. At that time neither of us gave much thought to how the church would change us.

It is common for a naive pastor to see only his or her influence on the church. It is naive for anyone to dismiss how life changes a person. However, after a person gains a few years of experience, the impact of the church and the conforming power of daily life become more apparent.

My friend said profoundly, "I believe God has always placed me in a church that has a knack for pushing the buttons that reveal my own struggles and inadequacies. But I have found that as I do my own soul work, God will teach me and provide me with the spiritual resources I need to lead that congregation."

Do your soul-work. It is one thing to give your external life to God, the difficulties, crises, and problems that trouble you. Give it all to God; it is a prayer that always comes down to "bless this mess." However, the mess is not just on the outside. Soul work opens your inner life to God's judgment, forgiveness, and transformation. Submit your emotions, perceptions, and desires to God. Often, prayer changes things because you are changed in prayer. This is the way God provides the resources you need for the challenges you face each day.

THE SOUL'S PURPOSE

In the unseen chamber, the craft of making sense of the world as well as the higher art of finding spiritual meaning continues relentlessly. The results shape the way you imagine and value yourself. Your imagined self may be a distorted figure of false potential and limitations or it may be the image of your true self in Christ. Your personal value may flow out of your life in God, your authenticity in Christ, or it may be warped by damaging demands and deforming wounds. Within the inner chamber your personal image and value are formed and reformed across the decades of your life.

The home of your soul may not look or feel like home to you. It may be discomforting to you. You may be tempted to plan a hasty retreat to the outer world. Yet this inner place is you, your eternal essence. To hide from your soul is to run away from yourself. There are many places to hide; you can hide from yourself in the expectations and demands that others place on you, in the timelines and deadlines of work, or in the pressing concerns of family and friends. You can even hide in a church pew under layers of pretentious spiritual fervor, religious rigor and rules, or showy goodness and false humility.

> *You can even hide in a church pew under layers of pretentious spiritual fervor, religious rigor and rules, or showy goodness and false humility.*

It takes courage and intention to face the essential and eternal you, your soul. Your challenge is to trust the soul's purpose, listen to God's inner wisdom, and make healthy choices. To know your soul is to know your ever evolving true self. To follow your soul's leading is to be your best in Christ.

There is a beautiful prayer in *Godspell*, a 1971 musical by Stephen Swartz. Robin Lamont sang the song "Day by Day." The original prayer, more than 900 years old, is a daily response to God's invitation to live true to your best.

> Thanks be to you, my Lord Jesus Christ,
>   for all the benefits you have given me,
>   for all the pains and insults you have born for me.
> O most merciful redeemer, friend, and brother,
>   may I know you more clearly,
>   love you more dearly, and
>   follow you more nearly, day by day.[4]

How to Enter the Workshop

To enter the workshop of the soul, you must set aside the tools of the outer life; the *calendar*, the *calculator*, and the *compass*. You are familiar with these tools and rely on them every day.

The *calendar* measures time in regular increments. It is concerned with appointments, deadlines, due dates, and delays. It is essential for organizing your life. However, there is no sense of eternity. It is all about here and now.

The *calculator* measures achievements and failures. It is an accounting tool for quantifying success, assessing setbacks, evaluating performance, gauging potential, and computing gains and losses. This is how you measure your progress. However, there is no sense of essence or the spiritual nature of life.

There is also the *compass* to measure where, whence, and whither. How far have you come and how far do you need to go? Where are you on the ladder of success? What is your strategy for the next advance? What are the contingency plans and alternate routes? Yet the present moment is lost, and the presence of God is neglected.

It is disconcerting to discover that the tools of the outer world do not function in the workshop of the soul. In fact, you must check them at the door before you enter. This is a hard lesson to learn. We gain and maintain our control with the calendar, the calculator, and the compass. To give them up on the steps of the soul is to give up control.

> *It is disconcerting to discover that the tools of the outer world do not function in the workshop of the soul. In fact, you must check them at the door before you enter.*

In the era before modern psychology, poets explained the working of the "psyche" or "soul" through great stories and myths. There is an old and epic poem from the seventh century that teaches a great lesson about entering the soul or inner life. It is the story of *Beowulf.*

Beowulf is a grand tale of courage, battles, and celebrations. For twelve years, the Danes suffer under the terror of a fiend named Grendel. Our hero, Beowulf, responds to the challenge to free the land from the beast. The inner meaning of the story is a challenge to move into your neglected soul and discover life from the inside out.

Our hero, Beowulf, travels to Denmark to fight the monster, Grendel. Grendel lives in a dark lake and comes out at night to kill and destroy. Beowulf fights and kills the beast, and then tosses the body in the dark lake. He is a hero. There is great feasting and celebration.

However, something else crawls out of the lake. It is Grendel's mother, and she is angry. The lesson is plain enough. In the work of the soul, it is not the problem in the outer world but the mother of the problem within (at the bottom of the lake, the bottom of your soul) that must be fought.

Grendel's mother lives at the bottom of a cold and dark lake where even the deer of the forest dare not drink. The lake represents the entrance to a long-neglected soul. In the story, Beowulf must descend to the bottom of the lake and battle Grendel's mother. It is a challenge to battle your own inner monsters, the monsters in the bottom of your soul.

Our hero jumps into the lake with the same weapons he used to win the battle on land. In the same way, we try to use successes, measures, and strategies to make sense in the soul. We think that our great achievement, accolades, and the applause of others will satisfy our inner life. It does not work. True enough, it can mask the inner pain, the inner monster, for a while, but, eventually, Grendel's mother comes out to seek her revenge. Eventually, our inner monsters reveal themselves and wreak havoc on our lives.

When Beowulf descends through the icy waters and blackness of the lake, the sword and shield of his surface life disintegrates in his hands. He is left defenseless and vulnerable. Yet at the bottom of the lake is a sword of light, the precise tool he needs to slay the monster within.[5]

When you enter the soul, you remain in darkness as long as you clutch the weapons of the outer life in your hands. It is an inner act of trust; turn loose of all you have. Turn loose of your achievement and failures. Turn a deaf ear to the praise and rebuke of others. Let it go and you will find what you need. You will discover the light.

> When you enter the soul, you remain in darkness as long as you clutch the weapons of the outer life in your hands.

*The people living in darkness have seen a great **light**; on those living in the land of the shadow of death a **light** has dawned* (Matthew 4:16).

*When Jesus spoke again to the people, he said, "I am the **light**
of the world. Whoever follows me will never walk in darkness, but
will have the **light** of life"* (John 8:12). *"I have come into the world
as a **light**, so that no one who believes in me should stay in darkness"*
(John 12:46). *In him was life, and that life was the **light** of men*
(John 1:4).

*So let us put aside the deeds of darkness and put on the armor of
light* (Romans 13:12). *For God, who said, "Let **light** shine out of
darkness," made his **light** shine in our hearts to give us the **light** of the
knowledge of the glory of God in the face of Christ*
(2 Corinthians 4:6).

THE TOOLS OF THE SOUL

To become an apprentice in the inner workshop of the soul requires extensive
training in the virtues of the spiritual life. The tools on the table in the workshop of the soul are *faith, hope,* and *love.*[6] These are the tools of eternity. They
probe the essence of life and give priority to the present moment, the eternal
moment, the moment you encounter God within.

The greatest of these tools is *love.* New life in the workplace of the soul
begins the moment you realize that the essence of your being is eternally loved
by God.

*At one time we too were foolish, disobedient, deceived and enslaved by
all kinds of passions and pleasures. We lived in malice and envy, being
hated and hating one another. But when the kindness and love of God
our Savior appeared, he saved us, not because of righteous things we
had done, but because of his mercy.* (Titus 3:3-5)

From love, faith and hope are born. Faith and hope act in the service of
love. God's gift of love is the fountain of your *faith,* even the faith that God
loves you. Faith's work is to put love into action. Whatever you do is in the
service of being loved, and loving others is an act of faith. Your essential value

is not something to be calculated in the plus/loss columns of the accountant's spreadsheet. You are an instrument of holy love set loose on the planet to do good as a living remembrance of God's love for all people.

Love creates *hope*. When you know you are loved, you envision all things as possible. The most difficult and heartbreaking truth becomes a partner of hope. Tragedy opens the possibility of new triumph. Deep loss is the seed of new life.

> *Deep loss is the seed of new life.*

Archibald McLeish wrote a modern telling of the story of Job, entitled J.B., that pits God and the Devil in a battle for the allegiance of a good man. When I was in college, I played the part of J.B. It was a disturbing role for me, a junior in college, to ponder the deep questions of life and death, good and evil, hope and tragedy.

It was during the darkest days of the Vietnam War. My draft number was high enough that I knew I would never be called. Not so for several of my friends. This background of war and death played in my mind as I learned by heart the lines of J.B., a modern Job.

I remember particularly the commentary of Archibald McLeish concerning the biblical story of Job. He said that it was not unusual for a person to lose everything. This happens in life. He went on to say that it is not surprising that God offers new life. This is what God does. What is most surprising is that Job took it, for along with new life comes the possibility of losing it all again.

Human beings are created for faith, hope, and love. One line from the play reads, "human beings are like old potatoes, stomp 'um deep enough and they grow."[7]

In the face of tragedy, time may not be on your side, but eternity is with you. Hope cannot always be tucked neatly into the pages of almanacs, date books, and schedules. Hope knows that whatever you have experienced of God's love, it is only a portion of what is to come. On the workbench of the soul, *faith* is the tool with which to face fear, *hope* is the partner of truth, and *love* is God's great gift.

This trio of virtues—faith, hope, and love—guided the life of Brother Lawrence, a wonderful man who worked in the kitchen of a monastery in France three hundred years ago. His wonderful book, *The Practice of the Presence of God*, has guided millions of Christ's followers. For Brother Lawrence, the trio of virtues is the essence of living life in Christ.

> In order to be sure we are doing God's will, we should simply develop an attitude of faith, hope, and love. We need not be concerned about anything else. It simply is not important, and should only be regarded as a means of getting to the final goal of being entirely lost in the love of God. We should desire to love Him as perfectly as we can, in this life and in Eternity. Many things are possible for the person who has hope. Even more is possible for the person who has faith. And still more is possible for the person who knows how to love. But everything is possible for the person who practices all three virtues.[8]

THE MEASURE OF SOUL SUCCESS

Authenticity is the measure of soul success. There are no compromises or half-hearted measures. The soul calls you to be the author of an authentic life, your life in God. Confront the truth about yourself, and embrace the challenge to be your best. Live true to your best in Christ.

The quest to be authentic—your true and best—is not an ironed-jawed determination to "be my real self" as if there is some static and fully formed person inside you yearning to be free.[9] Something is wrong with this concept. What is "real" and true about you is what you

think,

judge,

feel,

value,

honor,

esteem,

love,

hate,

fear,

desire,

expect,

and trust.

These dynamics of the inner life change constantly. There is no fixed, "real self" inside you. You are a human *being,* which means you are always *becoming* your true and best self or you are *becoming* a false and deformed self. You are not a finished product; you are an ongoing process. There is a workshop inside you, a place where the fragments of your life arrive, meaning is attached, and your growing, evolving self emerges. This workshop is the domicile of your soul.

Life comes to us in pieces, like a jigsaw puzzle tumbling out of the box or multicolored threads yet to be woven into a tapestry. You and your soul negotiate each fragment's meaning. This is your life experience. The result, for better or worse, defines you. Your perceptions, emotions, and motivations are shaped, reshaped, accepted, or rejected. As the years roll on, you have more experiences in life, encounter new depths of love, suffer more, pray more, and search for sense, meaning, and significance in all of it. You are relentlessly changing.

> *Life comes to us in pieces, like a jigsaw puzzle tumbling out of the box.*

When is a rose true to its best? Is it not living true to its best when it is contained in the seed? Is it not also true to its best when hiding in the soil and when breaking free as a small sprout? Is it not true to its best when it is a bud, then a bloom, and finally a withered flower preparing to return to the soil? There its chemicals and nutrients will strengthen the next seed, the rose for tomorrow. It is true to its best at every stage.

You cannot ask the rose to be in bloom all the time. Such a thing is not a living rose but a manufactured facsimile. It is a fake. It has no life. It does not have the "soul," the life essence, of a rose. Life is always in a process of transformation. At each season, the Soul of all life desires what is true to its best for that moment.

You have a soul. Indeed, you *are* a soul. Your soul's purpose is heaven's purpose: to bring your true and best in Christ to life in every season of life. Your soul is pleased when you are intent on living true to your real self, yet this does not satisfy the soul. It is good but not good enough. The soul presses on toward your best self. God smiles when you long for and learn to live true to your best in Christ. This is full life in the power and Spirit of God.

THE COST OF LIFE ON DEFENSE

Authenticity comes with a hefty price tag. To be authentic means you take on rather than avoid life's fears and pains. You don't need to create fear and pain; they are standard issue with each newborn. The question is how you will deal with them. Fear and pain are the gold mines of spiritual potential and growth.

While you shrink from the darkness, the soul perks up and is ready to burn the midnight oil in order to make sense of fear and pain, in order to find spiritual meaning, to hear, trust, and follow God in the midst of the problem. You pick at the problem, shovel though the debris, sweat and strain in search of the mother lode or at least a nugget of hope and truth. When you find it, you feel like yourself again.

At other times, the pain and fear distract you from your soul's calling. You feel compelled to camouflage your real self. You put up defenses. These defensive patterns provide immediate protection but eventually conceal the pure, spiritual ore. They are patterns that lead to self-deception. You lose touch with what you feel, believe, hope, fear, or desire at a given moment. You lose sight of who and what you are becoming.

Whatever the cost of authenticity, the price of living-on-defense is greater. It is a game of camouflage and deception played with torn maps, whispered lies, false clues and lost secrets. Burying your pain and fear is hiding from your own soul. You don't want to go down that road, and neither do I. But we do. A path of defensiveness leads to self-deception.

No one wants to be a fraud or live a lie, be a sham, a phony or hide from life. However, under enough pain and fear, we hide. We hide from the truth about us. We lose touch with our best. Defensive living turns patterns into ruts that are pre-determined by the past, the pain, and the people who dominated our lives. Why? Because we are dominated by what we fear or hate.

At the age of seventeen, I saw a younger boy lying on the grass in front of our high school. When I approached him, it was apparent he was on drugs. I talked with him for a few moments and attempted to say something about the love of God available to him. He sat up and looked hard into my face. Opening his fist, he showed me a collection of pills and said, "If I don't take these every day, I will die. You are too late with your talk of God's love."

To escape dealing with the hatred and fear, you set up defenses. Defenses serve as emotional and relational drugs that we believe we need in order to survive. The defensive posture serves two purposes, to be rewarded and protected. In one moment, you want both: to get on the radar, yet remain hidden under it. You want to be noticed and invisible. The motivating factors are to maintain control and protect your security. You feel impelled to control the sources of potential pain and rewards while insulating yourself from your worst fears and deepest resentments. Defenses attempt to create a life that is comfortable and filled with happy assurances.

Defenses come in many costumes and cover-ups. Here is a short catalogue of defensive postures and life roles that attempt to ease the pain, provide rewards, and protect from inner turmoil.

You might find yourself acting like a *child* who will not deal with life's problems and challenges. You shed personal responsibility. Is this you? Ask yourself,

"Am I creating problems in order to get attention?"
"Do I come off as fragile or incompetent in order to receive special treatment from others?"

Another defensive role is playing the part of the *messiah*, who is on a quest to fix everyone else's inadequacies and, thus, ignore his or her own. You substitute genuine compassion for the counterfeit currency of pseudo-concern that you use to broker relationships and enforce your power over others.

"Do I view the people I know primarily as people who need my help?"
"Am I trying to impress people with my self-sufficiency because I doubt my own abilities?"

A further cover-up is the role of a *control freak*. It is a cover for inward chaos. If you lack the courage to face your inner battle, you substitute controlling the outer world.

"Am I uncomfortable when someone else makes choices for me, no matter how insignificant?"
"Do I secretly believe that I know what's best for the people around me?"

There is also the *schoolyard bully*, who rejects the rules of fair play for intimidation and conquest. You subconsciously conceal weak or wounded self-confidence in a blustery display of pseudo-bravado and demands.

"Am I trying to prove I'm tough as a means of hiding my inadequacies?"
"Do I overwhelm others as a way to avoid hearing or facing the truth about myself?"

Fahrenheit 451 is the temperature at which paper burns. It is also the title of the famous book by Ray Bradbury.[10] It tells of a totalitarian society where books are burned by the government. Burning libraries is a dictator's oppressive way of defending himself against fear and pain in the soul of society.

> In 1933, the Nazis burned works by Jewish authors and other works considered "un-German." Throughout history, when emperors, kings, tsars, popes and dictators felt the need to defend their positions and power, they burned books. Often the ideas in the books unmasked the evil of the regime. When these frightened and angry leaders learned of books that expose their evil and prescribe what could be done about it, the writings (and often the authors as well) were put to the flame.[11]

To live in a defensive role is a book burning bon-fire of self-knowledge. You light the flame when you deny your own feelings, ignore your hopes, present a false front, or follow a path others have laid out for you rather than take responsibility for your own decisions. You lose sight of your potential, accept the limitations placed on you, react to the moment rather than respond with your best. You send out pity signals, work to make everyone else happy or become your own island, formed by a seething volcano of anger and surrounded by an icy sea of fear.

> *To live in a defensive role is a book burning bon-fire of self-knowledge.*

BECOME YOUR SOUL'S PARTNER

It takes an act of courage, confidence, commitment, and compassion to step out of a role of falsehood and break out of your self-made prison. It takes an act of integrity to seize your life, face the truth about yourself, and take the steps needed to get back on the path of living true to your best in Christ.

You are not alone in your struggle for inner freedom.
You have a partner who is an escape artist—your soul.
Your soul is the harbinger of your true and best in Christ.
Your soul is the conduit of the Spirit of God in you.
Your soul is the dwelling place of God on earth.

There is an eternal, uncompromising conspiracy at work in the world. Your earthly soul and God in His heaven have secretly planned to bring your true and best to life every day. Join the conspiracy! Sign up. As a full member, you pledge yourself to following a path of truth. On this, the soul will not negotiate. The truth is liberating. It is the truth about you. It is the truth about God. It is the truth of God's love.

> *Your earthly soul and God in His heaven have secretly planned to bring your true and best to life every day.*

At times the truth is stark and plain. At other moments, personal truth is elusive. Along the trail, there are places where you see clearly and know yourself truly. Yet the trail also moves through dark forests and uncharted lands where a true sense of self must be rediscovered. Your soul negotiates the varied and conflicting landscapes with unwavering loyalty to a single purpose: to live true to your best.

Everyone has a story, and God has a story, too. God's story, His Word, is made flesh in Jesus Christ. When God's story touches your story, your story is changed. The apostle Paul tells the essence of the mysterious story of God's love in Christ: Christ was crucified according to scripture, was buried and rose according to scripture. Paul goes on to explain the change in his life, a life in Christ: *"By the grace of God, I am who I am, and his grace to me was not without effect"* (1 Corinthians 15:10).

The soul has an eye for your best. It is a quest. It is what's best *in* you, *for* you, and *from* you at any given moment. Beyond the defensive walls that imprison your best is a journey of hope, wisdom, and grace. Each small, individual step that reveals your best in this moment moves you forward. It calls for and creates inner strength. You learn to attend to the needs of your inner life. Your life grows in authenticity, the authenticity of Christ Jesus.

The soul requests your partnership. Care for your soul. Pay attention to your inward life. Listen to your inner wisdom. Be faithful to your quest to live in God. God has called you to live in Him. Your soul is calling you to be a partner in this great vocation and spiritual venture.

All partnerships carry responsibilities. You are expected to make a meaningful and significant contribution to your soul's purpose.

> It is your responsibility to
> 1) Remain true to the Source of spiritual meaning,
> 2) Protect your eternal value, and
> 3) Strengthen your uniqueness.

These responsibilities comprise our acceptance to God's invitation. Our Lord taught us to live life in God when He taught us to pray, *"Our Father who art in heaven, hallowed is your name"* (Matthew 6:9). It is tempting to divide life into the secular and the sacred, the practical and the spiritual. God's name is holy in all things; He is our source of spiritual meaning in all of life.

Jesus also taught us to rest our eternal value in the kingdom of God's compassion rather than the rewards and recognition of the world. Pray, *"Your kingdom come"* (Matthew 6:10). Pray that God's kingdom will be the core of your being, the fountain of true value. Your eternal worth is not in your accomplishments or acknowledgments, but in the single fact that God's kingdom of love is advancing in your life and in the world.

Your uniqueness is found in God's creative gift of life, your life. God created you, not only in your mother's womb, but also through every experience that comes to you. Align the direction of your life on earth with Heaven's creative purpose. Pray, *"Your will be done on earth as it is in heaven"* (Matthew 6:10). Ask God to create His life in you.

It is to these three challenges we now turn our attention. To find spiritual meaning is to believe in, search for, and base your life in the love of God. To protect your eternal value is to return to the inward place of God's love, your inner home in God. To strengthen your uniqueness is to join the God who loves you in creating a life true to your best in Christ.

CHAPTER 3

SPIRITUAL MEANING

In a very real sense we are earthbound creatures, caught always
in the rigid context by which our experiences are defined.
The particular fact or experience which we are facing at
the moment, or the memory of other particular facts or
experiences from other moments—these are our openings,
these are the doors through which we enter into wider
meanings, into wider contexts.
HOWARD THURMAN[1]

The soul is the life force within you. The source of the soul's life is spiritual. To partner with your soul is to take responsibility to remain true to the Source of spiritual meaning, God Himself.

> You and I are called to live true to our best in Christ.
> You and I are born into life in this world.
> Therefore, our life in the world
> is intimately connected to our life in God.

Yet the temptation is to separate life into compartments, categories, and cubicles. There is a God-part and a world-part. There is the sacred and the secular, the eternal and the temporal. We work hard to mark and maintain the distinctions between the spiritual and the practical as described by Evelyn Underhill, a respected teacher of Christian spirituality.

> Most of our conflicts and difficulties come from trying to deal with the spiritual and practical aspects of our life separately instead of realizing them as parts of one whole. If our practical life is centered on our own interests, cluttered up by possessions, distracted by ambitions, passions, wants and worries, beset by a sense of our own rights and importance, or anxieties for our own future, or longings for our own success, we need not expect that our spiritual life will be in contrast to all this. The soul's house is not built on such a convenient plan: there are no soundproof partitions in it.[2]

Whenever we segment our lives into the spiritual and practical, our spiritual life suffers. The spiritual life, our life in God, demands priority. We are designed to live from the inside-out; our life in Christ is to guide the rest of life and all of life.

REWARDS AND EXPECTATIONS

The meaning of your life is rooted either in God or in something else. Not everyone embraces spiritual meaning as the core of life. But what else is there? There are five common alternatives, voices from the outer world bidding for the driver's seat of your existence. Each alternative binds the heart and spirit to tangible security:

Possessions—What I own determines my significance and security.
Power—What I control proves my worth and value.
Prestige—What I receive in accolades and recognition is my life.
Pleasure—What pain I avoid and enjoyment I find is life's meaning.
Performance—What I accomplish is the measure of my importance.

It is tempting to usurp the soul's urging for the spiritual by staking your eternal essence in material rewards and expectations. Great enterprises take advantage of this all too human weakness. They forge a corporate promise, a lasting covenant between the company and its employees: Remain loyal and competent and we will see that you are secure, comfortable, and have your share of the American Dream. For many people in years past, the promise delivered the goods, including large houses, secure retirement, and discretionary income.

> *It is tempting to usurp the soul's urging for the spiritual by staking your eternal essence in material rewards and expectations.*

Today, the promise has fallen on hard times. Fluctuating economies, volatile markets, and corporate dealings have stripped bare the old covenant. It has exposed a lifeless body of withered limbs with a marshmallow-middle. It is remembered in moments of nostalgic longing for the past or resentful outbursts decrying broken dreams, assurances, and guarantees that are broadcast on the airways of the press or in the protests of disenfranchised workers and investors. Today, any guaranteed pledge of security and comfort is wishful rather than certain.

An autopsy of the corpse of corporate promises reveals the cause of death: the deceased had no soul. The delivered goods were void of spiritual meaning. The contract was utterly tangible. A review of the fine print reveals no assurance of sacred significance. The promise was to bring comfort and security to life, not the power of life itself. Those who hung their eternal essence on the pledge were left wanting. Too late they learned there is no profit if you gain the world's goods and lose your own soul.

Take the lesson to heart: you dare not anchor the meaning of your life in the rewards and expectations of tangible success. You may strive to meet the demands and put forth enough effort to surpass the expectations. You

> *You may enjoy temporal success with its physical security and comfort, but, for the sake of your soul, be not beholden to it.*

may attain great rewards and recognition. You may enjoy temporal success with its physical security and comfort, but, for the sake of your soul, be not beholden to it.

THE SPIRITUAL AND PRACTICAL

The search for and enjoyment of spiritual vitality is the soul's natural habitat. However, one would never know it from the language of the culture. English contrasts "spiritual" with "natural," as if being "spiritual" is somehow "unnatural." It is a false dichotomy that reveals a false perception: to be spiritual is to be "other worldly."

We have met people who have so much heaven on their minds, they are of no earthly use. This can be a problem, but it is only a symptom of a deeper issue. The dichotomy that exposes the deeper rift is the one suggested by Evelyn Underhill, the chasm between the spiritual and the practical.

Practical issues, for the most part, are tangible. The tangible is known through the five senses: sound, sight, taste, touch, and smell. What is tangible can be measured, compared, catalogued, and accounted. The soul, your eternal essence, may consider these numbers or disregard them altogether. The soul's work is to make sense of what's happening and give it meaning. To paraphrase Albert Einstein, not everything that can be counted, counts.[3]

It is tempting to separate the spiritual from the practical. In doing so, life in God is dismembered from the practical decisions of daily life. Imagine the spiritual and the practical as two tiny cubicles in a small office. On one side of the divide you consider whatever your spiritual issues may be. On the other side you deal with the problems, pressures, and possibilities of getting on with the challenges of daily living. These are the concerns associated with possessions, power, prestige, pleasure, and performance. They are tangled troubles that simply won't go away. You must deal with them, and you must deal with them daily.

I am going to run out of money before I run out of month.
Why won't my family consider what I want for our vacation?
I am so weary of working hard without any recognition.
All I want to do is have some fun, and I've worked hard for it.
I have got to get this job done, or I just won't feel right.

Return to the image of the office: one cubical for spiritual meaning and another cubical for practical concerns. There is a divider down the middle. Which side of the office will receive the greater amount of activity? The practical wins every time because practical concerns demand relentless attention. How do we give spiritual life in God priority?

Change the image. Instead of two cubicles in an office, imagine two boxes. The practical concerns are in one box, and spiritual meaning is in the other. If you position the boxes side by side, you have the divided office. However, here is another way to think of it. Place one box inside the other. Put the box labeled "spiritual meaning" inside the box of "practical concerns." Thus, every practical concern is filled with spiritual meaning.

This image reveals that spiritual life resides within every event, decision, and challenge in daily life. Inside budget issues, family squabbles, office politics, pleasure trips, and sales goals are spiritual concerns. It also means that every event, decision, or challenge has a tangible, practical outward side and a spiritual, meaningful inwardness. A story from the life of Jesus demonstrates that outward-inward tension:

> When Jesus was approaching his death, he told his disciples:
> *Now my heart is troubled, and what shall I say? 'Father, save me from this hour?' No, it was for this very reason I came to this hour. Father, glorify your name!*
> *Then a voice came from heaven, 'I have glorified it, and will glorify it again.' The crowd that was there and heard it said it had thundered; others said an angel had spoken to him.* (John 12:27-29)

Was it thunder or an angel? It was both. It was practical and spiritual in the same experience. To discover spiritual meaning in your life and mine requires that we see the potential for spiritual meaning in all of life. It cannot be compartmentalized, cordoned off, or segregated. You cannot isolate your soul from the rest of your life; you cannot detach God from daily living.

Once we embrace the truth that life, at its core, is spiritual, that God has an interest in everything in our lives, we are faced with a new challenge. How do we pay attention to spiritual issues, tune in to God's voice, and respond in obedience? This is a matter of being inwardly willing to hear, trust, and choose to respond true to our best in Christ.

WILLFUL OR WILLING

The spiritual and practical are both found in the same experience. But which one commands priority? You must make the decision. To make practical concerns the first priority is to live from the outside in, while living from the inside out is true to your soul.

The key dynamic of the practical life is to be willful. In the external life you and I must exert our will. We must make decisions, express opinions, and even willfully choose to submit to the choices of others. Most self-help and motivational materials encourage you to exert your will, take responsibility for your life, stand up and be counted, and make something of yourself. All this is true and needed when dealing with practical concerns.

However, the spiritual life operates on a different principle. God designed it to function with vitality and health through a humble attitude of willingness. It is willingness to hear God's voice and respond with your true and best in Christ. You activate your spiritual life though surrender. Bring your desires, dreams, troubles, and turmoil to God; express them with passion. Exposing them in the presence of the One who loves you completely eases their grip, loosens their hold, and sets you at rest to surrender to the will of God. It is a strategy of surrender:

> *My heart is not proud, O Lord,*
> *my eyes are not haughty;*
> *I do not concern myself with great matters*
> *or things too wonderful for me.*
> *But I have stilled and quieted my soul;*
> *like a weaned child with its mother,*
> *like a weaned child is my soul within me.* (Psalm 131:1-2)

However, there is a danger here also. In some settings, the religious demand for surrender is so stark and inhumane that the unsuspecting Christian is left thinking he or she should have no desire, passion, or ever exert willpower. In this kind of dysfunctional religious community, "thy will be done" is a political ploy to control the will of others. God has given you a will, and He intends for it to be used with passion and compassion. You surrender your will to God in order for your will to be aligned with God's will.

> *In some settings, the religious demand for surrender is so stark and inhumane that the unsuspecting Christian is left thinking he or she should have no desire, passion, or ever exert willpower.*

In plain terms, practical concerns require that you exert an active willfulness. Spiritual meaning shapes life when you willingly surrender to God. Now you must choose: will you live from the outside-in, exerting your will over God, or live from the inside-out, aligning your will with God through spiritual surrender.

Option 1

Outside-In: Practical concerns take control. When tangible concerns run your life, you are in peril. This is like building your house on shifting sand (Matthew 7:26). Expectations and rewards offer little, if any, security. In themselves, they provide scant satisfaction.

When tangible concerns shape the spiritual meaning of life, you start down a dangerous path toward mind control, sorcery, or the nature religions of primitive societies that seek to appease the gods of thunder, mountains, or crocodiles.

In the Bible Simon the Sorcerer attempted to purchase the power of the Holy Spirit in order to increase his possessions, power, and prestige (Acts 8:9-24). His spiritual life, his soul, was given over and taken over by temporary and transient desires.

To be spiritually willful is to expect God to bend to your will.

Option 2

Inside-Out: Spiritual meaning shapes life. This is a life built *"on the rock"* (Matthew 7:24). When life in God is in control, the spiritual meaning of an event shapes our motivations, perspectives, and even our emotions. The soul's purpose is clear, to bring to life our true and best in Christ.

With this stance, you may transcend the clawing and clamoring of conflicting demands and needs in the practical world. Now, you can consider the greater, deeper issues; listen for the voice of inner wisdom; and respond in faith, hope, and love.

The Bible describes how Paul fell from his horse and was blind for several days. As a result, his concern was focused on the inner life, the spiritual life. It was not for power and prestige he longed, but for a personal relationship with God. Paul heard the call of God and answered (Acts 9:1-18).

This is an example of spiritual willingness and surrender. God's will is in charge.

Just as the tangible and spiritual live in the same moment, so, too, willfulness and willingness must be brought into harmony. But how? You must exert your will in the practical world. You must take responsibility for your life, your possessions, power, prestige, pleasure, and performance. You do this by choosing to live true to your best in Christ. You have a strong will, but a will that is guided, energized, and shaped by God.

To make this work, your will must consistently surrender to the will, the way, and the wisdom of God. In the spiritual core of life, there is only one stance: a humble willingness to be loved and led by Heaven's King. This is where the search for spiritual meaning leads:

I surrender my will to You, O God. I am willingly drawn into your presence. I willingly respond to your way and your wisdom for me. And I choose to use my will, the will You give me, to live true to my best in Christ each day.

God seeks to establish a home in your soul, a home where you are always loved. You arrive with your weapons and defenses, your choices and opinions, your accomplishments and possessions, your accolades and influence. Linger a while. Let your fingers loosen their grip and your mind ease its tension. Let your heart go. Surrender anew again and again and again.

A Christian teacher and mystic of the fifteenth century, Francisco de Osuna, teaches that God plays a game with the soul called "the loser wins," a game in which the one who holds the poorest cards does best. The Pharisee's consciousness that he had such an excellent hand really prevented him from taking a single trick.[4]

God will work His love, His hope, and His faith in you. You will emerge to live, act, choose, and engage your will in faith, hope, and love. You move inward and then outward, inward and outward. This is the rhythm of spiritual living. This is Christian authenticity.

OPPORTUNITY AND TRAGEDY

Can you hear the voice of God when you are tucked away in your soul's home? Can you discern the spiritual meaning inside the clamor of life? Here is an example: imagine a career advancement opportunity. The practical component is the evidence found in the job description, compensation package, strength of the corporation, and opportunities for continued advancement. It is a clerk's task to gather practical information. You are the clerk, and you

> *You have a fiduciary responsibility to your soul and your life.*

must do your due-diligence. You have a fiduciary responsibility to your soul and your life.

However, there is a higher function, a decision-making function that gives meaning and significance to your career opportunity. The spiritual significance and meaning of the event are negotiated in the workshop of the soul.

You, in your soul, must sort it out. You must make choices and decisions. You, in your soul must determine the spiritual significance of the opportunity. For example, here are three responses: "This will show my father I am a success." "This job matches my life's purpose." "It's not what I really want to do, but it's secure." Each response carries spiritual significance and meaning buried under the contract offer, the recruiter's promises, and the dissatisfaction with your current position. You must activate your will and make a decision. However, will you set aside the outer voices and willingly listen for God's wisdom?

Heaven's voice, echoed in your soul's purpose urges you to draw near to God and go forth to live true to your best. What is true to your best is always *something more*. The final decision is more important than the pay package, the window office, the executive workout room, or the advancement potential. It is *something more* than proving yourself, using your talents, or even engaging your passion. It is your spiritual surrender, your willingness to hear, trust, and follow God's wisdom.

The *something more* is not above you, beyond you, or away from you. Spiritual meaning is *within* you. It is the source and sustaining power of your true and best self. Your soul pledges its allegiance to the spiritual life within you. It is ever present in the workshop of making sense and finding meaning in life. It is the energy of spiritual strength, soul-strength, which centers your life. It is the surrender strategy.

Consider another example: You suffer a tragedy. The tangible information comes from doctors, lawyers, bankers, and financial advisors as well as family, friends, and foes. The meaning you ascribe to the calamity (your willingness to surrender to God's wisdom) and the actions you take based on the meaning (your willfulness in alignment with God's wisdom) encompass the spiritual issue. How will you, in your soul, negotiate the meaning?

The meaning determines your perceptions and motivations: "I am a victim" or "I will overcome." Will you disdain this tragedy as life's curse or embrace it as God's blessing? The clerks and accountants cannot answer this question. They calculate it like a batting average or a return on investment. But the meaning of your pain (your vision of your life after loss) must be worked out within your soul. You must exert your will, make a choice, and move on in life. Are you willing to hear God, trust God, and follow Him? Negotiate carefully.

A SPIRITUAL EAR

How can you hear the spiritual meaning in everyday experience? When I was a child, my Sunday school teachers had a ready answer: read the Bible and pray. True enough, but I didn't find it very helpful. The Bible was confusing, and prayer was but a ritual of words that didn't make much sense.

In this situation, prayer and Scripture can become another tangible source of security and reward. It is a way to bolster prestige, improve performance, and increase power. After all, if as a child I could quote a scripture, people were impressed and would listen. There are adults who bolster their prestige in the church like Pharisees in the days of Jesus, because *"they love to pray standing in the synagogues and on the street corners to be seen by men"* (Matthew 6:5).

It is possible to treat your spiritual life like another tangible asset; remember Simon the Sorcerer. However, to live from the inside-out requires a humble, willing soul. It calls for patience and persistence. It is not a technique, a tool, or a trick. It is simply learning by consistent practice how to come into the presence of God in order to hear His voice and be revitalized by His love.

First—Answer God's Call. God calls you to live your life in Him. Ask yourself the following two questions:

1. How can this experience open my soul to God?
2. How can I respond in a way that is true to my best in Christ?

Willingly search the Scripture and pray for an answer to these two questions. Read the Bible with these two questions in mind. Pray for the insight and determination to live true to your best.

Let me give you a suggestion about reading the Bible. Mark Twain quipped, "It ain't those parts of the Bible I can't understand that bother me, it's the parts I do understand."[5]

Read the parts of the Bible you understand and seek to understand the more confusing parts based on the portions of the Scripture that are clear and plain. Begin your journey with what you know and what is clear to you. Allow God to lead you to deeper understanding and truth. Cling to that truth. Remember that a relationship is two-sided. As you are drawing near to God, He will faithfully guide you.

Second—Relate to God as a Person. Many of us were taught to think of God as a collection of attributes or characteristics. This fosters an image of God that is distant, cold, and uncaring. We are taught that God is infallible, unchangeable, impassive, and infinite. There may be a partial measure of theological accuracy in these propositions. However, God is more mysterious, more personal, and more intimate than attributes and characteristics can describe. Squeezing God into attributes creates the image of a "watch-maker"[6] who set the world-a-spinning and then let it go. God is so much more. He cannot be contained in a theologian's description.

It takes an event, a great event, to reveal the wonderful mystery of God. That event is the incarnation of God in Jesus Christ. God did not send a description of Himself. He came, personally and in human form, to live with us! God is a person, a spiritual person. In Jesus, God took on human form: *"taking the very nature of a servant, being made in human likeness, and being found in appearance as a man"* (Philippians 2:7-8). He makes His home *in* us.

When you pray, talk to God as a friend talks with a friend. It's natural for you to do most of the talking. But if you learn to sit quietly, as if you were sitting with a best friend, you may sense an inner nudge, a feeling of assurance, or a thought that is beyond your normal frame of reference. You are learning to hear the voice of inner wisdom. God is speaking.

Third—Embrace the Challenge of the Journey. Knowing God and building your life on spiritual meaning is not always a "feel good" proposition. To remain true to what gives life spiritual meaning is to wrestle with life's deepest concerns and battle inner enemies.

The medieval map makers did not know what was in central Africa. Over the unknown they affixed the phrase, "Here be dragons."[7] As they reached the edge of the map, they wrote, "Beyond this place lie monsters." Below are four questions that expose dragons, monsters, and beasts you will meet on the inward journey:

How do I restore my inner commitment
when I have betrayed my own integrity?

How do I renew my inner confidence
when I have lost faith in life's purpose?

How do I rekindle my inner courage
when I have been assaulted by fear?

How do I revive my inner compassion
when my trust has been broken?

When you come face to face with your inner ghosts and goblins, God has not deserted you. Indeed, you are drawing closer to God. He places the light of truth in your heart. It shines against the lies and falsehoods that seek to cage you in defeat. God is determined to remove all obstacles and impediments in your relationship with Him. He invigorates your soul in Christ.

AN EVIL CONSPIRACY

God and your soul are in cahoots. They are determined that your true and best self come to life every day. However, there is another conspiracy at work in the cosmos, an evil conspiracy. Forces afoot in the world connive to distract and disconnect you from your soul-life, your spiritual center.

> *God and your soul are in cahoots.*

Your soul recognizes the voices that plot to steal your inner vitality. Their strategy is to separate you from your source of spiritual meaning. The voices promise recognition and rewards, comfort and security. They talk as if you could *"tell this stone to be bread" (Luke 4:3).* It carries the false promise that *"it will all be yours" (Luke 4:7)*. The temptations are old and deadly. They promise that if you reject your soul's purpose and conform to their wishes,

> Everyone will love you and admire you.
> There is an easy, effortless shortcut to all you desire.
> Compromise today and you can have all you want tomorrow.

The harmful voices speak with seductive generosity in order to gain your loyalty. Once you are beholden to them, the voices turn and growl with intimidation. They threaten the loss of your bread and belonging. You trade your soul for the security and acceptance you crave. At this point, your soul is in crisis.

Your soul will not accept defeat lightly. Your soul is committed to another way—a path of freedom and love. It is the voice of spiritual truth echoing inside you.

> People may use and abuse each other today,
>   but God's love is forever faithful.
> Life may be hard and harsh today,
>   but God's love is forever faithful.
> Choices may be complex and painful today,
>   but God's love is forever faithful.

Your soul is created for God's dwelling. Your soul has pledged allegiance to God. You must partner with your soul. You must choose to surrender willingly to God's way and wisdom. When you do, and as you continue to do so, your soul determines to live in alignment with what brings spiritual meaning to life.

THE SOURCE OF LIFE

You can know that you are *loved* by the God of the Universe. In traditional Jewish communities in Israel today, when a young man reaches bar-mitzvah or a young woman bat-mitzvah, the whole community turns out onto the streets. The child, now an adult, is lifted on strong shoulders and carried through the village. The father is in front of the procession, dancing, singing, and shouting, "This is my beloved." God, your Father, dances and sings before all creation: "You are my beloved child; you are the one I love."

You can know the spiritual meaning of *hope* in Christ. It is God's way to go beyond what we have experienced. The wonderful Scottish minister, James Stewart, expresses our hope in Christ.

> What we have seen and learned of God up to the present is not to be the end of our seeing nor the sum total of our learning; that whatever we have found in Christ is only a fraction of what we still can find; that the spiritual force which in the great days of the past vitalized the church and shaped the course of history has not exhausted its energies and fallen into abeyance but is liable at any moment to burst out anew and take control…God is promising to do wonders for you he has never done before, so that there will be more jubilant doxologies, more exultant hallelujahs…There is no limit to the creative love of God, and no end to the redeeming grace of Christ.[8]

You can know *faith* that enriches your daily life, strengthens your most important relationships, and advances you toward your God-given potential. There is faith in what God has done *for* you on the Cross of Christ. There is faith in what God does *in* you through the Spirit of Christ. And there is faith in cooperating with the Father's will to bring your true and best in Christ to the challenges of life.

> *Spiritual meaning brings a deep sense of belonging to a larger truth. It is connecting to the source of life in God.*

Spiritual meaning brings a deep sense of belonging to a larger truth. It is connecting to the source of life in God. As spiritual meaning fills your soul, you begin to perceive, receive, and cherish your life as a gift. You have a growing awareness that your personal truth is sustained in the great truth of God's love. Your personal best flows from God's best. You are at home in God. God is at home in you.

CHAPTER 4

ETERNAL VALUE

It's a lot worse to be soul-hungry than to be body-hungry.
A KENTUCKY MOUNTAIN WOMAN ASKING FOR HER GRANDDAUGHTER
TO BE ADMITTED TO BEREA COLLEGE HIGH SCHOOL (CIRCA 1900)[1]

Your soul's purpose is to hear the voice of God and respond true to your best in Christ. As such, your first responsibility is to embrace the spiritual meaning of life by receiving God's love and surrendering to His wisdom. Spiritual meaning is not primarily intellectual but relational, a relationship with God in Christ.

> At a revival service in 1887, a young man stood and spoke from his heart. He had just begun his life in Christ and did not know much about the Bible. However, he was determined to move forward with Jesus. He confessed that there were many things he didn't understand, but then declared "…but I am going to trust, and I'm going to obey." John Sammis, a lyricist, heard of the testimony from a friend and transformed the simple words of faith into a beautiful hymn:

Trust and obey for there's no other way
to be happy in Jesus than to trust and obey.[2]

The second responsibility you shoulder is to protect your relationship with God as the source of your personal and eternal value. How you think of yourself and what you feel about yourself have great impact on your life.

My master's work at the University of Missouri was in a relatively new topic at that time, self-esteem. The professors and psychologists believed that the most important issue in life was what you imagine about yourself, your self-image. Your experiences and choices shape your sense of self-worth, and your self-worth shapes your choices and perceptions. The theory seems to bear out in life.

I picture a man who always worked hard, helped others, and made a positive difference. Now he is old, struggling with illness, and unable to do what he once easily accomplished. He battles his own sense of value.

Consider the school principal who is under enormous pressure to raise the standard test score results, yet, despite all the plans, efforts, and energy, test scores drop. She feels devastated and disempowered.

There is a financial advisor who was accustomed to winning all the sales awards. Now the market has changed. The prizes and praises go to others in better markets. He tells himself he is still competent and a go-getter, but the speech in the mirror is less convincing each day.

Think of parents with a troubled child, an employee who is a casualty of downsizing or resizing, the worker who is reprimanded by the boss, the student with the low grade, the job applicant who is rejected, or the couple who lost their home in a financial crisis. When what we *do* is devalued, we feel devalued as human beings.

> *Our personal value is dangerously dependent on our success or failure in the world of tangible and practical rewards and punishments.*

In the same way, when what we accomplish is valued by ourselves and others, our sense of worth and self-respect increases. Our personal value is dangerously dependent on our success or failure in the world of tangible and practical rewards and punishments.

Each of us is engaged in the soulful challenge of evaluating our worth, establishing our value, and determining our esteem. The question is: What is the measure? Here is the truth: the world considers your abilities and accomplishments as the ultimate and only source of personal value. In this world, you are worth what you can produce and provide.

The specific measure of expectations varies with the setting, circumstance, and people involved, but the measure is always external. The measure is also a moving target. Like a desert shape shifter, you are never sure with what you are dealing. Yet it always comes down to "What have you done for me, what have you done for me lately, and what will you do for me next?"

It is a harsh and demanding voice that insists on full attention and effort. It is not a voice that makes requests, but commands: "If you want to be worth anything, do this and be that."

LOVE WITHOUT STIPULATIONS

In this reality, it is no wonder the psychologists conclude that the way we think and feel about ourselves is so influential. However, there is another voice and another source of personal and eternal worth: How do you think and feel about God? Do you fear Him and stand aloof, or do you trust His eternal and infinite love for you? Do you think He loves you because you love him, or do you open your soul, believe, and receive His mysterious and unconditional love for you?

> In a small country church on a cold Sunday evening, the crowd was so small that when the pastor opened the service in his usual manner, saying "Welcome, beloved," a woman in the second row blushed.
>
> When we realize that we are utterly and thoroughly loved by God Himself, we should blush. We are drawn into His compassion. It is not what we do that causes God to love us, but what God has done in Christ that woos us to Himself.

Some Christians emphasize the judgment of God as the antithesis or opposite of His love. This is a false dichotomy. God's judgment flows out of His love. When well-meaning Christians disconnect the judgment of God from His infinite and eternal love, people are driven away from Him, not drawn toward Him.

> If my children fear me, hate me, or ignore me, whatever good judgment I might have for them is lost on cold hearts and barricaded minds. Yet when my children know I love them, and I love them no matter what, they hear my heart and are open to my wisdom and good judgment even when it contradicts their own judgments and choices.

When we know and are consistently renewed in God's love for us, we are open to the inner voice, the voice of God's wisdom and good judgment. We also think and feel differently about ourselves. The root and nurture of our value, our ultimate and eternal value, are held in the compassion of the Lord of Heaven.

When well-meaning Christians disconnect the judgment of God from His infinite and eternal love, people are driven away from Him, not drawn toward Him.

The physical expression of God's love is Jesus Christ; the *"Word became flesh and made his dwelling among us"* (John 1:14). Jesus is the fullness of God in human form. The incarnation of Christ reveals God's compassion. The sacrifice of Christ on the Cross displays the eternal love of God for you and me. An image that captures this wonderful gift of grace is *"Lamb of God"* (John 1:29, 36).[3] In Christ, God has come to us, to our suffering and our sin. Now He invites us to come to Him and to come honestly and completely.

> Just as I am, without one plea,
> But that Thy blood was shed for me,
> And that Thou bidd'st me come to Thee,
> O Lamb of God, I come! I come!
> Just as I am—Thou wilt receive,

Wilt welcome, pardon, cleanse, relieve.
Because Thy promise I believe,
O Lamb of God, I come! I come!
CHARLOTTE ELLIOT, 1835 [4]

MARY AND MARTHA

Your soul echoes God's word: "Your eternal value is fixed in God's love for you." This is the foundation for your esteem and worth. Your ultimate worth is not proving yourself by your contribution to the world or even to the advancement of God's kingdom, but receiving the intimate knowledge and experience of God's love for you. The wonderful New Testament story of Mary and Martha describes it.

Jesus travels to the home of Mary and Martha, a home that is familiar, comfortable, and open to Him. He arrives with His disciples which puts a strain on preparing a meal. The scene is a classic distinction between proving personal worth or resting in God's love.

Martha prepares the meal for the large crowd. She frets and works, works and frets. Her sister Mary doesn't lift a finger to help, but remains seated at the feet of Jesus, listening to His every word.

Martha is distracted, worried, and upset. These are the symptoms of measuring personal worth by accomplishments. She demands that Jesus do something about Mary. Jesus replies, "*Mary has chosen what is better*" (Luke 10:42).

In the story, Mary points to a life that finds eternal value in the love of God; she listens and responds to His word. Martha, on the other hand, is consumed with proving her worth by getting things done.

You and I are a combination of both sisters, Martha and Mary. The demands of the kitchen are real and relentless. The need to rest life in the presence of God is eternal. It is tempting to think of the story in terms of balance.

But the story is not about balance. It is about choice and priority. Where does your personal and eternal value rest? Is your self-regard completely vested in meeting demands and expectations, or do you rest your worth in God's love?

Everything in the tangible world conspires to gain control by chaining your worth to meeting its ever shifting demands. We live in a world that orders and requires lunch to be served on time; it demands and expects sales goals to be met, projects to be completed, classes to be taught, meetings to be held, plans to be followed, results to be obtained, and progress to be maintained and monitored. In short, the world scales your value on what you contribute, yet you and your soul are to live by another measure, the full measure of God's perfect love for you.

We all want to make a contribution. We want to make a meaningful difference. We want to do something of value and be someone of value. Your soul knows that your contribution, your gift of value, shifts and flows throughout your life. You must do your best. Your gifts, talents, skills, and abilities are valued and needed. Your achievements are worthy of recognition. However, your inner value must not be enslaved to your abilities and accomplishments. Your soul seeks to root your eternal value in eternal love, in hearing, trusting, and following God's Living Word of love, Jesus.

THREE EXTERNAL MEASURES

You and I must deal with the external scale of measures, the world's demand and expectations. This is life as we find it. It is woven into your job and your family. Let's look at the necessity and danger of dealing with the world's measure of your worth and value. It is one thing to make a valuable contribution. It is something else to hang your ultimate worth on it.

> It is one thing to make a valuable contribution. It is something else to hang your ultimate worth on it.

For all people, there is an uneasy relationship between a sense of personal value and the ability to get things done. We judge ourselves and others judge us. When our abilities and achievements are met with recognition and rewards, the tendency is to equate our personal value with what we accomplish. However, when the situation changes, when our talents and training are rejected, when our services are no longer required, when we fall on our faces in failure, we question our personal worth. We are chained to measures of esteem that wage war on the spiritual essence and meaning of life.

The external measures are familiar to us. We deal with them all the time. They are used to determine our salary, rewards, prestige, and acceptance. They influence and sometimes dictate the way we think and feel—our emotions, our motivation, and our perception of reality. The measures are a combination of 1) relationships, 2) achievements, and 3) power. In personal terms: Do I please people? Do I reach my goals? Do I maintain control?

These three measures mark the way others measure us as well as the way we measure ourselves. Depending on circumstance and personality, one or another of the measures takes priority, for example, maintaining control or getting the job done. Then the situation changes, a new person is involved, and we discover that pleasing the new manager is now the key measure.

The priority we place on a particular measure may agree or disagree with the way someone else is making a judgment. If we agree with her choice of measure, we use terms such as "caring," "persistent," or "a go-getter"; if we disagree, we use another set of terms, such as "people pleaser," "obsessive," or "control freak."

The various combinations and labels are not the point. In each case, the measure of worth is external. It is the way we judge ourselves and the way others judge us. The measures determine rewards and punishments, yet no matter how the measures shift, the essence remains: pleasing people, reaching goals, and maintaining power.

Managing the impact of these measures on our inward and outward life is a spiritual issue. At times we are good at it. We maintain ourselves with inner strength and outward composure. Then, in a single event, it is all transformed. A relationship sours and vengeful words cut deep. We drop the ball; the project falls into disaster. Events spin out of our control; we can't get on top of it.

Feedback comes from those around us in two forms: first, do this and, second, be that. Helpful and harmful voices advise or rebuke: "You should have done this; you ought to do that; try to be more confident; try to be less arrogant."

At times the feedback is helpful and welcomed. Often it is painful and harsh. Clear, actionable feedback is essential for improvement. You must improve to make a valuable contribution. This is a worthy and good thing. We must all seek to learn from our regrets and build on our successes. In the best case, you review the event, receive feedback with integrity, gain insight, and improve. In a worst case, which is all too common, you duck the issues, defend yourself, or deny the problem.

Managing External Measures

How do you manage the inner turmoil that ensues? How do you judge yourself? How do you think through how to think about yourself? There are three levels to consider.

Level 1: *What I've contributed*—my relationships, achievements, and control. A scale from good to bad is applied to all we do: making or missing sales quotas, raising positive or prodigal children, managing or mismanaging finances, receiving or losing a promotion, growing fat or staying thin, completing or abandoning a project, pleasing or displeasing the boss, creating happiness or hard feelings in the family, and on and on and on. In a life without a spiritual center, personal and individual value is attached to this scale. It is untenable and treacherous. Organizations cast judgments on this scale. But we know that life is not this simple. People are complex and life is uncertain. To deal with it, we move to the next level.

Level 2: *What I think of my contribution*—my perspective and evaluation of my relationships, achievements, and control. Self-esteem is a genuine need for human beings. However, when I am dependent on myself alone to provide for my own esteem, I am in a dangerous predicament. My tainted perspectives and flawed evaluations determine my sense of personal value. I may overvalue what I have done; I move it too far up the scale toward good. Or I may devalue what I have done by moving my estimate toward the lower end of the scale. In the first case, friends talk behind my back, and in the second, they counsel, "don't be so hard on yourself." In either case, the deep human need to be loved and valued "just as I am" is missing. It takes more than a personal measurement of our contribution. This pushes us to the third level.

Level 3—*What I think **you think** of my contribution*—my estimate of your perspective and evaluation of my relationships, achievements, and control. At this level, we are looking for affirmation and forgiveness from one another. When we succeed, whatever the task or challenge, we long for some measure of recognition. When we fail, we yearn for the gift of forgiveness, understanding, and acceptance that restores our dignity and worth. All too often the voices around us (and within us) answer our yearning with "We affirm you, but let's see what you do next; we forgive you, but just barely." When this is the single or primary feedback for determining our value as persons, it is precarious. It is a target at the end of a field of fog.

The outer world shackles your worth to how well you handle relationships, produce results, and manage the situation. It is tempting to allow these measures to be ultimate, eternal, and final. It is a psychological and spiritual prison. Your worth is dependent on the latest numbers, results, rumors, successes, complements, criticisms, or failures.

FALLING PREY TO HUMAN JUDGMENT

Do you find yourself, on occasion, addicted to rewards and recognition, the organization's pins, plaques, and prizes? Families have their own version of rewards and punishment. You long for love, acceptance, and forgiveness[5] but find that it comes with strings attached. You internalize the patterns of judgment and use them as the scale of your own value. When given control, these measurements at work and home form manacles that restrict your best self and hold hostage your true self. They clank, rattle, and echo off concrete walls of solitary confinement in unrelenting whispers:

> *Families have their own version of rewards and punishment. You long for love, acceptance, and forgiveness but find that it comes with strings attached.*

Everyone must love me.
I must do it perfectly.
I'm not good enough.
What if I can't do it again?
What if there is someone with more talent?
Am I being passed over?
People are criticizing me unjustly.

The whispers grow into nagging concerns that dance in your head through sleepless nights. Give way to them and they open a dreaded closet of fear, depression, and self-effacement. Devilish screams fill your head with accusations:

You are useless.
You are inadequate.
You are worthless.
You are rejected.
You are such a disappointment.

These are the voices of a co-dependent relationship between personal-esteem and personal-contribution. The cacophony of inward anxiety overpowers the quiet voice of the soul's truth.

Yet in the clamor is a still, persistent voice. It comes without charts and graphs, without calculation or stipulations. It is a whisper older than the earth, yet fresh as the first cry of a newborn. It is a single, persistent utterance, relentlessly bearing its word: "God loves you, God loves you, God loves you."

Paying the Price

However, we are conditioned and trained to hear and respond to pleasing others, producing results, and maintaining control. It is these voices that command our attention and tempt us to trade our authenticity for a fleeting moment of effectiveness. When we feel we have fallen short, the voices speak words of fear and pain.

What is our response? It is predictable. We frantically seek ways to drown out the voices of fear and pain. We look for distractions. We will do anything to rid the mind of them, at least for a while. We try another glass of wine, more late-night television, or perhaps a new combination from the medicine cabinet. Modern wonders provide such convenient escapes.

Use with caution. When we are powered by the voices of fear and pain, it is a trap for addiction. Regard the warning label: continued use could be habit forming in your life and harmful to your soul. It can breed dependence on toxic relationships, dysfunctional behavior, moral failure, emotional blackmail, or chemical dependence.

If the discontent widens, you learn to fake enthusiasm, pretend to be fully engaged, and counterfeit an acceptable measure of commitment. Yet the charade cannot bridge the gap between the life you are living and your spiritual core. You could describe such a person as a spiritual zombie.[6] The Afro-Caribbean belief in voodoo recounts stories of reanimated bodies that serve as mindless and soulless workers for a great sorcerer. Consider the image as a metaphor of daily existence out of touch with the spiritual center of the universe. Look at the freeways streaming into any major city at eight o'clock on Monday morning. How many go through the motions of work and life like soulless beings! In this state, what happens to personal value? It is left in the fickle and unfeeling judgments of "What have you done for me; what have you done for me lately; what will you do for me next?"

An early symptom of this spiritual state is expressed in T. S. Eliot's *Murder in the Cathedral*: "The last temptation is the greatest treason / to do the right deed for the wrong reason."[7] It happens because we are angry, stressed, or afraid of the measurements that are used to judge us; indeed, the means by which we judge ourselves. We put in an appearance or do enough to get by. We convince ourselves that "what's good for me is good for everyone." We front a high calling and grand ideals while hiding a selfish, resentful, or malicious agenda. Or we fulfill the expectations and demands of others despite the incongruities with our authentic best.

> *You learn to fake enthusiasm, pretend to be fully engaged, and counterfeit an acceptable measure of commitment.*

We do this because we are obsessed with the drive to measure up, make the grade, or beat the record. We do this because we fear the punishment of losing our position or possessions. Beneath the turmoil, there is yet a more devastating state: We lose touch with the spiritual meaning of life. We may speak of God's great love, but we do not experience it. It is not the foundation of life, nor is it the bedrock of our eternal value.

If you find yourself headed down this road most traveled, heed the call of God that quietly echoes within. Return to the center of life. It is not a matter of maturation, learning from mistakes, but transformation, turning your life toward God. The New Testament writer Paul makes it clear:

> *"Do not conform any longer to the pattern of this world, but be transformed by the renewing of your mind. Then you will be able to test and approve what God's will is—his good, pleasing, and perfect will"* (Romans 12:2).

RESTING IN GOD'S LOVE

Rather than building personal and eternal value on external measures, you can rest your personal worth in the love of God. This way of living is spiritually and authentically human.

The tangible measures of rewards and punishments—our ability to please people, produce results and maintain power—are always with us, surrounding us, tempting us, and battling against our spiritual center. Here is the painful truth: it is an ever present enticement to shift personal value from receiving God's love to proving our own worth.

We must live in the tangible world that is impressed with "What did you do for me?" The demands and expectations are weighted down with requirements and mandates. In the rush and stress of the day, we move our stance from resting in Heaven's compassion to lusting for outward signs and symbols of approval, success, and power.

Sometimes the shift moves slowly, and other times it takes place in a flash: we attempt to build our eternal value on doing and being good enough, quick enough, bold enough, smart enough, educated enough, rich enough, attractive enough, sophisticated enough, normal enough, happy enough, and on and on and on.

How can we maintain our spiritual center, our eternal value in the love of God? How do we rest and protect our ultimate value in the compassion of the "Lamb of God?" How can we consistently live the words of the song, "Just as I am, I come"?

First, make choices that align with your soul's purpose. Set your limits and boundaries. In this daily dance, allow the music of heaven to take the lead. Ask, "How does this situation, this success, or this regret open my soul to God? How does this honor, failure, or routine bring my true and best in Christ to life?"

Expectations and demands do not go quietly into the great abyss, never to trouble you again. No indeed, the voices of requirements, rewards, and punishment continue their clamor like a brass band that's off key or a percussion section without a beat. You and I are not tone deaf. We hear it. Yet there is another song, a melody deep within. It is the soul's melody of eternal love, God's Word set to the music of life.

> *The voices of requirements, rewards, and punishment continue their clamor like a brass band that's off key.*

God's Word is Jesus. Say *love* and think *Jesus.* The love chapter of the Bible, 1 Corinthians 13, is a beautiful description of God's love. Take the word *love* and replace it with the name of Jesus.

> Jesus is patient, Jesus is kind.
>> He does not envy, He does not boast, He is not proud.
>> He is not rude, He is not self-seeking,
>> He is not easily angered,
>> He keeps no record of wrongs.
> Jesus does not delight in evil but rejoices with the truth.
>> He always protects, always trusts,
>> always hopes, always perseveres.
> Jesus never fails.[8]

It is a lovely image—dancing to the quiet music of love while the clamoring noise of the world goes on around you. I cling to the picture. But I don't always find it true to life. At times, more than I care to say, the noise of demands and expectations overwhelms me. You and I have to deal with the daily requirements of life.

How can we manage the pressure, frustrations, and conflicts, yet still dance in step with the symphony of the soul? Is it possible? Yes! Is it easy? No! It takes soul-work and soul-strength.

Here is a way to begin: Choose to do no harm to your soul's purpose. Analyze the expectations and demands made on you. Don't calculate them just in terms of your bread and belonging, but anticipate their consequences on living true to your best in Christ. Set your boundaries by asking questions that identify limits:

> Are these demands unreasonable?
> Will they harm my true and best self?
> Do they disengage my spiritual life?
> Are they out of sync with my values?

If the answers are *no*, then roll up your sleeves and work hard. The boundaries are in place. You are within the proper limits. Put all you have into it. Work for the glory of God. You can be confident that you and your soul will find the spiritual meaning in it. Choose to live in step with the soul's purpose. This is the place to start.

In a letter to the Christians in Galatia, their founding pastor, Paul, wrote the words that detail a life resting in the Spirit of Christ: *"...love, joy, peace, patience, kindness, goodness, faithfulness, gentleness and self-control. Against such there is no law...Since we live by the Spirit, let us keep in step with the Spirit"* (Galatians 5:22-25).

Second, intentionally cultivate intimacy with God. God's love is not simply cerebral, but heartfelt. It is not a logical proposition, but a stirring in your soul. Much Christian thinking today is too head-bound and not enough heart-free. To know God is to know him at a level that is personal and intimate. In the opening pages of the bible, we read that *"Adam knew Eve"* (Genesis 4:1).[9] This was not an exchange of resumes. It was physical intimacy. Paul exhorts us to passionate, spiritual intimacy: *"I want to know Christ"* (Philippians 3:10).

> *We must intentionally find the place where we are moved and swayed by the compassion of God.*

Our passions are moved and swayed by the clamor around us, by the measures placed on our lives. We must intentionally find the place where we are moved and swayed by the compassion of God.

A young girl once got in the habit of leaving her house every morning and going for a walk in the deep forest around her.

One day, her father asked, "Why do you go each day into the deep forest?"

"Why, to search for God."

"But don't you know that God is everywhere?" the father observed. "God is the same here in this house. God is the same wherever you are."

"Yes," answered the wise young girl. "But I am not the same wherever I am."

I need and you need times and places to walk with God, to experience His love, to exchange hearts with Him. Continually return home to the path of God's love. The world, each day, pulls you away from your true value to tangible measures of your worth.

Your soul is a faithful partner. Your soul is perceptive and patient. The word you need waits to be heard and to set you free. Can you learn to be still and know God loves you?

Quiet yourself, both outward and inward.
Seek out your sources of spiritual comfort.
Be still and listen to God's inner wisdom.
Open your soul to receive Heaven's love anew.

Reconnect with your inner life. Turn to the songs, the scriptures, the stories, and the memories that recall and reconnect you with heaven's compassion. Your soul is an echo chamber that vibrates with an eternal good word: God created you; God adores you; God cares for you. God's word from creation, galloping across galaxies, leaping through the ages, directing His life message to you, reverberates in your soul: *I will make my home in you.*

The first female author in the English language is Dame Julian of Norwich. She was a woman with a great soul that celebrated the grace of God in all things. In her writings, there is a beautiful sentence that could be a heart prayer for every Christian: "You are made, loved and kept by God."[10]

Dame Julian's phrase helps us re-center the soul, re-focus on what matters, on what is eternally true. The hurry and worry of daily life lures us away from our foundation. We need to return intentionally, to remember the love of God. Jesus took bread and a cup, offered it to his disciples, and said, *"do it in remembrance of me"* (1 Corinthians 11:24-25).[11] Receiving communion, the Lord's Supper or Eucharist, is not merely remembering the facts in our heads, but re-experiencing the gift of His love in our hearts.

The bread and the cup teach us that we need to rest and consistently rest again in the graceful love of God in Christ. The noise and demands of the world tend to *dis*-member us from our true value. We need to *re*-member the love of God in Christ.

Third, walk the path of humble prayer. This is the way of eternal affirmation and forgiveness. This is the deep hunger, the soul-hunger we crave.

When we succeed, it is good and right for us to appreciate one another, praise one another and even *"take great pride"* (2 Corinthians 7:4) in one another. When we fail, it is also good and right for us to *"admonish one another with all wisdom"* (Colossians 3:16), *"encourage one another"* (Hebrews 10:25), and *"forgive as the Lord forgave you"* (Colossians 3:13). But there is more, so much more.

Bring each success and failure to God's altar, to the place of love. You find this place down the path of humble prayer. At the end of the path, there under a green arbor, Jesus Christ waits to meet you. Humbly place your success and your failure in his hands. This is the way of a humble soul. Let's understand humility. David Steindl-Rastx writes:

Today, humility is not a popular virtue, but only because it is misunderstood. Many think that humility is a pious lie committed by people who claim to be worse than they know themselves to be, so that they can secretly pride themselves in being so humble. In truth, however, to be humble means simply to be earthy. The word "humble" is related to "humus," the vegetable mold of top soil. It is also related to human and humor. If we accept and embrace the earthiness of our human condition (and a bit of humor helps), we shall find ourselves doing so with humble pride. In our best moments humility is simply pride that is too grateful to look down on anyone.[12]

Grateful humility is a joyous thing. Carry your success, your accomplishment, your glorious deeds down the path that winds by still waters and green pastures.[13] Place it all at His feet. He will adore you, love you and remind you that He loves what you have done: *"well done, my good and faithful servant"* (Matthew 25:21). Yet His love for you is far greater, deeper, and more wondrous. In the presence of Eternal Love, you gain a grand perspective. God was with you all the time, working to bring your true and best in Christ to life. Praise Him.

There is also *sorrowful humility*. We have moments of regret, lament, and failure. Walk the humble path. Follow the switchbacks that cut a trail through the shadows of deep valleys. Carry the disappointment, the mistake, the transgression in your hands. When you see Christ waiting for you, you see the sadness in His face and the love in His eyes. Place it at His feet. It will serve as top soil for growing in Christ. But first, He will step over it and embrace you, hold you, and whisper in your heart, "I love you, still."

Paul describes this spiritual transaction in these words:

"...your sorrow led you to repentance. For you became sorrowful as God intended and so were not harmed by it in any way ... Godly sorrow brings repentance that leads to salvation and leaves no regret, but worldly sorrow brings death. See what godly sorrow has produced in you: what earnestness, what eagerness ... " (2 Cor 7:9-11).

This humble sorrow brought into the presence of God's love changes us (the word *repent* means change). We are different. We are new. We are energized. Our true and best are restored and released. Now, praise Him, again.

OPEN YOUR HANDS

Your responsibility in partnership with your soul is to protect your ultimate value by resting and abiding in God's love. The world will tug and pull at your value, trying to convince you that your ultimate worth depends on what you can produce and prove. You and I must return to our rest in God's love again and again. This is the power of prayer. Prayer changes us. It reminds us and re-binds us to God's love.

Spiritual reminding and re-binding are prayer and praise. It is a prayer of surrender. Turn loose. It is a prayer of love. Receive. It is in humble prayer and praise that you are ushered into God's presence: "Praise God from whom the blessings flow."[14]

Remember the image of palms down and palms up. Hold out your hands. In one hand are your accomplishments, and the other carries your failures. Turn your palms down. Let go of everything. Breathe your prayer of humble surrender. Now, turn your palms up. Receive the adoration, the forgiveness, the love of God anew.

CHAPTER 5

PERSONAL UNIQUENESS

"But by the grace of God, I am what I am."
THE APOSTLE PAUL

Following World War II, land developers produced tracts of houses,[1] each dwelling was like the one next to it. G.I.'s and their brides moved in, babies arrived, and daily life ensued. Almost immediately the look alike "cookie-cutter" houses began to take on personal and distinctive characteristics. The yard and flower beds, curtains and house paint, room additions and renovations contributed to the uniqueness of each home.

It was a long, painful journey from the hedge rows of Normandy to the track houses in the new suburban world found on the edge of great American cities. It was an arduous and amorous task to turn a tract house into a home, a speedy wedding into a lasting marriage, and youthful passions into a healthy, loving family.

I imagine the Creator of all things slipping up behind you and whispering in your ear, *"What kind of life do you want to create?"*[2] It is far better than the careless question, "What do you want?" It is too tempting and easy to compile a list of wishes as if that was a vision for a life worth living, as if God's role is that of celestial Kris Kringle.

God asks, "What kind of life do you want to create?" You and I must pause and reflect. The answer to this question involves effort and grace. It requires cooperation and long term commitment. This is the third requirement in the partnership with your soul. You must take responsibility for your uniqueness, the life you will create with God.

The soul takes hold of the question with glee. This is something to work on and work with. The answer to the question is not an idle wish, but an expression of heavenly hope. Hope demands patience and persistence. It is working and waiting. It is a dream shouldered as a duty.

The Apostle Paul describes the fulfillment of God's will in two phrases that heighten both the apostle's work and God's grace: *"I worked hard ...yet, not I, but grace at work in me"* (1 Corinthians 15:10).

Paul worked, pushed, persevered, struggled, and gave his best and his all: yet he knew it was God who transformed, guided, energized, rescued, and loved him into His will. His challenge is to *"work out your own salvation ...for it is God who is at work in you"* (Philippians 2:12-13). You are saved for a purpose; work it out, for God is working in you.

Creating life, your life, whether on a grand scale or in the daily grind, is a task the Lord chooses to undertake with you. He works for you, in you, and through you. When aligned with God's call and will, we shine like *"stars in the universe"* (Philippians 2:15). You and I can say from the depths of our being, *"By the grace of God, I am what I am"* (1 Corinthians 15:10).

What kind of life do I want to create? It is not the question we ask seven year old, "What do you want to be when you grow up?" but the reflective inquiry of a mature adult who understands that life is large and precious, constantly changing, and full of problems as well as potential. The question is

"What will I create out of this moment, this problem, this opportunity, this day, this week, this year, this one opportunity to live?"

With God as your partner, you can seize the greatest opportunity or the darkest night and choose to find purpose and meaning in it. You create something of it. The Creator is at work in you.

> *With God as your partner, you can seize the greatest opportunity or the darkest night and choose to find purpose and meaning in it.*

What kind of life do you want to create? You have three options.

First, you may avoid the question. Live your days as a problem solver rather than a purpose finder. Many people do.

Second, you may delegate the question to others and live in line with their answers. Your life will soon be yoked to someone else's agenda.

Third, take responsibility for your life and answer the question with complete honesty as you surrender to the wisdom of God, who is your creator and your guide.

It is the means of following your spiritual path. What do you want to create of this relationship, this challenge, this one life you have? In each situation, look for the path that is true to your best in Christ:

> ➢ Is it true to who I am?
> ➢ Does it align with my best?
> ➢ Does it engage my spiritual life?
> ➢ Does it express my authenticity?

If the answers are *yes*, then it is time once again to roll up your sleeves and work hard, love deeply, laugh loudly and live fully. Put all you have into it. God has called you to the challenge. Be confident that you and your soul have embarked on a unique path of God's wise will for your life.

Your Quiet Purpose

The industry of personal and professional development seminars addresses the need to "create your life" with a life-vision. It is a statement of personal goals and desires, the "things I must do before I die." For some, the life-vision awakens sleeping passions and potential. These seminars feature stories of world class athletes, humanitarians, and those who have overcome difficult obstacles. Such stories challenge us to lift our heads out of the daily jungle of living and reconsider our lives' dreams. They confront us with the need to be accountable for our lives, set goals, and live intentionally. This can be a helpful experience for many people, but I challenge you to think at a deeper level.

In business settings, both in-depth retreats and keynote addresses, I have often guided people in the development of a life-philosophy. The process includes an exercise that surfaces core beliefs and values. To use a common business term, it helps individuals discover what is below the bottom line. For many people, this experience is insightful and opens the door to meaning, value, and purpose. They come to see that life can be more intentional rather than coincidental. They discover that their lives' dreams are personally significant and can be brought into alignment with their deepest beliefs and convictions regarding family, friends, and doing something for the good of others. A life-philosophy is the foundation of a life-vision. However, there is something else, something deeper still.

You have a quiet purpose within your soul. It is quiet, yet persistent. It is often unseen, yet pervasive. It is part of you whether your life-vision is grand or simple, whether your philosophy is well thought out or you simply feel your way along.

Your path may be grand: You may respond to God's call and leave one continent for another as did the Apostle Paul, who left Asia-minor for Greece, crossing the line between Asia and Europe: *"During the night Paul had a vision of a man of Macedonia standing and begging him, 'Come over to Macedonia and help us.' After Paul had seen the vision, we got ready at once to leave for Macedonia, concluding that God had called us..."* (Acts 16:9-10).

However, your path may be simple: The Apostle Paul wrote to the people of Macedonia with a clear call to a simple life, a life that has been lived out by generations of good Christians who are following God's unique purpose for their lives: *"Make it your ambition to lead a quiet life, to mind your own business ...so that your daily life may win the respect of outsiders ... "* (1 Thess. 4:11).

Your life may be lived out in a grand scheme or along a simple path. You may follow a life-arching vision or faithfully respond to sequential callings. For you, life's plot may unfold neatly and in a timely fashion. Or it may be full of unexpected twists and turns. Here is the lesson: The deep commitment is not to the path or the plot, but to God's purpose, the quiet purpose Heaven weaves into your life.

Your quiet purpose is something God has created in you. It is something that is awakened in the presence of God, and it is nurtured by His love for you. The quiet purpose is a response to God's love by extending His love to others. Your quiet purpose remains rather consistent across the years of your life, even as roles, duties, and specific callings come and go. Through your quiet purpose, God works in you to create your life.

In conversations with many people, I have discovered that they can identify a persistent sense of quiet purpose. I ask them to reflect on how they naturally extend the love of God to others. Some people are very practical while others are almost mystical in their answers. Others tend to focus on more nurturing acts of service while a certain group devises and implements plans and achievements for the greater good. Here are several examples of quiet purpose:

- ➤ I just care about people whatever I am doing.
- ➤ I serve people in a way that improves their lives.
- ➤ I want my home to be a healing place for all who come here.
- ➤ I help people face the truth, even when it is painful.
- ➤ I want to support others from the sidelines.
- ➤ I want to build something that makes a positive difference.
- ➤ I am passing on a legacy of love.
- ➤ I have a message that I must share.

A quiet purpose involves nurturing people, serving in a practical way, advancing a cause, or opening spiritual reality for others. The quiet purpose is true to your best in Christ.

Jesus described the quiet purpose as being the salt of the earth and the light of the world. Salt does not do anything except be true to its nature. Light is true to its best, not when it is hidden but when you "...*put it on its stand and it gives light to everyone in the house. In the same way, let your light shine before men, that they may see your good deeds and glorify your Father in heaven*" (Matthew 5:15-16).

A quiet purpose may not produce amazing and inexplicable events. It may not change world history. But it will give birth to vitality and sustain authenticity in you. And it may lead to some grand scheme of greatness and wonder beyond what you can now imagine. Regardless, living out your quiet purpose is like dropping a pebble into a still pond. The ripples continue long after the pebble has disappeared.

> *Living out your quiet purpose is like dropping a pebble into a still pond. The ripples continue long after the pebble has disappeared.*

Thomas Merton, a man who lived authentic spirituality, writes: "The requirements of a work to be done can be understood as the will of God. If I am supposed to hoe a garden or make a table, then I will be obeying God if I am true to the task I am performing. To do the work carefully and well, with love and respect for the nature of my task and with due attention to its purpose, is to unite myself to God's will in my work."[3]

LIFE WITHOUT PURPOSE

In my college years, I held a retreat for a group of teenagers in Canada's Maritime Provinces. It was the dead of winter. Ice, snow, wind, and deep cold enhanced the sense of isolation.

The religious retreat center had a number of posters on the walls in almost every part of the building. One caught my eye and has lived in my heart all these years. It read, "Jesus went about doing good. It is disconcerting to me that I am content to simply go about."

To "simply go about" your own business, about your own concerns, and about your own problems and challenges is to lock away and lose your true and best self. The quiet purpose flows from authenticity. And, the quiet purpose, whatever the particulars, is always "doing good," and doing good for others brings glory to God. *"For we are God's workmanship, created in Christ Jesus to do good works"* (Ephesians 2:10).

Imagine a grand scheme, a drive to be the best, win the prize, realize the dream, without doing good for others, without reflecting the light of God, without being the salt that preserves goodness and flavors the blandness of daily existence. Jim, a long-time friend of mine, told me his personal story of outward success without an authentic sense of quiet purpose:

He had reached a pinnacle in his skyrocketing career. He had reached the top, literally. The awards banquet spotlighted his achievements, and as part of his reward, he had the top floor penthouse suite in the hotel.

The ride on the elevator to the penthouse was interrupted only once when it stopped on the eighth floor where he said goodbye to a couple of men who were also in sales. He received a final congratulation from his co-workers as the elevator door closed. He resumed his ride to the top, lost in his own thoughts. As the numbers of the floors flashed by, a series of new thoughts surprised his mind: "How did I get here? How did I really get here? What have I done? What has happened to me? Who am I? What am I becoming?"

The room at the top had all the anticipated elegance in furnishings and subdued lighting as well as the expected distractions of the latest electronics, whirlpool, and in-room bar. But he was struck by something else, something unexpected. The immense size of the room released the feeling of emptiness in his soul.

Turning to a full-length mirror by the door, my friend looked at his reflection and said aloud, "I don't know who you are, but I am pretty sure I don't like you."

What kind of life do you want to create? Henry David Thoreau wrote in *Walden's Pond*, "Most men lead lives of quiet desperation." It is a tragedy to go to the grave with your song yet unsung, with your quiet purpose never voiced.

It is also life's triumph, love's triumph, when you live true to your best in Christ, following your path with deep commitment to God's quiet purpose for you. Here is the wonder of it: Your faithfulness as you trust and obey advances God's great vision for His world and His kingdom.

GOD'S PURPOSE FOR YOU

What a wonderful offer. God, the creator, chooses to partner with you in the creation of your life. You and I would do well to respond, "Lord, what would you like to create of my life?" This is the search for God's will. Stephen Bryantl provides insight:

> The word "will" as in "God's will" comes from a Greek word that carries feeling and even passion. When we say "What is God's will?" we are asking, "What is God's deep, heartfelt desire for our lives and our world? What does this God who loves us want for us above all? What is God committed to accomplishing on our behalf no matter what the cost?" [4]

> *What a wonderful offer. God, the creator, chooses to partner with you in the creation of your life.*

When I was young, I debated and discussed and at times had meaningful dialogue concerning the will of God. It is natural to do so when life presents too many choices, choices that cannot be avoided: "What will be your major? Who will you date seriously? Where will you apply for work or graduate school?" It was comforting to think that some right combination of decisions would send life rattling down the right track. Like most young people in my religious tradition, we considered this right set of decisions to be God's will.

That was several decades ago. Through perspective and maturity, my own fumbling and failing, as well as mountain-top experiences, I have come to hear, understand, and experience God's will as an extension of His invitation to live in Him. This is the foundation of the inner life. As we respond in faith to God's gracious invitation, we come to treat life, all of life, as sacred. We root our lives and rest our souls in His love. It is His will to be our God. In the spiritual mystery of the life, death, and resurrection of Jesus, the door opens to life in God. The resurrected and glorified Christ makes the offer: *"Here I am! I stand at the door and knock. If anyone hears my voice and opens the door, I will come in ... "* (Revelation 3:20). His will is two-fold; He desires that you live *in* Him and *through* Him.

First, His voice calls us to know Him intimately, to live in Him. It is His will that we place our eternal self-hood in His love. The tangible world pulls us away, but we must intentionally and persistently return to our inward home in God. It is a relationship He wants with us. It is the Spirit of Christ, God's Spirit with us that reminds, restores, and revitalizes.

Second, His voice calls us to live true to our best through Him. It is His will that we cooperate with Him in creating a life that is true to our best in Christ. He wants us to know who we are in Christ, how He has uniquely knit us together, that we may be a light in darkness and that He shines through us in our generation. It is our quiet purpose that He guides and matures us for His glory.

In my tradition, at least in my youth, the emphasis was on the *second* voice: "what am I to do *through* God." However, set adrift from the first voice, living in God, His will degenerates into "what will I do *for* God." This is not a partnership in creating life. This is a truncated existence, an attempt to appease the celestial CEO. This is a self-made-man who worships himself as his own creator. It is a spiritual façade concealing inner emptiness.

God wants to create full life for you and me. It is life *in* and *through* God.

It is a grand project. We so quickly look at outcome rather than process; we look at results to the neglect of relationship. When a father and son build a tree house together, it is not just the tree that is changed, but the relationship of father and son. When Jesus called his twelve disciples, it was into a relationship: *"He appointed twelve ... that they might be **with** him, and that he might **send** them ..."* (Mark 3:14). The first call is to friendship with Jesus, spiritual intimacy and union, to live in God.

> We look at results to the
> neglect of relationship.

If you ask God, "What kind of life do you want to create for me?" the Lord's first and lasting answer is "I want a living and loving relationship with you." This has been God's plan from creation. He created a perfect place where He would walk and talk with Adam and Eve *"in the cool of the day"* (Genesis 3:8).

His desire is to be our God, and we will be His people.⁵ This is the path of full life. This is Jesus declaring, *"I have come that you might have life and have it to the full"* (John 10:10). The source of all life is God. Jesus gives us His life that we might have life in God. This is the kind of life God wants to create in you. God is intent on creating, nurturing, and developing a love relationship with us. He will be our God, and we will be His people.

> God's people were slaves in Egypt. He heard their cries and came to save them, to *"take them as my own people;"* (Exodus 6:7) they were to be *"his treasured possession"* (Deuteronomy 7:6).
>
> When the nation of Israel was led into exile, God repeated His purpose: *"I will be their God, and they will be my people"* (Jeremiah 31:33, also Ezekiel 11:20).
>
> The people returned to the land of Israel and began to rebuild the nation. Again, God reminds them that *"they will be my people, and I will be faithful and righteous to them as their God"* (Zechariah 8:8, also Zechariah 13:9).
>
> With the birth of Jesus, the purpose of God not only continued but expanded to include all people: *"I will call them 'my people' who are not my people"* (Romans 9:26, also Acts 15:14).
>
> God's purpose is a reality for us today; we are His and He is

ours: *"But you are a chosen people, a royal priesthood, a holy nation, a people belonging to God, that you may declare the praises of him who called you out of darkness into his wonderful light. Once you were not a people, but now you are the people of God; once you had not received mercy, but now you have received mercy"* (1 Peter 2:9-10).

The Bible closes with an image of the day when our relationship with God will be complete and eternal, the day when heaven and earth are one, *"And I heard a loud voice from the throne saying, 'Now the dwelling of God is with men, and he will live with them. They will be his people, and God himself will be with them and be their God'...He said to me ...'He who overcomes will inherit all this, and I will be his God and he will be my son'"* (Revelation 21:3, 7).

It is an awesome and holy thing to create life with God. God creates a quiet purpose within you that flows from your relationship with Him. It is uniquely yours. Your being and doing are aligned in His relationship with you. God creates a life that is true to your best. He calls for your commitment and perseverance.

UNIQUELY AUTHENTIC

God creates from the inside out. In the simplest of terms, your uniqueness is in who you are as a person and what you do with your life. It requires both, doing and being. There is no hope, no vision, no purpose served unless you put your heart into it. For example, a teenager resentfully sits down to a family meal. Mother requested that the family should "be together for dinner." The angry adolescent has other plans, quickly gulps down his food, and bounds out the door. He does what is required, but his inner being did not come to the table.

Consider the middle manager who is ordered to provide "conflict training for the team to deal with buried tensions and disagreements in the group." An outside consultant is brought in, attendance is mandated, and the series of conflict training seminars commence. In a follow-up meeting the manager eyes everyone on the team and declares with a note that disavows contradiction: "I think we are all doing much better. Does everyone agree?" His piercing tone silences any objection. He provided conflict training, he accomplished the assignment, but his inner *being* did not participate.

For your authentic uniqueness to take on significance, you must put your heart into it. There are businesses, schools, and organizations around the world seeking ways to help, encourage, cajole, demand, monitor, and measure whether people are "fully engaged." They want them to be "committed," to have the right "dispositions," or receive an "attitude adjustment." They are not doing this for the souls of their employees, but to advance the organization and the enterprise.

God has another plan. For the sake of your life in Him, He engages your soul in discovering and carrying out your unique calling, your quiet purpose, to live true to your best in Christ. Your *being* and *doing* come out of a loving relationship with God. Below is a description of aligning the inward and outward life:

- ➢ Being is living in God; doing is action in the world.
- ➢ Being is finding spiritual meaning; doing is applying spiritual meaning.
- ➢ Being is God's call of love; doing is my characteristic response.
- ➢ Being is restoring my inner life; doing is investing my energy.
- ➢ Being is focused on the present moment; doing is focused on the outcome.
- ➢ Being is resting in God's compassion; doing is service to others.

TRUE TO YOUR BEST

With alignment in God's will to live *in* and *through* Him, your quiet purpose comes to the surface. Your quiet purpose is lived out through your God-given talents, gifts, and graces. Living true to your best appears in a variety of forms. It may be tied to special abilities or skills. You may be excellent at managing time and resources. Some people produce results by motivating others with confidence and optimism. Others make their contribution by confronting tough issues and facing harsh realities.

You may be the person others depend on to get the job done. Or you may make a measurable difference as you courageously embrace change. Some make their contribution by rallying others to work for a better future while others provide the quiet gift of practical service.

You fulfill your quiet purpose through your unique abilities, talents, and gifts. Your relationship with God unites your "being" and "doing" in a way that is true to your best in Christ. Your true and best brings lasting value to others. Maya Angelou, a great African American poet, shares her wisdom, "I've learned that people will forget what you said, people will forget what you did, but people will never forget how you made them feel."[6]

It is not just your gift, but the way you give it.

It is not just the action you take, but your attitude as well.

It is not just your results, but the quality of your character.

It is not just your work, but the way you treat people.

It is not just your success, but the wisdom you share.

Living true to your best inspires those who feel defeated. It showers significance on the ones who feel worthless. You help people feel secure instead of vulnerable and loved rather than rejected. You help others change their perspective, emotions, and motivations. You help them hear God in their own souls.

This is the life God wants to create with you from the inside out. It is founded on a loving relationship with Him. It is motivated and directed by the quiet purpose He places within you a purpose He nurtures and nudges by His Spirit. It is lived as your being and doing are true to your best in Christ. God is fully committed to you. What He requires is your full commitment to Him.

WISHIN' AND HOPIN'

What kind of life do you want to create? It is not a question of idle fancy. This query demands dedication and passion. It is more than longing; it is a pledge. To long for a large sum of money, for a new home, for better health or better days can easily degenerate into a wish. A wish looks for a path that sidesteps pain and effort. It is a yearning for something bad or uncomfortable to go away. It is a craving for something grand and pleasurable to appear magically. The longing seeks a fanciful way to bypass tears, sidestep sweat, and avoid shedding blood.

I have asked many business groups, "If you had one wish, what would it be?" The most common answer is consistent across the country. People say, "I want to win the lottery." It is America's image of living on a wish.

People wish upon a star, a birthday candle, or a coin in a fountain. Wishing is a childlike response to life's obstacles. It can and usually is innocent and playful. You wish your favorite ball team would win the series. You wish for a raise that will solve your money troubles. You wish for a new car, a new house, or a new life.

> *Left to fester and ferment, a mentality of wishing draws you into the role of a victim.*

Left to fester and ferment, a mentality of wishing draws you into the role of a victim. The early symptoms are envy, blame, or a feeling of entitlement. Wishing for a life you don't have is not an act of creation. It is an escape, another mechanism of defense against the fears and pain of life. It is a sad thing to waste life upon a wish. The lingering handicap of wishful living is often the result of limiting voices first heard in childhood and then echoed in the adult interaction of family and work.

"You are not good enough."
"You are not smart enough."
"You will be hurt again."
"You are a disappointment."
"You deserve your pain."

It is a mystery, a mystery of truth that *the voices of false limitations often mark the spot where genuine hope lies buried.* Hope does not avoid pain and effort but takes them as comrades in the act and art of creating life. It embarks on a path of blood, sweat, and tears, but also goodness, mercy, and joy.

Think of it: your hope for today, tomorrow, and eternity is in Christ. In your pain, failure, and disappointment *"God has chosen to make known…the glorious riches of this mystery, which is Christ in you, the hope of glory"* (Colossians 1:26-27). The music of the first stars of creation reverberates in your soul: You are created by God, you are loved by God, and you are kept by God.

The soul brokers a meeting between you and the Almighty. The agenda is clear enough: What will you create with your life? To meet with God for such a discussion is both fearful and wonderful.[7] For that is how you are made and how life is formed. This will take spiritual courage and commitment. It takes faith. The One who loves you, who created you, wants to get His hands on you, *"like clay in the hand of the potter"* (Jeremiah 18:6). You willingly surrender: *"We are the clay, you are the potter; we are the work of your hand"* (Isaiah 64:8). It is here your hope is born.

Hope is unique. The soul will have no cookie-cutter dream, no paint-by-number vision. Your best hope is born in your unique truth: talents, traits, friends, family, personality, tragedies, and victories. It is your story. Wishing for another story will harm you. Accept your own story. In it, you find your greatness.

Here is another mystery of truth: *your pain and failures point to your potential.* Personal pain marks the path of deep passion. The closed door opens new possibilities. Your broken heart is the means of bringing healing to others. You see it. It is the hand of God at work on your behalf. It is not that God caused the pain and failure, but God takes it as it is and creates something wonderful of it.

It is not God who creates calamity. There is evil in the world and the human heart. There are always those who see God's fingerprints on the fuselage of a downed airliner or a crumpled car in a ditch. This is eternal nonsense and evil deception. God is both great and good. He can do all things; all He does is good. You cannot separate these two truths. Neither can your mind hold them together. In the face of your personal tragedies, pains, and disappointments, it makes no sense. Yet the soul is up to the challenge. Fueled with God's love, great faith, and lasting hope, the soul makes sense of it. The soul finds the spiritual meaning in it.

To nurture your hope is to walk where the trail blends your talents and traits with your pain and passion. In this place hope declares, "I know what I must make of my life, for I see what God is creating in my life." Your soul is not a slick marketer who manufactures a product to meet the world's demands. Your soul points toward a hope from God, both terrifying and magnificent. You see the potential.

> *To nurture your hope is to walk where the trail blends your talents and traits with your pain and passion.*

These mysteries of truth require practical care: **hope matures through boundaries and limits.** False voices would limit your potential. True wisdom engages limits that make the dream possible. What you want to create with your life must be faithfully wed to what you need to live true to your best in Christ. In every challenge, true limits and boundaries identify and implement what is needed to create the life you envision. It requires pain and effort.

To succeed in one endeavor necessitates neglecting another. On the path of your true potential, you can do great things, but you cannot do everything. You must limit time, energy, and resources by focusing on your true path. It takes structure, organization, habits, routines, and discipline to realize your hope. This is what you need. Now, make it specific for your life, the life you and God are creating.

> ➤ What do you need to keep yourself motivated when it is tempting to give up?
> ➤ What do you need to develop the skills and strength required to fulfill your calling?
> ➤ What do you need to delay gratification in pursuit of living true to your best in Christ?
> ➤ What do you need to follow through rather than give up in the face of hardship?

When hope is grounded in your true potential and boundaries provide genuine support, you are living and growing true to your best.

The look alike houses of the post war building boom gave way to an expression of uniqueness in each home. The uniqueness reflected a vision of life and family. Uniqueness turned the house into a home. Do not conform to a life stunted in the tangible, beholden to expectations and demands, or controlled by false and evil voices. Look on the love of God, surrender to Him and be changed: *"in view of God's mercy...be transformed"* (Romans 12:1-2).

God, our gracious and loving Father, gives us the gift of Himself, God in Christ. We can live as authentic Christians. The meaning of life is rooted in His love. Our personal value is found in Him. And the uniqueness of your life and mine is the path of our calling. These are God's gifts to His children.

But what if the child wants the gift but not the Father? What if the child demands the inheritance and then wastes it in a far off country? This is the story of the prodigal son. I know the story. I was a prodigal. I know the *soul crisis*. We will explore it in the next section.

PART 2

SOUL CRISIS

Give us this day our daily bread,
Forgive us our trespasses
As we forgive those who trespass against us,
And lead us not into temptation,
But deliver us from the evil one.

MATTHEW 6:11-13

CHAPTER 6

SOUL CRISIS

God is foolishly in love with us, it seems he has forgotten heaven
and earth and all his happiness and deity, his entire business
seems to be with me alone, to give me everything to comfort
me; He gives it to me suddenly, He gives it to me wholly,
He gives it to me perfectly, He gives it all the time
and He gives it to all creatures.
Why are you not aware of it? Because you are not
at home in the soul's inmost center.
MEISTER ECKHART (1260—1328)[1]

When my divorce became public knowledge, it was a devastating moment. There had never been a divorce in my family, and the family did not know what to do with me. For months, I did not hear from them. Some people I had known for years seemed to respond with concern and interest. Sometime later I discovered that they were primarily gleaning information to enlarge and embellish as they gossiped across the phone lines. The people at work were very gracious, supportive, and kind, but many did not know what to do or what to say. I felt isolated.

There had been times, indeed many years, when my life both inward and outward were aligned, open, genuine, and true to my best in Christ. God had worked through me to touch the lives and encourage the souls of many people. However, something happened to me, something deep and painful, that resulted in a broken home and marriage. Still, the brokenness was even deeper and more pervasive. My spiritual home, my inward dwelling place with God, had been dismantled.

I had a home that was not my own, a place to go and be welcomed as family. My friends, Rod and Cindy, provided what I needed most: quiet times in a safe place. It was a four-hour drive from my work to their house. I made the trip so often it became a routine. When I left work on a Friday evening and headed toward their home, a change came over me. I called it my "ten mile limit." When I was ten miles away from work, ten miles closer to my friends, I started feeling better, thinking more clearly, and growing in strength.

Rod and Cindy accepted me. They let me talk and cry. They allowed me to be uncertain and ambivalent. I found enough quietness to touch my deepest feelings, enough safety to be transparent. I remember one incident particularly.

It was Christmas. I had nowhere to go, at least no family home. I learned that people who are not your family can take care of you. Rod and Cindy invited me to their house for Christmas. It was a beautiful dwelling in southwest Michigan, fully decorated for the season, and the season packed with joy and celebration. They followed a schedule of family gatherings. Food, gifts, stories, and laughter abounded.

In the midst of this revelry, I showed up. I was a mess. I cried incessantly and pined away and carelessly wandered off without warning. My presence was the antithesis of the season. My divorce had been finalized two months earlier. People I had known for years broke off contact.

I had received a heart-breaking letter of judgment and rejection and felt ashamed and exposed. That year, I had winter without Christmas.

It was a sad, frightening experience to realize that I had lost touch with God's presence. I had lost not only my marriage and family, but also my inner home in God. It was my soul's crisis. I know that God longs to make His home in you and me. This is the grand story throughout the whole of the Bible, that the Lord of Love desires to be our God and we are to be His people. This is authentic life from the inside out.

Your spiritual home is the repository of spiritual authenticity. Your spiritual home is the inward place where you are true before God and yourself, and you choose to be your best in Christ. To be at home in spiritual authenticity is to be honest and open with God and yourself about your inner life and your choices. To be at home in your soul is to submit your inner life to the loving judgment, forgiveness, cleansing, and healing of God in Christ.

The Bible begins with a picture of our first parents, Adam and Eve, living in a beautiful home, the Garden of Eden. They rejected God's loving truth and choose to follow Satan's lie. They ate the forbidden fruit, realized their failure, and hid from God. They lost their home. The whole of the Bible is the story of God calling us home again.

Through Abraham and three generations of his dysfunctional family life, God called them to come home. For generations, the people lived in Egypt, yet God brought them out and to the land, the home, He promised. Through kings and prophets, God persistently called them to spiritual authenticity, a kingdom, a home for His people. In a grand moment, the greatest moment in history, a baby was born. Jesus made His home with us and offers God's home to all people. The last chapter of the Bible is a picture of Heaven descending to earth and God's people, at last, are safely at home in God.

It was a Sunday evening ritual in the church where I grew up. We almost always sang the same verse of the same hymn after the pastor's message. It was a continual reminder that we all need to quiet our hearts, open our souls and come home again to Christ.

> Softly and tenderly, Jesus is calling
> Calling for you and for me.
> See on the portals He's waiting and watching,

Watching for you and for me.
Come home, come home
Ye who are weary come home.
Earnestly, tenderly, Jesus is calling
Calling, "Oh sinner, come home."[2]

On the family room floor in Rod and Cindy's home, under the Christmas tree and before the open fire, I formed a picture of what I desired, a picture of home within me and around me:

I want a place to speak the truth and live in love.
I want a place to stand tall and fall on my face.
I want a place that protects my limits and my dreams.
I want a place to be alone and with you.
I want a place to laugh aloud and cry in silence.
I want a place to hush the rush and fan the flames.
I want a place that hears my whisper and echoes my shout.
I want a place to face my worst and be my best.
I want a place to be utterly real and utterly fearless.
I want a place that takes me in and sends me out.
I want a place to speak my mind and listen to my heart.
I want a place of peaceful sleep and inner renewal.
I want a place to speak my fears and find my courage.
I want a place to live the truth and die in love.

THE BATTLE: AUTHENTIC VS. EFFECTIVE

To live with spiritual authenticity is a challenge; at times it is a battle. The battle has been described as the contest between good and evil, light and dark, the King of Heaven and the Prince of this World. These are cosmic descriptions of the eternal struggle for your soul and the soul of humanity. But, how are we to understand this in our daily life and our inner life?

The common tradition in my faith, especially as a child and possibly for the faith of any child, was to turn the spiritual battle into a set of rules and reg-

ulations, a set of *dos and don'ts*. You could be sure you were on the side of good
as long as you followed the rules. If you broke
the rules, you were easy prey for the evil one.

> *To live with spiritual
> authenticity is a
> challenge; at times
> it is a battle.*

In my adult struggle to deal with my broken life, I needed more than theology that was
truncated into a list of behaviors, *dos and
don'ts*. I knew it was possible to follow rules
and still live in darkness. A person can do the right thing outwardly and be
filled with anger and evil on the inside. I needed a more personal and meaningful way of understanding the battle in my soul.

I discovered a way of expressing the conflict. It is two words: *authentic* and
effective. You and I want both. To be authentic is to follow the soul's purpose,
to be true to our best in Christ. We want to be *authentic* in personal relationships, our quality of character, the pursuit of a life mission, and our growth in
mature wisdom. God's presence, echoing in our soul, calls and creates our true
and best in Christ, our spiritual authenticity.

You and I also want to be *effective*, to have productive working relationships, to do a good job in our assignments, to accomplish our professional and
personal goals, to meet or exceed required expectations, and to acquire a
reward that will make a meaningful difference for ourselves and those in our
care. Effectiveness is the ticket to bread and belonging in this world. It is the
means of advancement and practical security.

Many times authenticity and effectiveness
go hand-in-hand. Imagine the faces of the
people who make a positive and meaningful
impact on your life. Are they not authentic?
Authenticity revives relationships, enlivens
courage, energizes confidence, and restores

> *When you are forced to
> choose between
> authenticity and
> effectiveness, you are in a
> battle for your soul.*

perspective. Authenticity is essential to healthy relationships. It is effective to
be straight up and real. When faced with a challenge of integrity, success is
choosing what is true and best.

However, there is another scenario that is also true to life. There are situations when authenticity and effectiveness are at odds. You cannot imagine
how living true to your best will produce the desired result; the truth offends

people in power; mature wisdom is rejected as too costly; toxic relationships rule the family; duplicity is the norm in the sales office. When you are forced to choose between authenticity and effectiveness, you are in a battle for your soul.

Will you compromise your authenticity for the sake of expediency?
Will you ignore your values to satisfy someone in authority?
Will you cheat your integrity to bring home the contract?
Will you put your health in harm's way to reach the goal?
Will you bury your better judgment to go along with the boss?
Will you sacrifice your true and best for bread and belonging?

This battle for the soul is a crisis for all people of faith. You want to live true to your best in Christ. You desire to be authentic; you want who you are to be in alignment with what you say and do. This is integrity. It is not a convenient world for spiritual authenticity. We will look at this battle through 1) the results of research, 2) practical experience, 3) spiritual dynamics, and 4) the promise of Christ.

RESEARCH RESULTS

I was a lead member of a research team at Ashland Theological Seminary,[3] Ashland, Ohio, that studied the emotional and spiritual vitality and weariness of ministers. It was a three-year study with over a hundred pastors, both men and women. Our method involved multiple interviews, psychological assessments, interventions and observations. The study became the foundation for a Lilly grant that funded an ongoing seminar, retreat, and mentoring program in spiritual and practical leadership for ministers.

We discovered that the practical and frustrating struggle these ministers faced was to be effective in managing and leading the church while at the same time to be genuine in their spiritual and relational life. The majority of the ministers we studied felt they were not winning the battle between effectiveness and authenticity. They were prey to unhealthy relational patterns, over-dependency or co-dependency, and a lack of satisfaction in their spiritual lives.

After several years of study, I presented our findings at the National Convention of the American Association of Christian Counselors in Nashville, Tennessee. The room was packed with clergy—men and woman—as well as therapists who work primarily with clergy. I presented the battle between effective and authentic. I know it had been my battle, and I knew it was the struggle of many of my brothers and sisters in the ministry.

Appreciation for the presentation was heartfelt. Many remained in the room after the seminar, lining up in order to talk with me. Finally, the line got down to one gentleman who was obviously waiting to be the last to speak with me. He introduced himself and said he was here with his wife, the counselor in the family. He was attending the convention with her, but made his living in the corporate world. I asked him why he selected this particular seminar, and he said it sounded interesting. Then, he said he had something to tell me: "I know you studied ministers, but what you described is the way it is for everyone. Everybody I know is fighting the battle of being effective while trying to remain authentic."

PRACTICAL EXPERIENCE

For me, the practical experience of the effective/authentic conflict entered my soul through the window of personal transparency. I find something wonderful about speaking from my heart, sharing my emotions, perceptions, and motivations with openness, transparency and vulnerability.

At a coffee shop I overheard an exchange between a regular customer and the proprietor as they discussed a mutual acquaintance.

"He is the most authentic person I know," observed the shop owner.

The customer responded, "Isn't that refreshing?"

We applaud personal transparency. It often encourages transparency in others. Yet it can also be a point of attack on the inner life. *First,* modern life moves too fast for authentic transparency. When people ask "how are you," they do not mean they actually want to know. The pace of modern life out strips the purpose of the soul.

> The pace of modern life out strips the purpose of the soul.

You are rewarded for moving at a pace that meets expectations but leaves the tender connections between your inner and outer world strained and frayed. The whirl of demands leaves little time to inquire into the well-being of your own soul, let alone the soul of your friend or spouse.

Second, it takes wisdom to be authentically transparent in the world. External transparency must be appropriate to the situation. Inappropriate self-disclosure carries lasting consequences. Only the youngest child or most ill equipped adult does not put a monitor between mind and mouth. You should not speak every thought or follow every impulse. To do so is not true and best, but childish, foolish, and selfish. Wise expressions of transparency require compromise and negotiation; it means being appropriate for the situation.

You swallow an opinion for the sake of friendship. You tell yourself to "let it slide" in order to keep the peace. You agree with authority in spite of misgivings. The normal give and take of life requires compromise. Great and common wisdom teaches the necessity of negotiation: Lose the battle to win the war; choose the right moment.[4] It is right to speak the truth, but we should *"speak the truth in love"* (Ephesians 4:15). Danger threatens when these practical and external negotiations lead to internal compromise.

Third, there are toxic people who take advantage of your moments of personal transparency. They use your openness to target your vulnerability. They read feelings, doubts, and hopes, then spin them in ways that promote their own agenda. They cannot be trusted. Jesus warns, *"Do not give dogs what is sacred; do not throw your pearls to pigs. If you do, they may trample them under their feet, and then turn and tear you to pieces"* (Matthew 7:6).

The world is vested in effectiveness rather than authenticity. In some situations and with some individuals or organizations, authentic people are *"like sheep among wolves."* Jesus understood the battle: *"Therefore, be as shrewd as snakes and as innocent as doves"* (Matthew 10:16).

Authentic transparency *requires* wisdom. The core of authenticity is to know yourself and to know God, but that doesn't mean it is necessary to let others know everything about you right now. Be authentic and in wisdom choose when, where, how and to whom you will be transparent.

> *Fear is the battle field on which you fight for your soul.*

But, when does all this—the speed of life, the careful negotiations, the toxic people—become a threat to spiritual authenticity? Fear is the enemy. You were transparent. Someone took advantage of your openness and hurt you, broke your confidence, twisted your meaning, or belittled you. You opened your heart and someone poured poison into it. Danger approaches when the practicalities of personal transparency cultivate inner anxiety. Fear is the battle field on which you fight for your soul.

SPIRITUAL DYNAMICS

To compromise spiritual authenticity is to turn from light to dark, from good toward evil. It is a path that saps spiritual vitality, harms relationships, leads to a compromise in character and to a loss of purpose, your soul's purpose. This is soul crisis. Confront the crisis with a combination of inner courage and mature wisdom.

> *When driven and pursued by fear, concealing yourself from others may eventually lead to losing touch with yourself and hiding from God.*

Fear drives you away from your true and best self. Fear pursues you through the seductive power of falsehood. When driven and pursued by fear, concealing yourself from others may eventually lead to losing touch with yourself and hiding from God. Being false to yourself inevitably means being false to God. This is what happened to Adam and Eve, who *"hid from the Lord God"* (Genesis 3:8). The purpose of the soul is under attack.

You ignore your inner wisdom.
You ignore emotional warning signs.
You can no longer name your motivation.
You betray your heart's values.
You break your deepest principles.

How does this happen? How do we lose touch with our authentic self? It is not in a moment. It is a creeping falsehood that eats like an undetected cancer. We ignore the signs and avoid the doctor. We don't want an honest diagnosis for fear the news is bad. We look the other way and the cancer grows.

Some look the other way by clinging to their own perspective as the one-and-only valid point of view. Inward falsehood arrives as they turn a deaf ear to God's wisdom expressed through the insights and actions of others. They hold to their own viewpoint and motivation, not because it is best, but because it maintains their sense of power. In doing so, they turn a deaf ear to the soul. The self-deception achieves the goals: It temporarily protects from pain and provides fleeting comforts and pleasures. It is a false promise of a shortcut to success. Engage in a little larceny. Betray a few friends. Set aside the greater good for personal greed. In a little while the way of fools looks like the great, wide way to all desires.

Others risk their authenticity with an opposite strategy. Inner fears and falsehood are drowned out by the expectations and demands of others that blare at an unhealthy level of decibels. They abandon their individuality and become enmeshed in the needs and emotions of family members, friends, or authority figures. They cannot hear or will not listen to their own voice. They settle for what it takes to get by rather than flourish. They maintain their rewards and meet expectations at the sacrifice of their true and best self. They drown out the voice of God's inner wisdom.

The soul's priority remains steadfast: *Authenticity is a prerequisite to effectiveness.* The soul chooses to make genuineness the main concern. The soul is committed to healthy choices, life-giving choices. But these decisions are seldom easy or clear.

The battle for spiritual meaning in life does not take place on a mountain top of clear vision and obvious options. The soul's struggle for spiritual meaning takes place in the dark valley of shadows, swamp, and fog where choices are unclear and confusing. In the dark valley, attacks and challenges to your true and best self do not announce themselves. They simply show up. They are uninvited opponents in the midst of the unstructured mess you are trying to sort out. At that moment, the problems are so real that the battle to maintain spiritual meaning is often relegated to the sidelines or perhaps unheeded altogether. It is easy to justify: "I will solve the problem and then get back to my soul matters."

> *The soul's struggle for spiritual meaning takes place in the dark valley of shadows, swamp, and fog.*

However, all solutions are temporary. Most problems don't stay solved. Solutions evolve into other problems. Solving problems requires reason and compromise, but the more threatening menace, the danger in disguise, is the problem within the problem. It is not just the external compromises but the inward ones that signal the warning. It is tempting to compromise spiritual authenticity, values, uniqueness, and the spiritual center of life. Inward compromise drains inner strength and vitality.

This is soul crisis. Spiritual meaning is lost in a desperate search for temporary solutions. Uniqueness gives way to the demanding, commanding and conforming powers and pressures of daily stress. Personal worth and esteem totter on the tipping rock of producing results.

The soul will compromise the effectiveness of a solution, but a healthy soul, as God intended, will never compromise spiritual authenticity. However, the reverse is the dangerous temptation, to compromise spiritual authenticity for the sake of an effective reprieve. The price seems reasonable. Be careful. Read the small print, "Your interest rate and service charges may change without notice."[5]

TO TURN ASIDE FOR A MOMENT

The soul crisis is individual, but it is also epidemic. In glass buildings and factories, public schools and parishes, the demand is the same: "Do more with less." The effective/authentic conflict is expanding. Note this observation from *Fortune* magazine:

> Executives generally aren't an introspective lot, but at the dawn of the new economy—with no job security or clear career path, with more responsibility and less certainty than ever—stressed-out managers increasingly are turning inside for answers.[6]

You take a job that suffocates you, carry out an order that grates against good judgment, or put up with toxic relationships that slowly drip poison into your soul. You turn away from the uniqueness of your calling.

> The conference room was lavishly furnished with the trappings of success and authority. Wood paneling, leather chairs, crystal wine glasses, and original paintings portrayed success and power. The room was empty of people except for a woman in a tailored suit and her consultant who wore an off-the-rack sport coat.
> Rain drops splattered against the large window panes and slid downward under the force of gravity. The droplets joined together to form a chaotic collection of interesting rivulets, ever shifting from right to left, left to right, but always downward, downward, downward.
> She sighed. Focusing on the rain drenched window, her eye followed one drop as it slid on the window pane, first this way and then that, until it disappeared from view. Still staring at the window, she reflected on her own journey: "I turned my face away from my dream for only a moment. I promised myself that I would get back to it. That was twenty years ago."

It seems impossible to go back again. One compromise leads to another. The next decision is easier. The third becomes a pattern. In time, a person loses touch with the inner life, the soul.

You choose the path of effectiveness at the cost of your authentic self. You are quite reasonable to protect your bread and belonging, meet expectations, and gain rewards. However, when you compromise what is inside you, you place the soul's purpose in peril. There is something more at work here. You have responsibilities as your soul's partner. Take stock and assess your contribution to the partnership:

> Am I neglecting the source of spiritual meaning in my life?
> Am I placing my eternal value in harm's way?
> Am I abandoning my unique calling in order to fit in or stand out?

When you negotiate with your soul, negotiate carefully. All is on the table. Your soul will not surrender your true and best in Christ. Christ is with you, in you, and for you.

THE PROMISE OF CHRIST

To come home, home to God, home to your soul, is a journey that begins with spiritual awakening. Jesus crafted an eloquent story of the lost coming home. It is the story of the *Prodigal Son* (Luke 15:11-24). It begins as a story of running away from home.

A certain man had two sons, and the younger of them said to the father, "Father, give me my portion of the inheritance." The father divided his wealth between his two boys.

And not many days later, having gathered all his new riches, the younger son went abroad to a far country. There he scattered his wealth and lived riotously. He spent all he had.

There came a great and prolonged famine on that country. With no money left, he had no bread to eat and no place to belong. With no other alternative, he became a servant to one of the citizens of that country. His employer sent him to the fields to feed the pigs.

The young man was so hungry and discouraged that he was willing to eat the same husks he was feeding the hogs. But the employer would not allow it. The young man wallowed in misery.

The story is about our relationship with God, our Father. The young man wanted the Father's blessings but not the Father's home. To adapt Douglas

Steere's image, this is like trying to water a broomstick in the hopes of grow-ing a tree, or tapping into a telephone pole in order to gather sugar for maple syrup. What is the source of real life? Is it a relationship with God or employment in a far country? The young man learned a harsh lesson: The world loves you only when you can effective-ly meet their desires and needs.

> *God loves you, period!*
> *He loves more than*
> *you love and before*
> *you love at all.*

God loves you, period! He loves more than you love and before you love at all. God's love is the meaning of the story. The father loved the son, but the son was not aware of it; as the African proverb says, "When God speaks He does not wake up the sleeper." The son had to be awakened. He needed a spiritual awakening. He had to find his spiritual senses. The story continues:

> As he thought about his situation, he came back to himself. He said, "How many servants of my father have a superabundance of bread, and I am here perishing in hunger!"
>
> The young man's spirit rose within him. He declared, "I will go on home to my father and will say to him, 'Father, I have sinned against heaven and against you. I am no longer worthy to be called your son. Let me be one of your servants.'"

I find the words of Isaac Pennington, a spiritual writer of several hundred years ago, true to my own experience: "There is that near you which will guide you; O, wait for it and be sure that you keep to it."[7] God speaks in our wounds and calls to us in our pain, but the wounds and pain I refer to are far more than physical. They cry out against a pattern of living and call for a source of real care, everlasting love that, as written in the 23ᴿᴰ Psalm, *"restores my soul."*

I have found that it is a gift of grace to recognize God's voice in the pain. Pain is a powerful motivator. It truly drives to distraction. The spiritual chal-lenge is to pay attention. Attention must be linked to action, the action of obe-dience. Without knowing the full measure of his father's love, the son began the journey home.

He rose to his feet and started for home. While he was still a long way off, his father saw him. His father had been watching and waiting for his return. The father looked at his condition and was moved with compassion. He ran to him, hugged and kissed him.

The son began to give the speech as he had prepared it; "Father, I have sinned against heaven and against you. I am no longer worthy to be called your son."

But his father interrupted him. He said to the servants, "Bring the best robe and clothe him. Put the family ring on his hand. Get sandals for his feet. Kill the calf we have been fattening. We will have a feast because my son who was dead is alive again. He was lost and is found. And, the celebration began.

The word *prodigal* means extravagant. The word describes the son's wasteful behavior. Yet, the word also portrays the father's lavish love. It was an extravagant love. Jesus gives us the story of the father's love as an image of God's love. Augustine has a beautiful thought: "We come to God by love, not by navigation."[8] It wasn't the careful speech worked out among the hogs, but the open arms and extravagant love of the father that brought the boy to life again. Notice:

> ➢ Our Father's love looks beyond past hurt.
> ➢ Our Father's love runs to restore us.
> ➢ Our Father's love is quick to forgive.
> ➢ Our Father's love celebrates our return.
> ➢ Our Father's love resurrects our relationship with Him.

The tale of a father and his prodigal son is a story of crisis, soul crisis that leads to spiritual awakening. Spiritual awakening is realizing you are lost and God is looking for you. It always results in greater love for God and greater love for people. An awakening is a grand thing. It is worth celebrating. It is the start of a new day.

> *Spiritual awakening is realizing you are lost and God is looking for you.*

A Dark Night

However, if a new day has dawned, it means you have endured a dark night, a night in which you fought the battle for your soul and won. It was a 3:00 AM moment. I felt utterly alone and abandoned as I sat at the kitchen table. I did not "feel loved" or worthy of love.

In a book of spiritual readings where I found comfort on many occasions, I turned to the words of a writer from the Greek Orthodox Church. He is not a model of excellence in the eyes of the church for he was banished as a heretic. Some of his writings are at the point of offensive. Still, the short piece I read that dark night at the kitchen table was used of God to whisper in my soul, "I am with you."

> My prayer is not the whimpering of a beggar or a confession of love. Nor is it the trivial reckoning of a small tradesman: Give me and I shall give you.
>
> My prayer is the report of a soldier to his general: This is what I did today, this is how I fought to save the entire battle in my own sector, these are the obstacles I found, this is how I plan to fight tomorrow.
>
> My God and I are horsemen galloping in the burning sun or under drizzling rain. Pale, starving, but un-subdued, we ride and converse.
>
> "Leader!" I cry. He turns his face towards me, and I shudder to confront his anguish.
>
> Our love for each other is rough and ready, we sit at the same table, we drink the same wine in this low tavern of life.[9]

The crisis of the soul must be faced to live true to your best in Christ. It is a spiritual awakening that comes after fighting through a dark night. It is facing fear and pain. It is turning away from spiritual distractions, paying attention, and responding to God's call to come home.

How do we lose touch with our inner home? What are the stages? What are the emotions and thoughts that tear us away from our home in God? And, how do we find the path that leads us home? These are the questions we take up in the next chapter.

CHAPTER 7

A LOST SOUL

"They'll take your soul if you let them, don't you let them."
CAROL KING[1]

A startling verse of scripture describes the humanness of Jesus: *"Because he himself suffered when he was tempted, he is able to help those who are being tempted"* (Hebrews 2:18). Jesus knows our points of vulnerability; it is when we are threatened with the loss of our daily means of support, our *bread*, or our relationships at home and work, our *belonging*.[2] Our daily means and the relationships that maintain our earthly existence, our life-style, comfort and survival are portals that expose us to potential threat and temptation. We do not risk our bread and belonging lightly. We all find their potential loss intimidating. This threat is the ground of temptation exploited by the evil one.

It is with a clear and deep understanding of our humanity that Jesus taught us to pray:

> *Give us this day our daily bread,*
> *And, forgive us our trespasses*
> *as we forgive those who trespass against us,*

And lead us not into temptation
but deliver us from the evil one.

A malevolent conspiracy wages against our souls. It attacks through the
tantalizing and titillating offer of rewards and
security, of bread and belonging, if we but sacrifice our authenticity, our true and best in
Christ. It is a fearful thing to discover that
many of those around us want only what we
can produce for their benefit. It is true of all
organizations most of the time. It is also true
of many families and friendships.

> *It is a fearful thing to discover that many of those around us want only what we can produce for their benefit.*

We must consider the enormous pressure on those in the public arena.[3]
Politicians, ministers, and community leaders who conduct their work in the
public eye place their true and best self in a pressure cooker. Their constituents
demand respectable authenticity that conforms to the expectations of the
crowd. However, the scrutiny and criticism that come with the job require an
appearance of effectiveness, whatever the cost. This tension sets up an inner
battle. The casualties are those who side for appearance of success to the detriment of their inner life.

You and I experience the same tension and temptation. For us, the "public platform" may be the workplace or a holiday gathering for the family rather
than a national spotlight. The same enticement to set aside authenticity for
appearing favorable and effective is present, persuasive, and powerful.

THEY WILL STEAL YOUR SOUL

The behavior patterns and motivations that undermine authenticity creep into
friendships and partnerships. This battle is played out in the relationship
between manager and employees, husband and wife, and parent and child. It
is a dark force in human relationships. The world does not always cooperate
with those who choose to live authentically. The grim reality is that organizations, many family members, and most individuals are interested in our

authentic selves only as long as authenticity produces the results that meet their expectations and align with their personal agendas.

It is a tragedy to lose our inner home, to lose touch with our soul's purpose. It is a tragedy to come to the place where we cannot distinguish our true and best self from a false and disfigured imitation. The spiritual meaning, eternal value and unique purpose of life slip from our souls. In its place is codependency on the rewards and expectations the world places on us. This is the battle between spiritual authenticity and the appearance of effectiveness.

Slowly, almost imperceptibly, we lose our grip. A classic picture of the subtle loss of the inner life is the story of the frog in a pan of boiling water:

> The frog is placed in the water. The water is in the pan. The pan is on the stove. The stove is slowly, ever so slowly, warmed from room temperature to tepid to hot and boiling. As the temperature increases, the frog does not notice nor try to escape. The web-footed water animal has an internal thermometer but no thermostat. Its temperature matches its surroundings. It has no mechanism for controlling an internal response to the danger. It remains unaware of the threat as it is boiled alive.[4]

The frog's story was lived out by a young man who finally realized he had betrayed his integrity: "How did this happen to me? I am a good person. I had no idea what they were doing. I trusted the wrong people. They took advantage of me, used me, manipulated and betrayed me. Now, my life is in ruins."

It is tempting to blame. Plenty of blame is available to spread around. Our true and best selves are under attack. The water is hot and growing hotter. Fault can be found in authority figures, family members, and enemies of all descriptions. Culpability—the blows, pain, and harm others have inflicted on us—may be catalogued into "intentional harm" and "unintentional harm," those that "calculate" their evil and those that are merely "clumsy" in human relationships. It all hurts and with each wound the temperature rises.

The battle is on. Blame may help sort out what's happening. It reveals part of the picture, but blame does not change anything. We are still in hot water.

The frog's story is a sad one. The lesson: Blame is a thermometer without a thermostat. It monitors without management. It reports without shouldering responsibility. However, in the soul's battle we are not members of the press, just reporting the facts. We are in the mêlée.

It is ever so tempting to complain that the world is not as it ought to be, that we are the victim of some malicious plot, that people are cruel and heartless. And, to some degree, this is accurate. Such is the reality of a fallen world. The wounds we have experienced, the betrayal, the abuse churns up strong emotions of pain, anger, and vengeance.

A reality check: We must take responsibility to deal with our emotions. We cannot stamp them down, bury them under our work, or hide them in the inner life. We need to express them in order to be released from them. However, simply exploding in anger will not set us free. In fact, it will probably complicate our situation and increase the power of the vengeful emotions.

Perhaps you and I share a religious background that did not acknowledge angry feelings, or, if the feelings were recognized, they were labeled as sinful. Anger is not sin; it is emotion. Anger, like all emotions, sadness, fear, or love, naturally seeks expression and action. It is what you do with your emotion that is healthy or harmful. Feeling vengeful does not mean you must act with vengeance. However, vicious feelings will smolder if you stifle them. In fact, the vengeance is likely to slip out in acts of gossip, inappropriate self-disclosure, or worse.

> *Express your vengeance and act out your rage in the safe presence of Heaven; it is essential for spiritual health and authenticity.*

There is another way: bring your complaints to God. Shout and stomp, weep and wail, complain and lament, express your vengeance and act out your rage in the safe presence of Heaven; it is essential for spiritual health and authenticity. Express your emotions fully and with freedom in the safe presence of God.

The book of Psalms includes a small group of poems that express anger, rage, and wrath.[5] Each of these angry psalms is a prayer, an unusual yet important kind of prayer. In this kind of prayer, you feel the depth of your emotions, express them to God, and believe He will cleanse and heal you. Each lament expresses emotion and faith. Psalm 109 is a lesson in how to express your rage in prayer.

First, tell God what has happened. Tell God the personal and painful details. *"O God …wicked and deceitful men …have spoken against me with lying tongues. With words of hatred …they attack me without cause. In return for my friendship they accuse me …they repay me evil for good and hatred for my friendship"* (Psalm 109:1-5)

Second, fully express your anger and rage. Note that it is safe to express the most vicious feelings in the presence of God. *"Appoint an evil man to oppose him …let him be found guilty …may another take his place of leadership …may his children be fatherless and his wife a widow …may a creditor seize all he has…for he never thought of doing a kindness …he wore cursing as his garments"* (Psalm 109:6-20).

Third, trust God's purpose and peace. Express your rage until you are emotionally spent, until you reach the bottom of your soul; praise will rise from within. *"But you, O Sovereign Lord, deal well with me…out of the goodness of your love, deliver me. For I am poor and needy, and my heart is wounded within me. They may curse, but you will bless…I will greatly extol the Lord; in the great throng I will praise him"* (Psalm 109:21-31).

In the presence of God, it is safe to express your deepest and darkest thoughts and feelings. Trust God with them. Empty your soul before the Lord of Compassion.

THE STEPS OF SOUL LOSS

Losing your soul is not a moment, but a process. It comes in increments like the frog in boiling water, but this is only part of the story. You are not a cold-blooded amphibian. You are a human being with warm red blood pulsing through your veins. You have a soul that signals a parade of warnings. Los-

When you ignore the cries of the soul, you place your true and best self in mortal danger.

ing your soul is not an inevitable tragedy, but the commission of a crime. If you ignore a baby's cries for attention, you will be arrested. When you ignore the cries of the soul, you place your true and best self in mortal danger.

The hermit built a cabin. The cabin was in a lost valley several miles west of Anchorage, Alaska. Anchorage was preparing for a heavy, early snow. Winter was about to pounce. Through a small radio, the hermit heard the forecast. Fear flushed his face. The wood for his winter fire was not cut. He would freeze.

Immediately he took up his chainsaw and attacked last season's fallen trees. Some were still too green to burn now, but would be suitable in the months ahead. Others were dry and ready to provide the life saving heat he needed. All of them needed to be cut, stacked and covered before the storm buried the valley in a merciless blanket of wintry weather.

A problem was quickly apparent. The saw was dull. Sharpen the saw and the job could be accomplished, but the storm was approaching. Dark clouds crawled over the mountains and tumbled into his valley. Was there time to sharpen the saw? Would it not be better to cut with a dull chain? He fired up the saw.

The work was slow and exhausting. The saw jammed in the green, fibrous aspens and fir logs. The dry ones were on the bottom of the pile. A sharp chain would make short work of it. The hermit hesitated between sharpening the saw and the sight of the storm on the mountains. He cursed the dull blade and shivered in the cold wind. The first snowflakes fell.[6]

With each step toward soul loss, the symptoms are more malevolent. The soul sounds its warning and gives instructions—sharpen your saw, strengthen your inner self, hold to what gives life meaning. But your attention is captivated by the storm, the demands, and the expectations. A cold wind whistles through your lonely valley.

Your soul continues to call out. It begins as a gentle reminder to pay attention. It becomes a frantic shout of distress, "come home." Consider the alarms and warnings, the symptoms and signs at each step in the downward cycle of a lost soul.

Step One: Relationships Suffer. Outwardly, you look energized and effective. In dealing with people you are polite, but there is an air of superficiality that wasn't there before. Your inner life is weary and stressful. Your private world is showing signs of confusion and the soul's neglect. You are draining your inner strength.

You are effective, but there is a subtle diminishing of inner vitality. As spiritual lethargy progresses, you react with insensitivity and ungratefulness that is out of character. You are focused on performance to the detriment of the people around you. You don't see it. Friends and co-workers offer excuses because they know you are under a lot of pressure.

Your inner life absorbs the stress, but rather than release it in spiritual care, you retain it and compound it. You hold to slights, nicks, and emotional surface abrasions that don't heal as quickly as they once did. You are more vulnerable to criticism. Relationships at home and work pay the price. Tension and conflict grow. A misspoken word has the potential for creating misunderstanding. People are more guarded around you. You either ignore the emotional isolation or appreciate being left alone. It is not an authentic solitude you seek, but an escape.

Life is out of balance. Listen to your inner wisdom. Attend to the soul's work: you need self-care. Take responsibility for your physical, emotional, mental, social, and spiritual well-being. What restores your inner vitality? What re-ignites your inner passion? Do something for the body and the mind, and do something to nurture your soul. How? Use imagination with reverence.

Stir the soul with imagination. Fly a kite. Attend the opera. Walk the beach and explore the tide pools. Go line-dancing. Browse through a bookstore. Read the Scriptures. Read poetry. Read for fun and inspiration. Go horseback riding. Parachute from a plane. Play the piano. Experiment with a new recipe. Curl up in a chair to watch the fire on a rainy night. What did you like to do as a child? What do you wish you could do now?

Soothe the soul with reverence. Linger in front of a little altar. We have little altars[7] around us: photos on the piano, the shells from the beach on the windowsill, the painting that brings to life a lovely memory, the sight of children at play, or the glory of a setting sun. Speak to God from your heart, as to a friend. Listen to the silence. Little altars are places that remind you of God's gracious presence in your life.

Good self-care opens a path to good soul-care. Without it, you are more likely to take short dips into self-indulgence. You eat too much, drink too much, sleep too long, or play the part of your favorite vegetable on the couch. It's easy to rationalize. There seems to be temporary relief, but the inner vitality is not there.

> *Good self-care opens a path to good soul-care. Without it, you are more likely to take short dips into self-indulgence.*

If you disregard the soul's alarm, you deplete your inner strength faster than you replenish it. You self-indulge rather than take responsibility for your well being. You can justify the indulgence. It has a look of effectiveness, but it is not true to your best. The physical indulgences do not replenish your inner being. You find that before long you indulge yourself mentally and emotionally, nursing slights as you toss in your bed, justifying anger as you argue your case with the bedroom ceiling.

Stage Two: Character Suffers. You vacillate between following the inner words of wisdom and submitting to the pestering clamor of pain. In your outer life you continue to be effective, but you are beginning to appear less capable and more harassed. Your response to people, especially those close to you, becomes either to evade or to command. Your inner life is under pressure. You are vulnerable to your own emotions and thoughts. You start to ruminate. A torrid of fearful, angry, or depressive thoughts flow through your mind, and you are not able to stop them.

In your private world you rationalize by stacking up perceptions and cultivating emotions that justify your motives and actions. You look for ways to release the stress and abate the fear through excessive work or play. You are a workaholic or play-aholic. You are losing touch with your inner life. You sense that you are not yourself.

Your behavior patterns begin to change. The truth is tainted and promises forgotten. Breeches of integrity are justified, excused, or accepted as needful. You still perform at a high level, but a seething, foaming discontent is boiling away inside you. Sometimes people in this stage avoid relating to others, including family. Others defend themselves with a demanding attitude. You may find that you do both.

You do not realize that to your closest friends and co-workers you are exposed. They see what's happening, but you don't. Your unconscious goal is to keep family and friends at arm's length so that they cannot or will not confront you.

In your inner life, you are depressed, fearful, or angry when goals are not met. You sail the sea of blame, pointing out the flaws of others or accusing yourself of not working hard enough, long enough or well enough. You take on too many problems and demand unrealistic results from yourself and others, but you will not look at the problem under the problem—something is troubling your soul.

Criticism, even when shared in love and justified by your behavior, is almost intolerable. Negative thoughts rush through your mind like a train you cannot stop. Over and over you rehearse the same problem, the same criticism, the same sadness, the same failure or the same worry.

Something is missing. At this point it takes more than replenishing inner strength to set you aright. To self-care must be added self-insight. Look at the truth, your personal truth. The soul guides your search through the gift of spiritual-awareness. It is your story, your wounds, your fears, your traits and your talents at work here.

Confront, conquer, and learn from your regrets. Regrets are particularly difficult, especially if you come from an environment where regrets were not a source of learning, but only a matter of blame and control. Either you learned to ignore your regrets, or you learned to be overwhelmed by them. The healthy choice is to wrestle with them. What's happening in you? What's causing it? What can you learn? What can you do to take responsibility to restore your true and best self?

Get in the ring and wrestle with your regret. Choke the truth out of it and learn the lesson you need, the lesson God wants to teach you through your regrettable action. When you have learned the lesson, toss the regret out of the ring and get back to the task of living true to your best. This is self-insight.

> *Get in the ring and wrestle with your regret. Choke the truth out of it and learn the lesson you need.*

However, self-insight is not an attractive pastime. Self-avoidance is the way of least resistance. You keep your eyes on the faults of others rather than digging into your own character flaws. You certainly don't want to dig out the fears crammed into the fractures and fissures in your character.

To compensate, you make resolutions. You determine to be different. You beg forgiveness and are certain you have turned over a new leaf. It works for a while, but the problem under the problem lingers. To keep yourself distracted, you lean harder and longer on other and outer means of support.

You turn a blind eye to what is happening and seek new pain killers. A parade of pleasure producing and pain repressing distractions displays its seductive charms: a dangerous but titillating relationship, larger doses of stimulants or depressants, or irresponsible actions that fire the nerves. Each keeps your face turned away from your soul's cry.

It seems effective. It feels helpful. It is just that the effects is fleeting. Like swatting at a swarm of flies, the distractions are only useful as long as you keep swatting.

Stage Three: Purpose Suffers. At this point, you respect wisdom but obey pain. Something is wrong. Outwardly, you are able to keep up with work, family, and the demands of life most of the time, but dysfunctional behaviors inhibit your effectiveness. You carry a heavy load of pain for which you pay a considerable price.

> *At this point, you respect wisdom but obey pain.*

People who know you and care about you muster the courage to confront you. They see that something is wrong. You respond by being defensive or explosive.

Your inner life is flooded with danger. Thoughts, feelings, and motivations are painful and problematic. It takes more and more energy to resist. In your private world you are secretive and may be immoral in your actions. You are losing the ability to resist the power of impulse. Addictive and dysfunctional behavior wraps its thorny vines around you.

Your purpose in life is embroiled in a battle with momentary impulse. Your approach to tasks at home and work is unfocused and reactionary. Plans are always in turmoil, and strategy is ever changing. You don't know what you want; you just know that want, need, and desire coax you down a seductive path of emptiness. Whatever you do is unsatisfying. The chaos on the inside might be revealed in excessive perfectionism or frazzled disorder. You are just barely able to hold it together.

Often you are defensive in your conversations. Excuses, blame, and fault finding abound. You may turn the blaming inward, but you do so not to take responsibility but to prove that you can't do anything about it. You confess that you care, but "can't help it." Secretly, you wonder if perhaps you don't care after all.

At other times you explode. Anger wells up. You cannot control it. You speak your mind only to discover that your mouth was not connected to your brain. You break things. You strike out at the furniture, the wall, or the people you love. If it is not a physical blow, it is an emotional strike that is cruel. It sickens you. For a moment you are remorseful. You care and want to do something about it, but the impulse passes and you retreat into ignoring or justifying your actions.

Your true and best self is in mortal danger. The soul screams for attention. The path home is reclaimed by discovering and determining life's meaning and purpose. Friends and family fully believe that all you need is a resurgence of self-discipline—simply do what is necessary or sensible without needing to be urged by somebody else. True enough; but you cannot discipline what you do not know, and you do not know yourself. You have lost touch with your true and best self. The inner power of spiritual meaning and divine purpose is lacking.

Rufus Jones, a great soul who mentored many people in the inward way, describes this state: "a lower nature dominates us and spoils our life." It is what the Apostle Paul experienced: *"For I have a desire to do good, but I cannot carry it out. For what I do is not the good I want to do; no, the evil I do not want to do—this I keep on doing"* (Romans 7:18-19).

"The most solemn fact of sin is its accumulation of consequences in the life of the person," writes Rufus Jones. Sin is aiming at what is false and marred rather than what is true and best; it is turning your back on the spiritual meaning of life and living only for the temporal. Each sin wears at your inner life like water falling over sand stone; it carves and molds your nature. Jones concludes, "It weaves a mesh of habit. It makes toward a dominion or as Paul calls it, a law of sin."[8]

Paul concludes his description of life under the habit or law of sin with this insight: *"So then, I myself in my mind am a slave to God's law, but in the sinful nature a slave to the law of sin"* (Romans 7:25). It is not self-discipline that breaks the law of sin, but turning and trusting the power of God in Christ to make all things new. The most potent words to express it are repentance and conversion. It is what E. Stanly Jones termed "Victory through Surrender." It is not surrendering to the impulse of sin, but to the presence, power, and love of God. It is with hope Paul turns to the source of salvation: *"What a wretched man I am! Who will rescue me from this body of death? Thanks be to God— through Jesus Christ our Lord"* (Romans 7:24-25).

Your life's meaning must be rediscovered. It is a religious rebirth and a personal awakening. For everyone it is a spiritual moment. It is a moment when the spiritual meaning of life determines your life's direction. You are re-awakened to your soul's purpose. You are rejuvenated in God's love. This is conversion; God reclaims your soul and you take up your soul's purpose.

You are not alone. The love and power of God are present and available. In your soul, cry out for help. You struggle against the chains of pain and fear that hold you. In a moment of trust, the change, the conversion begins. Jesus explains the dynamics of conversion: *"I tell you the truth, unless you change and become like little children, you will never enter the kingdom of heaven"* (Matthew 18:3).

A man slipped on the edge of a cliff and would have fallen to certain death had he not grabbed hold of an exposed root protruding from the cliff face. In desperation the man looked heavenward and cried, "Is there any one up there that can help me?"

God responded, "I can help you. Just let go of the root."

The man cried again, "Is there anyone else up there that can help me?"

Trust is bold and courageous. To surrender the root of falsehood, the root of brokenness, the root of sin's habits is a mighty act of faith in God's love. The invitation still stands: *"Come to me, all you who are weary and burdened, and I will give you rest. Take my yoke upon you and learn from me, for I am gentle and humble in heart and you will find rest for your souls"* (Matthew 11:28-29).

Conversion has a beginning, but it is also a way of life. It is trust in the love of God, surrendering to God's purpose, turning from old ways to new life. This is the work of spiritual determination, God's work in you. Now, you must work out the new life. You must set up

> *Conversion is not something that is done once and for all. It is a journey.*

the discipline, limits, boundaries, support, and accountability you need.

Conversion is the starting point of every spiritual journey. It involves a break with the life lived up to that point. However, conversion is not something that is done once and for all. It is a journey, even a painful journey. There are doubts and questions. We are tempted to turn back to our old ways. Martin Luther, the protestant reformer of the 16TH century writes:

This life is not godliness, but the process of becoming godly, not health but getting well, not being but becoming, not rest but exercise. We are not now what we shall be, but we are on the way. The process is not yet finished, but it is actively going on. This is not the goal but it is the right road. At present, everything does not gleam and sparkle, but everything is being cleansed.[9]

Through the love of God, you can live on purpose instead of on impulse. Re-ignite your true and best motivations. You cannot do it alone. Seek help. Join a group of faith-filled people, find a spiritual partner, see a doctor, talk with a counselor or spiritual mentor, and create a net of support under your high wire act of crossing to freedom. You need structured and empowering accountability. Your soul is on your side. You are not abandoned. The way is hard, but the way is open.

The hope offered through repentance and conversion is there. Yet there is also a sad and tragic side to the story. The adversary fights against the offer of new life. The common weapons are false pride or deepening depression. False pride screams, "I don't need your help; I don't want your help; I can do it myself." False pride is a pattern of fear and anger that hardens like marble. Be bold and brave. Ask God to break your façade and open your soul.

Depression is even more insidious. An evil thought whispers in your mind, "It will always be this way, always be this way, always this way, always." The evil brings an entourage of self-degradation. Rage against it. Fight against it. When bruised and battered, get up and fight on. Fight by repeating, believing, and envisioning, "I am created by God, loved by God, and kept by God." The soul fights with you to cleanse depression with inner confidence and purpose.

Whether it is the temptation of pride, the sickness of depression, or a combination of both, when you refuse the homeward journey, you slip down a slope of self-destruction. You are dragged along by a weight of painful anger, fear, and heaviness. The problem will not go away. It cannot be ignored. Your life as a spouse, a parent, an employee, and a friend is in peril.

Stage Four: a Lost Soul. The voice of inner wisdom is silenced. Pain and fear drive behavior. As you follow the self-destructive path, you lose respect for the person you have become. Your relationships with those around you are poisoned with disgust and apathy. Your inner life fluctuates between devastating, uncontrollable pain and inner numbness.

Masking the pain creates a pattern of dysfunctional behavior often expressed in physical or emotional addiction. It could be physical addiction to one or more of the big three: alcohol, drugs, or pornography. The more widespread addictions are power, sex, and money. For these, society has developed subtle, sophisticated, and acceptable addictive patterns. Perhaps your position in society allows for outbursts or irresponsible acts without negative consequences. Alcoholism is attired in business suits and cocktail dresses. Prescription pills are acquired from unethical physicians. Toxic relational habits are tolerated. Dysfunctional behavior maintains a tenuous semblance of order over the chaos. You say, "It's just me. That's just the way I am."

The dynamics of addiction provide insight into dysfunctional patterns of perception, emotion, motivation, and action. What may have started as useful methods of coping with life's struggles and tragedies has now become a habitual or addictive system that hides and harms your true and best self.

The addiction of dysfunctional behavior infests the personality with the harmful traits of avoidance and escapism: impulsiveness, dependence, deviousness, manipulation and self-centeredness. Underneath, it is all driven by fear. When is a pattern dysfunctional and addictive?[10]

> Have I lost the power to stop?
> Are the consequences harmful?
> Is it destroying my ability to function?
> Does the act of quitting cause pain and fear?
> Is it hiding or harming my true and best self?

Dysfunctional and addictive thoughts and actions cloud the way you understand life, set loose obsessive impulses and take your emotions hostage. This is a soul issue. You are compulsively self-focused, existing in a survival mode. The evil voice whispers with seductive malevolence, "Is survival worth

You trudge on, hip-deep in the mire and the mud that has no meaning.

it? Why not take a window for a door, a final pill for eternal peace."

It is a quagmire of apathy, cynicism, and desperation. You trudge on, hip-deep in the mire and the mud that has no meaning. You are destroying your soul purpose. This road is dark, dangerous, and a dead end. You have lost your soul. That is, you have lost touch with your soul's grand purpose.

GRACE SO AMAZING

> *There is a path home.*
> *Truth and hope are on*
> *your side. What is lost*
> *can be found again.*

However, even here there is a path home. Truth and hope are on your side. What is lost can be found again. What is forgotten can once more be remembered. The silent wisdom of heaven vibrates through your being if you but take time to be still and know.

On an 11ᵀᴴ century tombstone of a forgotten soldier from northern Europe is the epitaph, "darkness is my closest friend." It is the last line of the saddest Psalm in the Bible. The prayer of this lost soul begins,

> *O Lord, the God who saves me,*
> *   day and night I cry out before you.*
> *May my prayer come before you;*
> *   turn your ear to my cry*
> *For my soul is full of trouble*
> *   and my life drawn near the grave.*
> *I am counted among those who go down to the pit;*
> *   I am like a man without strength.*
> *I am set apart with the dead,*
> *   like the slain who lie in the grave,*
> *whom you remember no more,*
> *   who are cut off from your care.*
> (Psalm 88:1-5)

Something has died in you. Your true and best self has been denied and broken. But the echo chamber of heaven is still within you. Your soul's purpose will not be compromised. The soul's purpose survives. At the precise moment you discover and accept your loss, the soul journey begins. In the middle of the prayer, the lost soul questions God:

"Do you show your wonders to the dead?
Do those who are dead rise up and praise you?
Is your love declared in the grave, your faithfulness in Destruction?"
(Psalm 88:10-11)

The answer to each question is "Yes, yes, and yes!" The answer is not a human longing or a philosopher's conjecture, but a fact of history: Jesus died and Jesus lives. This is the foundation of Christianity: He lives. In Jesus Christ, God displays the power that brings death to life. In Christ, you can be raised up to your true and best self. Living true to your best is your daily praise to God. God's love is greater than any failure, falsehood, brokenness, or sin.

John Newton was a lost soul. He served on the crew of slave ships at the darkest time of the slave trade. It was here that he discovered in his own soul, the spiritual empowerment of God's mighty action in raising Jesus to life. John Newton was raised to a new life. He turned away from the slave trade and worked against it, inspiring and mentoring William Wilberforce who led the British Empire to abolish slavery. The first verse of Newton's famous hymn is his story:
> Amazing grace! How sweet the sound!
> That saved a wretch like me;
> I once was lost, but now am found;
> Was blind, but now I see.[11]

This is the love of God at work in you. You cannot do it alone. You need help. God's Spirit is inside you, and great souls are around you. It requires inward healing and systems of support and structure. It is also a lifelong journey that begins with an encounter, a spiritual encounter with God. What does it mean to encounter God? This is the subject of the next chapter.

CHAPTER 8

FINDING GOD

Late have I loved thee!
Thou wast within me, and I stood without.
I sought thee here, hurling my ugly self on the beauty of thy creations.
Thou hast called me, thy cry has vanquished my deafness.
Thou hast shone, and thy light has vanquished my blindness.
Thou hast broadcast thy perfume, and I have breathed it;
now I sigh for thee.
I have tasted thee, and now I hunger for thee.
Thou has touched me, and now I burn with desire for thy peace.
AUGUSTINE[1]

"I don't believe I lost my soul, but I stood on the cliff where I could have tossed it away." The statement was more self-revealing than I intended; indeed, surprise and anxiety filled my chest when I heard the words spill out of my mouth and roll across the table in the restaurant. The kind face of my dinner partner assured me with his acceptance. The gentleman was one of a half-dozen of the highest ranking elected leaders in my denomination.

He went on to tell me of the times of struggle and uncertainty in his own life and ministry. My self-disclosure was honored by the openness of his soul. We spoke of my divorce, my failings, and my deep yearning to come home to my true and best in Christ. He never pushed, but listened patiently, as a good pastor.

For a long time we talked about heritage, hope, failures, fears, recovery, release, and the loving grace of God. He asked me what I would like to do with the rest of my life. We dreamed of wonderful possibilities. He could have ended the conversation by assuring me that there is a place for me in the church. That would have been gracious and kind; but he went beyond that and told me, "Richard, the church needs you."

Could it be true? Does God love those who have faltered, failed, and fallen? Does God invite broken, bruised, and battered people into partnership? Does God restore broken lives into the service of His cause and His people? I treasured the words of my church's leader. In his words I heard the echo of a deeper word, the inward promise of God.

Across the dinner table, we had a spiritual conversation. These soul-to-soul encounters mark the trail that leads home. Such talks are reflection of and preparation for soul-to-soul encounters with God. This is a form of prayer. It is often through these spiritual conversations that God's Spirit, the Spirit of Jesus, is set free to transform us into the image of Christ. Authentic Christian spirituality is *living true to my best in Christ*.

> *To be true* is to be genuine, honest, open, and real about what I
>   1) understand and 2) feel at any given moment, and 3) what is
>   driving my thoughts, emotions, and actions.
> *To be my best* is to submit my understanding, feelings, and motives to
>   the acceptance, assessment, correction, cleansing, forgiveness, and
>   empowerment of the Spirit of Christ.

Spiritual conversations are potent because they are born out of spiritual struggle. When security is threatened, relationships are frayed, dreams are in jeopardy, or tragedy strikes, the soul battles to make sense of it and find spiritual meaning in it. We change because we struggle. It is essential to the soul's work. A soul-to-soul conversation, a soul-to-soul encounter with God is the right place for spiritual struggle.

> *We change because we struggle. It is essential to the soul's work.*

Here is the wonder of it: God initiates the conversation. God, in a mystery of grace and compassion, awakens the soul to His presence. He invites us to the table. Often His invitation comes at a crisis point in our lives. In crisis we are more spiritually attentive and open to a spiritual awakening. But it takes more than an emergency or a difficult predicament to bring to life the spiritual need within us, it also requires compassion.

In my spiritual exchange with my church's leader, I received his compassion. It was an expression of God's kindness. Compassion changes your perceptions, emotions, and motivations. It provides strength for the struggle. It is the ticket home for a lost soul.

CRISIS AND LOVE

No one changes because it is a good idea. We change for only two reasons: because we are in love or because we are in crisis. Deep, profound, and lasting spiritual change requires both.

Personal crisis appears when our bread or belonging is jeopardized. When "daily bread," the means of sustaining or enriching our lifestyle, is in jeopardy, it creates fear and anger. "Trespasses," our own and those of others who hurt us or the ones we love, makes us vulnerable and open to attack. These are moments of testing, of "temptation," when the "evil one" whispers false promises as he attempts to lead us astray.

The soul crisis is triggered when we respond to threats to our bread and belonging by continually choosing to appear effective rather than fight for authenticity. The outcome is predictable. Our perceptions are altered. Our motivations twist into a tangled web. Emotions harm rather than help our judgment. We neglect the needs of the soul. Self-indulgence characterizes our response. We are driven by inner pain, responding to impulse rather than living on purpose.

We must recognize the crisis and respond with a desire to change. But how do we come to perceive the tragedy of our plight? And what is the true and best source of our motivation to change? In our culture, we admire the people who lift themselves "by their bootstraps." Try to picture that image. It is just as impossible to lift yourself by your bootstraps as it is to "sit in a wheel barrel and wheel yourself"[2] around. The power to lift your life is with God and not due to your own grit.

At the age of 19 I was hired by a small church in upstate New York to be the pastor to youth for a summer season. I was a teenager myself. I lived in an upstairs bedroom in the parsonage. Looking back, I wonder what possessed the minister to hire such a young and inexperienced person.

Before appearing on the scene, I earnestly thought through and prayed about the challenge. I wrote down several key ideas and convictions as well as one verse of Scripture that would serve as a philosophy for my summer ministry. In fact, I found a cube (six-sided) and wrote one thought on each face. They were values and principles that guided my thoughts and decisions.

I have long since lost the little plastic cube. And I have lost the memory of what I wrote on five of the sides. But I remember the Scripture. It was the one that guarded my heart then and now. *"This is love: not that we loved God, but that he loved us and sent his Son as an atoning sacrifice for our sins"* (1 John 4:10).

The search for a lost soul does not begin with us, but with God. God is the initiator. He is like a woman sweeping the house in search of a lost coin. He faces the storms and dangerous trails of the mountains, listening for the bleat of a lost sheep over the roar of thunder. He is the father with a broken heart, watching, straining to see the first glimpse of His prodigal returning home (see Luke 15).

God, in Christ, sweeps the house, braves the storm, and searches for us in Jesus. Jesus came *"to seek and to save that which was lost"* (Luke 19:10). Jesus came as a human being, as a friend, as a teacher, as a preacher, and as a miracle worker. But there is more, so much more. He came as God, God in flesh, in human form. What are

> *God is amazingly like Jesus.*

we to conclude from this wonder? It is this: God is amazingly like Jesus. What we see in Jesus is what we find in God.

At the heart of the Christian faith lies the deep conviction that we can know and love God because God first loved and knew us. The one truly existent God, we believe, has been so poured out, so made known to us in Christ and the Spirit that we can respond with mutual knowledge, and in the awe and intimacy of love.

In terms of the universe, we see Jesus Christ as the personal and eternal Word of God, as creator and redeemer. In terms of his earthly life, we see the cross and the resurrection as the sacrificial climax and achievement, and as the axis of every Christian's understanding of history, from death to life. In terms of application, we see justification by faith and forgiveness as the pattern of God's grace coming as a gift to the undeserving.[3]

God's love does not come to you as a "good idea" to consider. God's love is a relationship with Him in which you follow a path toward your true and best in Christ. And it begins with His invitation: *"Wake up, O sleeper, rise from the dead. And Christ will shine on you"* (Ephesians 5:14).

WAKE UP

How do you land in the mire and mud? Sometimes you are pushed. Sometimes you fall because you strayed from the true path. And sometimes you walk in under your own power. It is useful to sort out how you got in the mud. However, the true goal is to get out of the mud.

She asked to speak with me privately at a break in the seminar. "Dr. Parrott, if what you are saying is true, and I believe it, I have to look at myself, at my life, and say there must be more to life than this." She was a success in all outward appearance. But beneath the surface was confusion and pain. She was taking an extended program that enhanced professional development. Before the first session was over, what started as professional became personal for her. "Right now, this program is not about improving my work; it's about working on me."

Her soul had cried out. She heard and responded. The soul is faithful. The soul journey begins when a person realizes there has to be more to life than this. For you, it may come like the tornado in *The Wizard of Oz.* You wake up and say, "I am not in Kansas anymore." It may come in more subtle ways as you reflect on your life and discover that you are not living true to your best.

> *It is useful to sort out how you got in the mud. However, the true goal is to get out of the mud.*

Your soul seeks to win your attention. It may be through a life crisis, a pattern of dysfunctional behavior, emotional pain, or an inner yearning for "something more." Wake up! Wake up and pay attention! Wake up and answer the soul's cry.

"When did life take on deeper meaning for you?" I have asked rooms full of people and the most common answer has been the birth of a child. It is a reminder that life is more than achievement and power, more than respect and recognition. Life is more than bread and belonging. There is a deeper meaning. When a new soul enters the world, it is a spiritual moment. It is a moment when a parent reconnects with the soul.

A newborn infant in your arms, particularly your own child, is a moment of magic and mystery. It is a spiritual moment. The tiny child peers out at life with wonder and awe. You see the soul of your living legacy in the tiny grip and wide eyes of your baby. It is a moment that reconnects you to a grander and higher purpose, power, and presence.

The soul aligns with spiritual reality. The soul works from an unquestioned assumption; your true and best self is rooted in spiritual meaning. Your soul has pledged allegiance to God. The soul crisis is a spiritual crisis: "There must be more than this."

SPIRITUAL AWARENESS

Jacob confronted his soul's crisis *"in a certain place where he stopped for the night because the sun had set"* (Genesis 28:11). The setting sun and the night were indicative of this young man's life. Jacob was on the run. He deceived his father, betrayed his brother, and abandoned his home for fear his brother would kill him. His mother, who was deeply involved in the plot, sent her son to her brother's home for safety. This story is all too human. It portrays a dysfunctional family wallowing in their squabbles, schemes, and sins.

Jacob left his home with no idea what would become of him. We can only imagine the thoughts, emotions, and images in his mind as he stopped for the night. With Jacob all alone and feeling abandoned to his misery, God awakened him to a greater reality.

In traditional fashion, Jacob made a bed on the ground using a large stone to rest his head. Thoughts lingered like the stars overhead, but eventually, his mind rested and Jacob fell asleep.

What follows is a dream sequence in the story. It is a miraculous, astonishing dream. He saw a stairway extending from heaven to earth. Angels, the messengers of God, traveled up and down the staircase. Above everything, God stood in majesty.

In the dream, God said, *"I am the Lord God who was worshipped by your grandfather Abraham and your father Isaac."* Jacob must have shuddered in fear; he had recently deceived his father with the goal of gaining his brother's inheritance.

The Lord continued, *"I will give you and your family the land on which you now sleep. You will have descendents that will spread over the earth in all directions and so plentiful that you will not be able to count them anymore than you could count the specks of dust.*

"Not only will I bless you; you and your family will be a blessing to all the people on earth. I will always watch over you no matter where you go. I will bring you back to this land. Have faith in me, for I will never leave you. I keep my promises" (Genesis 28:10-15).

When Jacob awoke from his sleep, he realized, *"Surely the Lord is in this place, and I was not aware of it"* (see Genesis 28:16).

"God is here and I didn't know it." This is the essence of spiritual awareness, to be aware and awake to what we cannot see, to what is most true and eternal. Spiritual awareness often comes to us through common, earthly pictures and images that open the mind and soul to God. At other moments, God brings His presence in ways and wonders beyond our ability to comprehend.

God is near and dear to us. The most common way God speaks to us is through our imagination, through the images, pictures, and incidents of ordinary life that open the soul to extraordinary and eternal meaning. We are *"sure of what we hope for and certain of what we do not see"* (Hebrews 11:1). We see the truth of God's love through the newborn baby, the setting sun, the smile of a returning friend, the kindness of a stranger, or the gift of forgiveness and grace.

The Bible is filled with wonderful pictures and images that bring God's presence and God's word close to us—He is our rock, our fortress; Jesus is the door, the good shepherd, and the bread of life. Jesus told simple and compelling stories of a good Samaritan, a rebellious child, and a mustard seed. These stories open our imagination to God's wisdom. God speaks through history in the epic events of Scripture, the exodus, the exile, the return, and the growth

> *Even the smallest and most normal events in life may awaken our spiritual imagination to the presence of God.*

of the early church. A spiritual awakening is when these pictures, stories, images, and events carry spiritual meaning for us and for our present moment. We know, "God is speaking to me."

Spiritual awakening is a moment when we realize that God is right here. He is closer than our next breath. God, the one who reigns over all, is at our side, indeed, in our hearts. We place our lives in His keeping. Even the smallest and most normal events in life may awaken our spiritual imagination to the presence of God.

During the 1640s in Britain, John Bunyan's soul came to life. Troubled by an inner war of doubt, temptation, and dread, he searched for assurance. A vision of God's gift of life came alive to him in a verse of Scripture and the image of a small coin.

One day as I was passing through a field ...suddenly this sentence fell upon my soul, "Thy righteousness is in heaven;" ...I saw with the eyes of my soul, Jesus Christ at God's right hand ...Now did my chains fall off my legs indeed ...Twas glorious to see his exaltation ...those four-pence-half-pennies that rich men carry in their purses, when their gold is in their trunks at home: Oh! I saw my gold was in my trunk at home! In Christ my Lord and Savior.[4]

John Bunyan eventually wrote the story of the Christian life in *Pilgrim's Progress*. It is a story of metaphors, analogies, and word pictures that fire the imagination. Our pilgrim, named Christian, carries a heavy burden. Yet when he kneels at a wayside cross, the heavy sack falls from his back and rolls into an empty tomb. You can see it in your mind and imagine it in your soul.

To see God and God's love in near and dear moments and meanings is spiritual awakening. God is my shepherd in the green valley, beside still water, on a dark trail, and at a table of plenty.

God is above and beyond us. There are other moments, unusual moments, when God brings His living word, His presence to us in ways that are beyond the mind's ability to understand. It is mystical rather than common place. This type of experience reveals God in mystery and wonder that cannot be verbalized. It is another way God brings us to spiritual awareness and awakening.

These experiences remind us that whatever our categories, our understanding, our mental mechanisms, the grandeur of God cannot be contained in them. Our metaphors and images cannot hold the vastness of God. These overwhelming moments are rare and beautiful. Like diamonds unearthed from dark, hidden places, they sparkle with unexplainable fire.

Blasé Pascal was a genius. He achieved fame as a mathematician, physicist, philosopher, and theologian, all within the span of twenty years. He considered faith in God as a "wager," calculating that if God does not exist, the skeptic loses nothing by not believing, but if God does exist, then the skeptic gains eternal life by believing. So, why not make the bet?

However, one winter day, all that changed. Pascal was awakened to the reality of God that was beyond his rational mind, his calculations and classifications. He writes:

In the year of Grace, 1654,
On Monday, 23RD of November, Feast of St. Clement…
From about half past ten in the evening until about half past twelve, *FIRE!*[5]

"Fire!" He had no words, no way to express the wonder of God's presence. There was no way to sort it out, catalogue it, or run it through a logic matrix. It was an awakening, an invitation that was beyond words.

His experience was unusual, certainly, but there is something here for all of us, for we realize that God is far greater than we can comprehend. The mind cannot get around it. It is beyond logic, beyond our ability to contain it in reasonable terms. We can only fling our lives into the great fire of His love.

> *God is beyond us, yet God is near us.*

God is beyond us, yet God is near us. His communication with us is earthly and heavenly. It is at the same moment ordinary flesh and eternal mystery. To fall back upon Jacob's dream, God speaks to us from both the top and bottom of the staircase. How can this be? God's essence, His word, became human and lived with us. This is beyond what our minds can fathom; it is closer than the skin that wraps our frame. Jesus said, *"I tell you the truth, you shall see heaven open, and the angels of God ascending and descending on the Son of Man"* (John 1:51).

SPIRITUAL STRUGGLE

The spiritual journey of Jacob was far from over. An awakening is just that, a wakeup call, but there is more; there is the spiritual struggle. For Jacob the next decades were filled with broken promises and dashed hopes. His mother never sent for him to come home. He had to assume that his brother was still bent on killing him. His uncle cheated him in business and in love, swapping out one sister for another on his wedding night. The years piled up and, eventually, so did Jacob's wealth.

In fact, Jacob did so well in business that his cousins were determined to ruin him and take back the family fortune. It was time to leave. He packed up his family, servants, flocks, and belongings and started for home. His uncle, now father-in-law, gave chase. At the same time, word came that his brother was moving an army toward him. His old, deceitful ways were catching up with him.

It was night. Jacob made a decision. He sent his family, including his servants and all his belongings, across the stream. Jacob was all alone.

He entered into a deep spiritual struggle. The Bible says, *"a man wrestled with him till day break"* (Genesis 32:24).

The man did not overpower Jacob, but in the battle, Jacob's hip was wrenched. What they talked about as they wrestled, we do not know. However, near dawn we know they had a conversation:

"Let me go, for it is dawn, said the man.

"But Jacob replied, I will not let you go unless you bless me.

"What is your name? the man asked.

"Jacob, he answered" (Genesis 32:26-27).

The stranger, whom Jacob came to see as the presence of God, blessed him with a new name. A name is a symbol of identity. Jacob became a new person that night.

The stranger said, *"Your name will no longer be Jacob, but you will be Israel because you have struggled with God and with men and have been victorious"* (Genesis 32:28).

As the sun rose, it was a new day in the land and a new day in the life of Jacob. He always remembered that night and that place where he *"saw God face to face"* (Genesis 32:30).

When you engage in a wrestling match with the Almighty, God has the upper hand. I remember wrestling with my son when he was only three years of age. It is the kind of play that parents and children enjoy. The contest strengthened our relationship. With Jacob, the contest, the struggle with God altered his relationship with the Lord of Heaven.

> *When you engage in a wrestling match with the Almighty, God has the upper hand.*

In all likelihood, our struggle with God will be worked out in lonely nights and in the company of trusted friends. It may not take place in one night, but over a longer period of time. But the outcome is the same: It is an *identity* change, a change in personal identity as well as how we identify with God.

Here is the spiritual dynamic that is at the heart of the spiritual life: Jacob came to know himself and to know God. The knowledge of God is so linked to self-knowledge that the two cannot be separated. John Calvin was a Protestant reformer of the 16TH century. Calvin understood the deep bond between your self-knowledge and your relationship with God. He writes:

Nearly all wisdom we possess, that is to say, true and sound wisdom, consists of two parts: the knowledge of God and of ourselves. But, while joined by many bounds, which one precedes and brings forth the other, is not easy to discern.[6]

This is the how the spiritual life works: To know God, you must come to know yourself. It is God's way. The struggle is to know the truth about yourself and to know God's best for you. Some forms of religion, Christian religion, attempt to teach the knowledge of God without self knowledge. It is also true that modern forms of psycho-therapy delve into self knowledge without regard for knowledge of God, the Creator of "self." Authentic spirituality is to know who you are and who God is.

The conversation that night was life changing for Jacob. Our lives change when we engage in conversations that open the soul to the knowledge of self and God. These are spiritual conversations. It is how we wake up, become aware of the presence of our Lord. In these conversations, private conversations with God and conversations with soul friends, we struggle to know ourselves and our Lord.

SPIRITUAL CONVERSATIONS

What is a Spiritual Conversation? A spiritual conversation is a very human event. It is also a divine encounter. It may take place in private prayer or in conversation with another like-minded soul. It need not be gut-wrenching or tear-drenched, yet on occasion it may. It need not take several hours or deep levels of meditation, but there are times when it should be demanding. Spiritual conversations cannot be measured by time and tactics. Openness that leads to inward change is the process and purpose of a spiritual conversation.

> *Openness that leads to inward change is the process and purpose of a spiritual conversation.*

A soul-to-soul conversation is when you set aside the duties of the day, the distractions of the moment, and 1) focus on discovering what is going on in your inner life right now, 2) listen for the guidance of God that often comes through personal questions and an enlivened imagination, and 3) submit your inner life, as it is, to the love of God as you cooperate with His Spirit in creating your life. Let me describe a spiritual conversation in five statements:

First, a spiritual conversation is a genuine and appropriate *revealing of the inner life*: personal perceptions, emotions, and motivations. In prayer, I share my inner life with God. It is also a conversation in which I share my heart with you and you share your heart with me. Together we listen for God's wisdom in each other as we are open to learn and grow in Christ. Most often, God's guidance comes in discovering personal questions rather than giving definitive answers. Trust the spiritual questions; God is speaking through them.

Second, a spiritual conversation employs the *language of the heart* rather than depending on the language of religion and theology. The Gettysburg address and the 23RD Psalm are in the language of the heart. It is the use of simple language, stories, and images that fires the imagination. God speaks through the imagination. The Psalms, the parables, the sayings of Jesus, and the great stories of faith ignite the soul's inner eye. Look and listen for God's wisdom.

Third, a spiritual conversation requires *listening for God's inner wisdom* as well as listening to each other. It is hearing the truth about yourself and courageously embracing moments of self-discovery. It is embracing Christ's words and work in you. The truth includes the good and bad, virtues and vices, ideals and transgressions. Parker Palmer describes it this way:

> I sometimes lead retreats, and from time to time participants show me the notes they are taking as the retreat unfolds. The pattern is nearly universal: people take copious notes on what the retreat leader says, and they sometimes take notes on the words of certain wise people in the group, but rarely, if ever, do they take notes on what they themselves say. We listen for guidance everywhere except from within.
>
> I urge retreatants to turn their note-taking around, because the words we speak often contain counsel we are trying to give ourselves. We have a strange conceit in our culture that simply because we have said something, we understand what it means! But often we do not—especially when we speak from a deeper place than intellect or ego, speak the kind of words that arise when the inner

teacher feels safe enough to tell its truth. At those moments, we need to listen to what our lives are saying and take notes on it, lest we forget our own truth and deny that we ever heard it.[7]

Fourth, a spiritual conversation is one in which we *safely express what is true about us*: our feelings, understanding, and motives. Again, Parker Palmer provides a clear image:

How we are to listen to our lives is a question worth exploring. In our culture, we tend to gather information in ways that do not work very well when the source is the human soul: the soul is not responsive to subpoenas or cross-examination. At best it will stand in the dock only long enough to plead the Fifth Amendment. At worst it will jump bail and never be heard from again. The soul speaks its truth only under quiet, inviting, and trustworthy conditions.[8]

Fifth, a spiritual conversation moves us toward *living true to our best in Christ*. It is a conversation in which we actually have the audacity to believe that God is at work in our souls, molding, shaping, and transforming our inner lives for His glory. *"And we, who with unveiled faces all reflect the Lord's glory, are being transformed into his likeness with ever increasing glory, which comes from the Lord, who is the Spirit"* (2 Corinthians 3:18).

SPIRITUAL MASQUERADES

Some conversations masquerade as genuine and spiritual, but are, in fact, false and empty. Each type of conversation is part of the normal day. Each has a place in our dealings with one another. However, these types of conversations are unable to produce authentic and meaningful spiritual connections. They employ spiritual language, clichés, or phrases; they rely on moral prerogatives, compliance, and capitulation, yet they result in shutting down the soul, an essential participant in an authentic spiritual conversation. Three masquerade costumes parade as genuine spirituality:

Conversation #1—Talk to the Hand. This is fully defensive. It is the most common form of conversation in a fast-paced world of expectations and demands. It is treating people as objects to be handled, managed, manipulated, used and sometimes abused. It is the level of clichés, such as How are you? How's your family? Where's the report? I like your outfit. Where have you been? I hope we get together soon. Pass the potatoes. It's really good to see you.

Spirituality at this level is relegated to a series of clichés or rituals without meaning, *"a resounding gong or a clanging cymbal"* (1 Corinthians 13:1). Religious routines and habits come and go without leaving any evidence of influence. You speak of spiritual awakening in empty phrases. You conform to an empty religious pattern rather than receive a transformed life.

Conversation #2—Tickle the Ear. You immerse yourself in other people's business rather than the business of your own soul. You try to figure out other people's inner lives without disclosing your own. You pass judgment while not revealing your own perceptions. This form of conversation has a place in the work-a-day world when it is necessary to complete tasks without authentic human interaction.

This type of exchange decomposes the spiritual life into a conversation piece, a series of talking points, and a lens through which to judge others. You exchange pat-answers, accepted responses, and approved rhetoric. These kinds of conversations are like manicured graves: They appear *"beautiful on the outside but on the inside are full of dead men's bones"* (Matthew 23:27). Nothing authentic or transforming is in these conversations; they are means of spiritual insulation.

Conversation #3—A Piece of My Mind. This is mutual discussion or debate in which you willingly reveal your opinions, beliefs, and judgments. Often the goal of such conversations is to justify your emotions, reactions, and decisions or make demands, give commands, or level expectations on others. Such a conversation "feels" spiritual because it conjures up emotions, perceptions and motives. However, these inner dynamics are hidden and unexplored or justified and defended. The soul is left out of the exchange.

This is a common level of conversation in the market place. It is the discussion of business, work, tasks, strategies, and decisions. It is fraught with misunderstanding. It is a negotiation between shadow and light; you calculate, "how much should I tell and how much should I hide?" This type of exchange comes home from the office and is the official substitute for intimacy in marriage. It is a means of speaking your mind, concealing your heart, and remaining on the defensive.

This is the surrogate language of authentic spiritual encounters. It is a form of discussion that is head high and heart weak. Ideas are thrashed about, debated, and discarded without an authentic exchange of heart and soul. It is the high road rather than the holy way. It is declaring and defending ideals, as if you were jumping for heaven, hoping to appear perfected (or at least somewhat better than others). It is proving that your way is right because others are wrong; *"you shut the kingdom of heaven"* (Matthew 27:13). Religion is relegated to spiritualized measures of morality and theological correctness.

SOUL-TO-SOUL ENCOUNTERS

While the above conversations impersonate genuine spirituality, there are two forms of conversation that move us into authentic spiritual dialogue and prayer. The *heart* conversation opens the door, and the conversation of the *soul* echoes the voice of God within.

Conversation #4—From the Bottom of My Heart. This is gut-level dialogue. In the head level conversation (conversation #3) you often feel that no one understands you. And they don't. You have not revealed enough of yourself to be understood by others. It is likely you do not understand yourself. You are more than your judgments, beliefs, and opinions. You have perceptions, emotion, and motivation. This is the deeper truth about you.

The true you is not a static and unchanging person. The true you is a collection of perceptions, emotions, and motives that constantly change. You are always changing. Your true self is what's happening in your mind and heart at this moment. Speaking from the gut level exposes your true self. To speak from the heart is to explore and express your emotions, motivations, and perceptions:

Emotions—How do I feel at this moment, and what's the root of that feeling?

Motivations—What is moving me to think, feel, and behave as I do?

Perceptions—How do I understand what is happening and why it is happening?

Your emotions and motivations are powerful forces that shape your perceptions, that is, your understanding of what is happening and why. These inner dynamics form the foundation of your opinions, beliefs, and judgments. In a gut-level conversation, you discover, explore, own, question, release, or embrace your perceptions, emotions, and motivations.

> *You must embrace and confess your true self before you can submit your true self to God's work.*

These heart-to-heart conversations are moments of authenticity that open genuine spiritual dialogue, the way of prayer. You must embrace and confess your true self before you can submit your true self to God's work. The soul works to transform an authentic moment into an authentic life.

Conversation #5—Soul-to-Soul. The soul-to-soul conversation moves from discovering what is true to creating what is best in Christ. It moves beyond intellect and emotions, beyond questioning perceptions and exploring motivations. The light of God's love is the soul's North Star. Your call is to work in allegiance with God's love to create Christ's best in you.

God is not content with behavior that conforms to the world's pattern of understanding, feelings, and desires. Embrace a journey of growing true to your best in Christ. Your soul responds to His invitation: *"Come to me ... Take my yoke upon you and learn from me"* (Matthew 11:28-29).

The soul pledges allegiance to God. God, the infinite source of love and compassion, loves you as you are. God applauds every step you take from darkness into light, inauthentic toward authentic, false into true, broken toward wholeness. God loves you as you are but is not content to leave you as you are. God actively shapes you in soul-to-soul conversations.

If your child fell off a bicycle and was suffering from a broken bone .d bleeding wounds on the sidewalk in front of your house, you would run to her instantly. You would love her exactly as she is. You would not tell her that you will love her again as soon as the bones are healed and the wounds have passed. You would love her just as she is.

But your love would not leave her on the sidewalk. Your love would determine to heal her wounds, mend her brokenness, and get her back on her feet. You would go so far as to want her to overcome her fear of the bicycle and teach her to ride again with greater skill and ability. When you do this, you are reflecting the image of our Heavenly Parent.

God brings His healing power and determination to the creative task of bringing forth your best. He does this by helping you honestly evaluate your perceptions, accept your emotions, question your motivations, and make choices that are true to your best in Christ. This is the work of God's Spirit in your soul.

I experienced a number of soul-to-soul conversations at the home of Rod and Cindy Bushy. In the powerful presence of validating relationships, my true and best self came back to life. I received compassion. I found acceptance. Acts of forgiveness and restoration healed the wounds. I remember the day, months later, when Cindy observed, "I'm beginning to recognize the Richard I know. Welcome back."

The soul-to-soul conversation is how the lost one finds the path home. It is how you listen for, hear, and follow the wisdom of God. You move out of crisis and into the soul journey. Marked with truth and hope, it begins the day you wake up to find yourself in exile. Freed from your prison, everything looks different. This is the beginning of life in Christ.

> *Where is the path? Look!*
> *It is under your feet.*

The soul journey is the topic of the final chapters in this book. God's people were freed from slavery in Egypt; we are freed from our spiritual imprisonment in sin. God's people found themselves in the desert, and we find ourselves learning to live a new life, life in Christ. It feels like exile from the world; but it is home for the child of God.

In exile, you speak the language of the heart and sing the song of the soul set free. You walk in the cadence of eternity and dance to the music of life. It is not your outside life with proper attire, time clocks, and practical matters that is at stake. It is your eternal life, your essential life, the place where you find your true and best. This is the soul's journey. Here you must let go and trudge on. Where is the path? Look! It is under your feet.

PART 3

SOUL JOURNEY

When you pray, go into your room,
close the door and pray to your Father who is unseen.
Then your Father, who sees what is done in secret,
will reward you.

MATTHEW 6:6

CHAPTER 9

SOUL JOURNEY

In the middle of my life's journey
I found myself in a dark wood
Where the true path was wholly lost.
Oh how hard a thing it is to embark
Upon the story of that savage wood,
For the memory makes me shudder with fear.

DANTE[1]

Moving day is not so bad when you are a child. The people who care for you go with you. For the most part, all the heavy lifting is done by others. A collection of your most cherished possessions, toys, stuffed animals, and pictures are in the small suitcase that you keep close at hand. Favorite treats are yours for the asking. There may be a few tears, but songs, games, and promises of new delights distract from the pain of loss. The new home or apartment is different, but the furnishings are familiar. Well known and comfortable patterns, foods, and interactions appear out of cardboard boxes almost by magic. The child relaxes. The old ways of living are all present and accounted for. Identity is intact. This kind of journey is relatively easy on the inner life.

Now imagine a different move. Robinson Crusoe found himself marooned on an empty island. What was familiar, comfortable, and cherished was gone. Alice fell through a looking glass and entered a land that was more frightening than wonderful. When asked, "Who are you," she replied, "I'm not sure." Self-identity was jeopardized. Think of Dorothy's anxiety after the tornado had passed and she saw a strange landscape and it was not Kansas. This is the experience of exile; you find yourself in "a dark wood where the true path was wholly lost."[2]

John Simpson, Foreign Affairs Editor for the British Broadcast Company describes the experience in the preamble of his book *Exile*:

> To be wrenched from home, family, everything pleasant and
> familiar, and forced into a world that is cold and hostile,
> whether the expelling agent is the Angel of God or Stalin's
> NKVD: this is the defining experience of exile. The word itself
> carries powerful connotations of sorrow and alienation, of the
> surrender of the individual to overwhelming strength, of years
> of fruitless waiting. It was Victor Hugo who called exile, "a long
> dream of home."[3]

The Bible often depicts our spiritual struggle and journey in terms of exile. The first parents, Adam and Eve, were banished from the garden of paradise. God's saved His people from slavery in Egypt and then led them on an arduous journey through the wilderness. Jesus battled Satan for forty days of fasting on the Mount of Temptation. Blinded on the road to Damascus, Paul experienced spiritual exile; in the light of Jesus, he questioned and revisioned everything. Deported and exiled to the Isle of Patmos, John the Revelator was lifted beyond the veil of physical experience and saw, in profound and provocative images, God's victory over evil.

AT HOME IN EXILE

Something in the experience of spiritual exile is counter intuitive; it goes against natural logic. The challenge of physical exile is to end the journey and go back to the place where we started; *"they are thinking of the country they had left"* (Hebrews 11:15). In the spiritual life, exile is a lifelong journey, an acceptance of the fact that the world around us is not our home. God's people are *"longing for a better country—a heavenly one. Therefore God is not ashamed to be called their God, for he has prepared a city for them"* (Hebrews 11:16).

I remember a beautiful spiritual that regained new popularity several decades ago. The lyrics express our longing for freedom from a world of pain and injustice.

> I'm just a poor wayfaring stranger
> A traveling through this world of woe.
> But there's no sickness, no toil or danger
> In that bright land to which I go.

The song is drawn from the story of God's people traveling through the wilderness toward the land of promise. The New Testament expands the theme into an image of life in Christ. In the world, we are sojourners, travelers journeying toward our home in heaven. The Bible expresses it in many ways:

> *"Live your life as strangers here …as aliens and strangers in the world"* (1 Peter 1:17; 2:11).
> *"Your citizenship is in heaven"* (Phil. 3:20).
> *"We do not have an enduring city, but we are looking for a city that is to come"* (Hebrews 13:14).

The spiritual gathers up the truth of Scripture and sings the hope we have in Christ:

> I'm going there to see my Savior;
> Who shed for me His precious blood.
> I'm just a-goin' o'er Jordan.
> I'm just a goin' o'er home.

For the Christian, to be born anew in Christ is to be born into a new and different life. The eternal love of God has taken up residence in our souls. Life has spiritual meaning. We live our lives on the sure rock of God's compassion.

Our calling is to live in Christ, with Christ, and through Christ. We know that there is more to life than what we see. We are *looking forward to the city …whose architect and builder is God"* (Hebrews 11:10). We are journeying toward that city.

To be born anew in Christ is to become an alien in the world. But we are not alone. Before we were born in Christ, Christ was born in this world. Before we began our life of spiritual exile, He was also exiled. Before we took the first step on the spiritual journey, Christ walked and marked the trail. He is here to lead us home.

To find a home in exile is the spiritual journey. It is two-fold: 1) to find our way home to God's Heaven and 2) to make a home in our hearts with God's Spirit as we continue the journey. The home in our hearts is where we meet with God. In the desert, the wilderness, we encounter the Presence of God. In the place of banishment we hear the inner voice and open our souls to God's soul. *"A voice of one calling: 'In the desert prepare the way for the Lord; make straight in the wilderness a highway for our God'"* (Isaiah 40:3).

The purpose of exile is to make us true to our best in Christ. It is both a moment and a process. There are moments when we become aware at a new level, when we surrender at new depths, and when God floods our lives with His Spirit. These are wonderful moments to be cherished, guarded, and lived out. There is also a process. God's chisel works on us, chipping away, scraping, digging at our fears and dysfunctions, smoothing out the rough places, and bringing to life each day the image of Christ in us. This is the work of the soul's journey.

MOSES IN THE WILDERNESS

Moses found a home in exile. It was not because he lived there, was married there, had children or tended sheep there. He found a home in exile because God found him.

He was born a Hebrew, the slave class in Egypt, at the time Pharaoh was depleting the power of his stable of slaves by killing the first born male children. Moses was rescued by his mother's clever plan, his sister's watchful care, and God's gift of grace. It was a wonderful scheme: make a small basket, tuck the baby inside, and send it floating toward the daughter of Pharaoh while she bathes in the river Nile.

Pharaoh's daughter saw the basket floating in the reeds that grew in the shallows of the river. The cry of the infant touched her heart. True, the baby was a Hebrew slave and a male child at that, but she could not, would not allow her father's cruel decree to be carried out, at least not for this baby. She became his protector.

Miriam, the baby's sister, watched from a distance. She knew the royal princess would call for a nurse maid for the child. What courage it took for her to step in at the right moment and offer, *"Shall I go and get one of the Hebrew women to nurse the baby for you?"* (Exodus 2:7).

"Yes, go," said the princess. Miriam ran home with the wonderful news. She returned to the palace with her own mother, the nurse maid. Thus, the mother of Moses had her baby boy back in her arms.

The child grew up in the opulence of the palaces of Egypt. Eventually, the daughter of Pharaoh adopted the boy. His life was filled with the best—the best education, feasts, and finery.

The years roll on. A lifetime slips by. Now, look at Moses as an old man. The clothes of fine Egyptian weave are replaced by the simple garb of a desert nomad. The memories of wondrous delicacies from the dinner table have faded. A simple fare is now his staple. Moses is no longer the grandson of Pharaoh. He is an old man of the desert who tends sheep.

A banished expatriate and refugee, he has left his old life in Egypt years ago, but he has not yet found a home, a spiritual home for his soul. True enough, a Bedouin family takes him in and treats him with kindness and hospitality. He marries one of the daughters. Yet when their first child is born, he chooses the name Gershom which means *"I have become an alien in a foreign land"* (Exodus 2:22). This is exile.

Why this transformation from Pharaoh's adopted and favored grandson to outcast? What happened? His deportation is the result of his dysfunctional anger and dominating fear. Here's the story:

One day, after Moses had grown up, he went out to where his own peo-
ple were and watched them at their hard labor. He saw an Egyptian
beating a Hebrew, one of his own people. Glancing this way and that
and seeing no one, he killed the Egyptian and hid him in the sand. The
next day he went out and saw two Hebrews fighting, He asked the one
in the wrong, "Why are you hitting your fellow Hebrew?"

The man said, "Who made you ruler and judge over us? Are you
thinking of killing me as you killed the Egyptian?" Then Moses was
afraid and thought, "What I did must have become known."

When Pharaoh heard of this, he tried to kill Moses, but Moses fled
(Exodus 2:1-15).

It began with uncontrollable anger. Like greed or lust or ego, it twists perspectives, mars motivation, and births irresponsible behavior. It is tempting
to focus on the painful behaviors that send people into exile: cruelty, betrayal,
theft, adultery, jealousy, and actions that kill the soul. These must be
addressed and rectified. However, the actions are symptoms. The cure comes
at a deeper level.

A driving force is beneath these dysfunctions. It is fear. Fear drives us off
the path of living true to our best. Fear separates us from spiritual authenticity.
It hides in deceit. It is a force that turns the inner eyes away from the truth,
the truth about failings as well as potential in Christ. Fear is a power used by
the evil one to disfigure what is best.

Fear floods the mind with empty questions and harmful imaginings. "What
if "[4] performs a marathon dances in the mind. The mind's eye sees threats and
seeks survival. We think there is no other way. We lose touch with who we are
and who we can become in Christ. This is exile without a home.

THE FIRE THAT CALLS YOUR NAME

Fear banishes Moses to the desert. Yet something about the desert, the place
of exile, is unknown to Moses. God lives in the desert. God finds us in the
place of banishment. The mountain of God, the home of God is in the
wilderness.

Now Moses was tending the flock … The angel of the Lord appeared to him in flames of fire from within a bush. Moses saw that though the bush was on fire it did not burn up. So Moses thought, "I will go over and see this strange sight" (Exodus 3:1-3).

The rabbis teach that there are really two miracles that day in the desert: The bush that burns but is not consumed and Moses who looked long enough to see a bush burning that was not consumed.

There is a fire in the wilderness of life, the broken time, the rocky path of failure, the place where we can remember only what we want to forget. I believe that we hear and encounter God in that place in ways we can never hear and encounter Him inside the walls of the palace.

The wilderness strips away the clutter of too many words, too many duties, too many

> *God finds us in the place of banishment.*

demands, and too many expectations. The cold cynicism that clings to empty speech, overwhelming obligations, and bitter disappointments melts in the heat of the desert. The wilderness creates simplicity: Quietness fosters curiosity and nurtures a sense of wonder. In the wilderness we learn to pay attention, spiritual attention.

Moses could have thought, "The bush is burning. This is trouble. I'll move the sheep on." But he did not move on; he stayed put and heard his name in the fire. *"When the Lord saw that he had gone over to look, God called to him from within the bush, 'Moses! Moses!'"* (Exodus 3:4).

When you encounter God, you hear your own name; you discover your identity in the heart of Heaven. The soul journey with God winds its way through your inner life, through your mud and mire, through your hopes and potential. God comes to you in your secret, private thoughts.

It is good to come to the wilderness by choice. Schedule times to be alone, exiled from the world, in order to talk with God. Make space in your life and calendar to have time away from the daily demands where you cultivate the art of focusing your spiritual attention.

Most come to the wilderness via crisis. Like Moses, our dysfunction and fear have brought us to the desert. It is the emptiness just on the other side of trying too hard for too long. We find it past the foothills of failure. It is just beyond the place called disaster. As it did Moses, fear drives us into exile. As it did Moses, love draws us to the flame.

We all have stories of how we got there: divorce, failure, rejection, tragedy, or shameful behavior. Whatever brings us to the wilderness, it is the place where we find God; it is where God finds us.

God Speaks from His Soul

To the world weary office worker, the stressed couple under financial pressure, or the frustrated souls imprisoned in the congestion of the freeway, there is something romantic about tramping off into the desert to find God. We imagine it; as soon as we arrive in the desert, as soon as we turn aside from the world, the desert will bloom like a rose. God will respond to our agenda. All will be right with the world. If that were true, we would have to enlist tour busses to shuttle the crowds, eager for a relaxing vacation spot with spiritual decor.

But that is not how it works. It is not as we desire but as God ordains. The desert is not an escape from the bustling noise and blistering pace of our outer lives. The desert sends us headlong toward our inner lives with all its anxieties, unrest and blindness. When there is calm around us, we become aware of the turmoil inside. It is here God speaks from the flame. Moses heard the heart of God.

> God revealed the compassion of his heart. The Lord said, *"I have indeed seen the misery of my people in Egypt. I have heard them crying out because of their slave drivers, and I am concerned about their suffering"* (Exodus 3:7).
>
> God revealed his plan to rescue his people. *"So I have come down to rescue them from the hand of the Egyptians and to bring them up out of that land into a good and spacious land"* (Exodus 3:8).
>
> God included Moses in his plans. *"so now, go. I am sending you to Pharaoh to bring my people the Israelites out of Egypt"* (Exodus 3:10).

God gave himself to Moses; God expected Moses to do the same. But Moses was frightened. Years of fear do not evaporate in an instant. Flaming shrubbery and heaven's grand schemes brought anxiety to the surface. This was part of God's treatment: Bring the fear out of the closet and face it.

> *This was part of God's treatment: Bring the fear out of the closet and face it.*

QUESTIONS THAT PROMOTE FEAR

Moses stammered and stumbled as he desperately looked for a way to avoid God, or at least God's plans for him. He tried a few questions. Fear uses questions to escape and evade. We are accustomed to these types of questions. Indeed, most of the questions we ask and most of the questions that are asked of us are shrouded in fear:

- ➤ Who broke the window?
- ➤ The test questions will determine your grade.
- ➤ What if they don't like me? What if I fail?
- ➤ Are you going to meet your quota this month?
- ➤ I have a few questions concerning your tax return.
- ➤ If you answer correctly, you have nothing to worry about.
- ➤ Whose fault is it, and who is going to pay for this?

The questions Moses posed to the Almighty were full of fear. First, he questioned God's logic: *"Who am I that I should go?"* (Exodus 3:11). Logic is a proven plan to escape personal involvement: It speaks from the head rather than the heart. God did not respond to the evasion. God heard the deeper issue in Moses' question: *"Who am I …?"* He saw the fearful soul of Moses begin to surface. The prince of Egypt had wasted decades in hiding. God's answer was direct: *"I will be with you"* (Exodus 3:12). Moses didn't grasp the wonder of this offer. Before him was an invitation to know God and to know himself as a new person.

Feeling backed into a corner, which can happen when dealing with the Almighty, Moses tried a second question. Specifically, he inquired, *"What if they ask me, 'What is his name?' Then what should I tell them?"* (Exodus 3:14). The question sounds a bit familiar. Moses was unable to conceal all his fear. Years before when he tried to settle a dispute, he was asked, *"Who made you ruler and judge over us?"* (Exodus 2:14). The wound of that day so long ago was surfacing. God's strategy was sound. Moses had played directly into His hand. Moses was facing himself. To know himself, Moses had to know God; to know God meant that Moses would come to know himself. God answered.

> *To know himself, Moses had to know God;*

God revealed his name. God said to Moses, *"I AM WHO I AM. This is what you are to say to the Israelites: 'I AM has sent me to you.'"* (Exodus 3:14.)

He told Moses his story, *"I am the Lord, the God of your fathers—the God of Abraham, the God of Isaac, and the God of Jacob"* (Exodus 3:15).

God exposed the mystery and gift of his soul. He promises to Moses and to those who meet him in the desert, *"I will be with you"* (Exodus 3:12).

God speaks from the heart with no small talk. He is a practitioner of free speech, and he expects the same from you and me. God will settle for nothing less than our true and best in Christ. To bring this about, he opens Himself to us, gracing us with His true and best, the Spirit of Christ, the Holy Spirit. He expects us to be open to Him.

No jet stream reaches to heaven in the desert, only hot winds, cold nights and the relentless sting of the blowing sand. The wind forces us to tuck our heads low against our chests, close enough to hear our hearts and face our inner lives. Here, in exile, God probes our souls with an invitation to cast our lives into His keeping.

Moses had one more inquiry. After questioning his own identity, "Who am I," and questioning God's identity, "What is your name," Moses questioned their relationship. Notice how God used the fear-filled inquisition of Moses to establish a relationship with him. The relationship was not what it would be one day, but it was a beginning. Again, the query is driven by fear: *"What if they don't believe me or listen to me and say, 'The Lord did not appear to you?'"* (Exodus 4:1.) The imagination of Moses was exposed. He envisioned the crowds disbelieving, shunning, rejecting, and disgracing him. God transformed his imagination with another kind of question.

GOD PROBES THE SOUL

Some questions flow from love. These questions open the soul as God inquires out of compassion. Even God's interrogations are expressions of eternal love. The source of authenticity for Moses is in relation to God.

> *Even God's interrogations are expressions of eternal love.*

God probed the heart of Moses much like we probe the heart of a good friend who is reluctant to open up. We ask questions. We ask, not to control our friend, but because we genuinely care. And God had a few questions for Moses:

"What's in your hand, Moses?" (Exodus 4:2). Moses is reminded that he has nothing. The palaces, the prestige, the power and wealth are all gone. He has nothing but a staff. As with Moses, the issue is not what we control, but what we place in the hands of God.

"Who gave man his mouth? ...Is it not I, the Lord?" (Exodus 4:11). God created the voice; God created Moses. And God's creative work in Moses was still in process. The Lord promises, *"I will help you speak and will teach you what to say"* (Exodus 4:12).

"What about your brother? ...He is already on his way to meet you" (Exodus 4:14). Moses was not alone in his exile or his calling. As with Moses, God has given us each other for spiritual support and friendship. Faith is not designed to be lived out alone. God works in the relationships of His people.

I have discovered that the fire in the wilderness is kindled by questions of love. Each question probes my soul. Loving questions stab at the coals and release the sparks of faith. Let me challenge you to think about this question: If you stood alone with God, what would He ask you? What are the questions God whispers in your soul? Explore the questions. Determine to give God an honest and complete answer. Responding to God's questions with authenticity opens the soul to healing and hope.

THE QUESTIONS OF JESUS

Jesus also asked questions. Many times He responded with a probing question rather than a direct answer. And he asked questions in love. They were not always tender questions, they were never easy questions, but they were questions that search the heart and soul.

Several years ago I sat with my New Testament and read the four Gospels straight through. I marked every place where Jesus asked a question. More than fifty questions are recorded in the conversations of Jesus. Let me share several of them with you.

Are you not worth more than the birds of the air? (Matthew 6:26)
Which of you being anxious can add a single hour to his life?
   (Matthew 6:27)
Why are you thinking evil in your hearts? (Matthew 9:4)
Do you believe I am able to do this? (Matthew 9:28)
Who do you say that I am? (Matthew 16:15)
What will a man give in exchange for his soul? (Matthew 16:26)
What do you wish me to do for you? (Matthew 20:32)
Why are you reasoning about these things in your hearts? (Mark 2:8)
Why is it you are so timid? (Mark 4:40)
Do you have a hardened heart? (Mark 8:17)
Why is it you were looking for me? (Luke 2:49)
Where is your faith? (Luke 8:25)
Why are you troubled and why do doubts arise in your hearts?
   (Luke 24:38)

What do you seek? (John 1:38)

Do you wish to get well? (John 5:6)

What have I been saying to you from the beginning?
(John 8:25)

Do you know what I have done to you? (John 13:12)

Do you love me? (John 21:15, 16, 17)

These questions, taken directly from the life of Jesus as recorded in the Gospels, are also questions for you, today. Allow them to be personal questions, directly from His soul to your soul.

First, choose one question for meditation. Read the list of questions.
Which one knocks on your heart's door? Select that question.

Second, read the question in the context of Scripture. What did it mean
to the person who first heard the question? Put yourself in his or
her place.

Third, take the question into your heart. Write it down and review it
several times each day.

Finally, answer the question with authenticity. Look within for your
honest answer. Tell it to Jesus. This is prayer. It is a conversation
with your Lord.

THE FIRE OF IMAGINATION

The questions not only open the soul, but also emblazon the imagination. God speaks to the inner life through the power of imagination, God inspired and guided imagination. In the imagination you envision what you cannot see in the world. It is *"evidence of things not seen"* (Hebrews 11:1).

We tend to confine imagination to human endeavors; a flight of fancy, a new innovation, a corporate vision, or a work of art. In the practical world, imagination inspires, entertains, and prescribes; what is a business plan except a detailed image of how we want to run the business. Leaders wanting to initiate change must make that change imaginable to their followers. This is the practical side of imagination.

In the spiritual life, imagination is a means of communication and faith. When God guides our spiritual imagination, we envision what is beyond our physical sight; we see what is unseen. Sanctified imagination also emboldens our faith, our confidence and commitment in Christ: *"being sure of what we hope for and certain of what we do not see"* (Hebrews 11:1). In the Bible, imagination is a Divine means of communication. God uses common things as well as wondrous miracles to stir the imagination.

Imagination and Miracles. Miracles are *"signs"* (John 20:30) that help us understand the Kingdom of God in our world and the future of the world. God reaches into the Kingdom as it will be and pulls a moment of awe and wonder into our world as if to say, "this is what it will be one day when the dead shall rise, the blind shall see and the hungry will be satisfied." We see the miracle with the physical eye; the eye of the soul envisions the "sign."

God stirred the imagination of Moses with miraculous wonders. God asked Moses to take the staff in his hand and throw it to the ground. The stick became a snake. Then God said, *"Reach out your hand and take it by the tail"* (Exodus 4:4). When Moses did, it became a staff again. What thoughts, what imaginings raced through the mind of Moses?

The spiritual imagination of Moses was transformed. No longer did he imagine the rejection of the people. Now, the eye of his soul pictured the power of God let loose on the empire of Pharaoh. For a moment he imagined God could use him to set the people free. The desert looked the same and the burning bush did not burn anymore. But faith was set afire in the soul of Moses.

Imagination and Daily Life. God used the stars of the heavens to help Abraham imagine the legacy of his family (Genesis 15:5). In a dream, Jacob saw a stairway to heaven (Genesis 28:12). We draw near to God through the images in the Psalms: a shepherd (Psalm 23) or a stronghold (Psalm 27). Through spiritual imagination, God invites us to hide *"under his wings"* (Psalm 91) and rest in Him as a *"weaned child with its mother"* (Psalm 131). The Prophets consistently roused the people through imagination. The images the prophets pictured allowed the people to see the unseen and hear the silent voice. Jeremiah spoke of a potter's wheel (Jeremiah 18:6). Amos heard the

Lion's roar (3:8). Zachariah pictured a gold lamp stand, a flying scroll, and a woman in a basket (Zachariah 4-5).

God moves in our imagination, also. He wants to give us images that reveal His wisdom and power at work in our world. For us, that is, most people most of the time, God uses common items and daily events to awaken the spiritual imagination. He uses simple moments to help us see the unseen and hear the silent word from Heaven. In this way, God kindles the prayer-filled fire of imagination.

It was such a confusing time for me. I did not know what to do, where to turn, or how to proceed. I went for a prayer walk in a large and heavily wooded city park. I found a bench at the edge of a clearing where I sat and mulled over the questions: Where do I go? What do I do? What's the next step? The true path was lost. I heard inner questions that were uncomfortable. Why is this so hard for me? What is holding me back? What is the inner source of my struggle? My head was pounding.

It was a day when the skies were fickle. First, clouds turned everything gray: trees, grass, and brush. Then, the sunshine returned. The colors were vivid. The sunshine also revealed the shadows, the points of distinction, the clear lines of dark and light. I watched the transformation three or four times before it took on meaning for me.

Across the clearing was a trail that led through a deep wood. When the clouds obscured the sun, the gray tones hid the trail from view. The sun would return. In the light and shadow the path was clear and plain.

God spoke to me in that little image. He guided my imagination and opened my soul to hear the wisdom I needed: "Richard, move forward only when the path is clear before you."

The image helped me and sustained me with good wisdom for several months. The power of imagination is a gift from God. Under His guidance, it is wisdom from Heaven.

I am obliged to provide a warning at this point. Imagination is powerful,

> *The power of imagination is a gift from God. Under His guidance, it is wisdom from Heaven.*

but it is not the source of power. The power is God. The evil one will try to use your imagination to distract you or deceive you. It is evil when imagination shuts down your true and best in Christ by imprisoning you in fear or fooling you into thinking it is your greatness that is the issue.

"If I want it and dream it, I can believe it and achieve it" is not Christian spirituality. For followers of Christ, we know that God uses our imagination to speak to us, comfort us, fill us with vision, direct our path, enlighten our understanding, and embolden our faith. However, it is God, in Christ, who is the center and sustaining power. The eye of the soul sees, hears, prays, and asks in His *"name"* (John 16:24), in full allegiance to the will, way, and wisdom of God.

JESUS AND SPIRITUAL IMAGINATION

Jesus used common images, things we can see, touch, and hear, to help us envision the unseen, touch the untouchable, and hear His voice. He told many stories and parables. A farmer scattering seed is an image of God's active word transforming lives (Luke 8:5-15). Little children depict the inner condition of God's Kingdom (Mark 10:13-16). As Jesus walked to the garden of Gethsemane, He stopped in front of the doors of the Temple. A grape vine was embossed on the door. *"I am the vine and you are the branches"* (John 15:1). Jesus speaks to you and me through our imagination, the inner eye of the soul.

> Open my eyes that I may see,
>   Glimpses of truth Thou hast for me.
> Open my ears that I may hear,
>   Voices of truth Thou sendest clear.
>   CLARA H. SCOTT[5]

Again, I must share a word of warning. You can catch yourself beginning to misuse the imagination when you either stretch the image beyond its meaning or hold onto it longer than is useful. To do so means that we are just on the edge of trusting the image rather than trusting the One who speaks to you through the image.

How can you learn to open your imagination in prayer? Look to Jesus. Start with the images Christ gave us in Scripture. The Bible is filled with images that confront and comfort us with truth. Jesus shared pictures and stories that stir the imagination. They are also images of God in Christ, the great I AM. As God spoke to Moses, *"I AM WHO I AM"* (Exodus 3:14), Jesus opens His heart and we find the heart of God in Christ. Jesus invites us to imagine Him as bread and light, as a door, a good shepherd and the true vine. He is life, truth, and the path of the spiritual journey.

> *"I AM the bread of life"* (John 6:35, 41, 48, 51).
> *"I AM the Light of the world"* (John 8:12; 9:5).
> *"I AM the door"* (John 10:7, 9).
> *"I AM the good shepherd"* (John 10:11, 14).
> *"I AM the resurrection and the life"* (John 11:25).
> *"I AM the way, the truth, and the life"* (John 14:6).
> *"I AM the true vine"* (John 15:1, 5).

Choose one image, one that rouses your imagination. Trust the Holy Spirit to draw your attention to the image you need to consider. Open the Bible and read the image in context. Think about what it meant to the people who first heard these words. Finally, carry the image with you in your mind. You may find it helpful to write it on a card and place it where you see it often. Trust God to bring the image to your mind and speak through it to you at just the moment you need to hear from heaven.

THE JOURNEY BEGINS

Jesus meets us in the desert, in the wilderness. His purpose is to present us to God, to help us find our way with God, and to make our home in God. When

He transforms our fear into love, we find a home in exile. God will question the soul and speak through our spiritual imagination. God is working in us, for us, and through us. For the journey we need three things:

First, we need to make healthy choices, choices that display, protect, and nurture our true and best in Christ.

Second, we will build an inward house of prayer, a place to lay bare the soul and find God's true and best, the Spirit of Christ, renewed and restored in us.

Third, we need to learn the art of holy listening. The spiritual life is not meant to be faced alone; we need each other.

In the final section of the book, ***Soul Journey***, we will examine each of these essential parts of the spiritual life.

CHAPTER 10

HEALTHY CHOICES

My chains fell off, my heart was free,
I rose, went forth and followed Thee.
CHARLES WESLEY[1]

To live true to your best in Christ is a great decision. It is your response to the love of God for you. Your true and best in Christ is also shaped by thousands of daily decisions, heart decisions, and, sometimes, hard decisions. It is choosing to let go of old patterns and ways that harm your soul's vitality. You choose to take hold of God's promise, and, in doing so, God fashions your identity in Him.

God gives you the choice; He gives you the ability to choose. There are a few profound moments when you choose to surrender at a new depth of consecration. There are many personal moments when you freely give a specific situation or a troublesome part of yourself to Christ. Each choice is accompanied by another chip of God's chisel that shapes your identity in Jesus. In this process, God asks for your cooperation, your free and heartfelt decision to live your life in Him.

At the University where I was employed, a colleague joined me for long walks. I talked and he listened. Stories poured out of me, stories of my past with its triumphs and tragedies, the good and the bad. Fear and confusion were constant companions. I simply did not know what to do.

My friend gave me his best insights, but I simply couldn't or didn't know how to begin. Sitting on a small bench in a little garden behind the administration building, he responded to my lack of understanding with a bit of frustration. He said, "Richard, when you don't know what to do, choose health."

It was a revelation for me. I knew how to choose: choose to meet the demands of others, choose to reach expectations. However, this was something different: "choose health." It was simple yet changed my pattern of life. Choose what brings life and health to the soul. Choose the courage to live true to your best in Christ.

It was what I needed. I also needed to learn how to make healthy choices, how to choose what keeps me alive in Christ.

THE GIFT OF CHOICE

The central, essential, and foundational event of the Bible's Old Testament is the Exodus: God delivered His people from the tyranny of Egypt's Pharaoh; God brought them into the wilderness to make them His *treasured possession* (Deuteronomy 7:6). The Bible is clear: God is not like Pharaoh. Pharaoh enslaves his people; God sets His people free. This is a truth that we must take deep into our minds and hearts. Over the centuries too many religious leaders, seeking to control the masses, have depicted God's way as a form of spiritual slavery.

God is not a slave master. Pharaoh controls his slaves. If Pharaoh gives a choice, it is an illusion on a stage of fear. He demands conformity and fearful obedience. God, however, sets His people free. God freed the ancient Hebrews from the shackles of slavery, the physical bonds of Egypt; God frees you and me from the dominion and law of sin that, as Rufus Jones observes, "weaves a mess of habit," the chains of evil. God is our champion, our liberator.

Oswald Smith, pastor, author, evangelist, and lyricist, was the founder of The People's Church in Toronto, Canada. In one of his most popular hymns, he expresses our praise and gratitude for the gift of freedom in Christ:

> 'Tis the song of the soul set free
> And my heart is ever singing
> Hallelujah! Hallelujah!
> The song of the soul set free.[2]

In a mighty act, God brought His people out of Egypt. Moses led them to the edge of the Red Sea. There was nowhere to turn; they were trapped. Pharaoh's army was in hot pursuit. Clouds of dust from advancing chariots billowed in the distance. When it seemed that all was for naught, Moses said to the people, *"Do not be afraid. Be still and see the deliverance of the Lord … The Lord will fight for you; you need only to be still"* (Exodus 14:13-14).

Moses raised the staff and stretched out his hand. All that night the wind blew. *"The waters divided, and the Israelites went through the sea on dry ground"* (Exodus 14:21-22). When the army of Egypt followed, the waves crashed together and swallowed them. God liberated His people. Safe on freedom's shore, the people sang what many scholars consider to be the first remembered and written words to be included in the Bible:

> *Sing to the Lord,*
> *For he is highly exalted.*
> *The horse and rider*
> *He has buried in the sea.*
> EXODUS 15:21[3]

Yet there is more. God's graceful gift of freedom is deep and eternal. He was not satisfied with taking His people out of Egypt; he determined to take Egypt out of His people. God is determined to remove the inward chains from our hearts as well.

Moses led the people out of Pharaoh's evil empire and into the wilderness. Guided by the memory of meeting God on the mountain, he led the people.

He was intent on going back to the holy mountain. It was there that the inward work of freedom would begin. And they needed the inward work.

True, they were out of Egypt, but the inner bondage, the soul of slavery lingered. It would require a generation to remove the inward chains. Although they were no longer slaves, they thought like slaves, looked at the world as slaves, and were motivated with slavish patterns of heart and mind. It takes time to learn to live free in God. It takes time to learn to choose health for the soul.

> It takes time to learn to live free in God. It takes time to learn to choose health for the soul.

The old ways had a grip on God's people. *After three days of freedom,* three days after crossing the Red Sea, three days after Pharaoh's army was drowned in the waves, God's people complain against the person who led them out of slavery: *"So the people grumbled against Moses, saying, 'What are we to drink?'"* (Exodus 15:24).

After *six weeks of freedom,* the people long to return to their slavery in Egypt: *"In the desert the whole community grumbled against Moses and Aaron. The Israelites said, 'If only we died by the Lord's hand in Egypt! There we sat around pots of meat and ate all the food we wanted, but you have brought us out into the desert to starve...'"* (Exodus 16:1-3).

After *three months of freedom,* they worship the image of an Egyptian god, Apis, a false god in the image of a calf: *"The people gathered around Aaron and said, 'Come, make us gods who will go before us.' Aaron ...made an idol cast in the shape of a calf ...Then the people said, 'These are your gods, O Israel, who brought you up out of Egypt'"* (Exodus 32:1-4)

In freedom, you are tempted to return to prison. You knock on the penitentiary door, pound the steel gate, and beg for readmission. There are jailers who are pleased to return you to your cell. The guards promise rewards and reasonableness. It's a lie; buyers beware!

Viktor Frankl wrote a deeply significant book entitled, Man's Search
for Meaning, about his own experience and the experience of others
in the Nazi concentration camp at
Dachau. He observed that some prisoners who yearned so desperately for freedom demonstrated a strange response
when at last the guards were gone and
the doors were open wide. They walked

> *You knock on the
> penitentiary door, pound
> the steel gate, and beg for
> readmission.*

into the sunlight, blinked nervously, and then silently walked back
into the familiar darkness of the prison.[4]

The first taste of freedom is in the wind and on your tongue. To wake up
in the wilderness is liberation. It also means that Pharaoh no longer makes
decisions for you; you are required to make your own choices. Choose health!

For Moses and the band of freed slaves, it was a forty-year journey, a spiritual journey. They had to come to know God and themselves. *"At the command of the Lord, Moses recorded the stages in their journey"* (Numbers 33:2).
Every step of the journey was logged. In the record, one phrase is repeated
more than forty times: *"and they journeyed"* (Numbers 33).

The spiritual journey lasts a lifetime. Here is a physical exercise that
helps sink this truth into your inner life. Read the phrase, "and they
journeyed," forty times. This works best if you read it aloud:

...and they journeyed ...and they journeyed ...and they journeyed
...and they journeyed ...and they journeyed ...and they journeyed
...and they journeyed ...and they journeyed ...and they journeyed
...and they journeyed ...and they journeyed ...and they journeyed
...and they journeyed ...and they journeyed ...and they journeyed
...and they journeyed ...and they journeyed ...and they journeyed
...and they journeyed ...and they journeyed ...and they journeyed
...and they journeyed ...and they journeyed ...and they journeyed
...and they journeyed ...and they journeyed ...and they journeyed
...and they journeyed ...and they journeyed ...and they journeyed

...and they journeyed ...and they journeyed ...and they journeyed
...and they journeyed ...and they journeyed ...and they journeyed
...and they journeyed ...and they journeyed ...and they journeyed
...and they journeyed! (Numbers 33:5-48)

This spiritual journey was designed to teach one lesson with every event and each step: *"This day ...I have set before you life and death, blessings and curses. Now, choose life"* (Deuteronomy 30:19)

In your old life, your old ways, your "slavery in Egypt," there were many people to play the part of "Pharaoh" and choose for you. In the world, the world that operates on demands, expectations, rewards, and punishments, if you do not choose for yourself, someone will choose for you.

You are set free. Learn to choose life and health for your soul. Don't take anything that is handed to you. Learn to question, probe, and choose. Your life is in Christ. It does not belong to anyone else.

The wilderness is the way, the spiritual journey in which you examine choices, consider decisions, cross-examine your perceptions, explore your emotions, and interrogate your motivations. If something is unwholesome and harms your life in Christ, set it aside. If something is healthy and enlivens your life in Christ, take it up.

> If something is unwholesome and harms your life in Christ, set it aside.

Let me be bold in my statements. Even the good word of parents, religious teachers, and old traditions and patterns must be taken up anew or set aside. God does not set you free from the slavery of sin in order to chain you in a slave camp of religious traditions, customs, and mores. Choose what keeps you alive in Christ. Choose this day! Choose life!!

There are four principles that guide healthy choices: *attention, validation, contemplation,* and *intention.*

ATTENTION: TRUTH AND HOPE

The currency of the marketplace is money; the currency of the spiritual life is attention. You make healthier choices when you focus attention on what God is doing inside you. God forgives your failings and imparts His Spirit. He heals your wounds as He opens new paths of life. He confronts your dysfunctions, yet envisions your potential. He unearths your painful past, while resurrecting a new future. Remember the old adage:

> Two men looked through prison bars
> One saw mud and one saw stars.[5]

Should we focus attention on the mud: our transgressions, poor choices, indulgences, dysfunctions, the "mesh of habit"? We must face the truth about our failings. Or should we center our attention on the stars: our new life, potential and possibilities? We must envision our hope in Christ.

> *The currency of the marketplace is money; the currency of the spiritual life is attention.*

Should we attend to our failures or our future, to our mud or our stars? Here is the answer: Focus on *the tension* between truth and hope. To let go of either side is spiritual danger. God works in the tension, moving our true self toward His best hope for us.

The epic poem, The Odyssey, follows the journey of a king returning home. Along the way obstacles abound in the form of tempting distractions, wondrous possibilities, hellish pathways, and personal monsters. The first monster encountered on his travels is the Cyclops: the beast with one eye. King Odysseus himself kills the creature. Danger attacks your soul if you view your life in God only with one eye, the eye of mud or the eye of stars.[6]

Your journey toward your true and best in Christ, your soul purpose, requires two eyes. With one you focus on the truth of your life. With the other, fasten your gaze on hope. To close one eye or the other mars your perspective and sends you off the edge of the map. A focus only on harsh truth or optimistic hope creates a personal cyclops.

To focus only on the mud is a sure path toward more mud. The thought, "I don't want to deal with this reality," screams inside you, pressing for relief and escape. "I can't do anything about it anyway" leads to a dead end of giving up or giving in. You look for escape from such painful truth.

In addition, avoiding truth in order to wish for a new tomorrow is a false path that doubles back on itself. You "wish upon a star." You persuade yourself, convince yourself, and believe in yourself. However, it is a covering rather than a cleansing. It soon becomes a pretense of inner freedom grounded in your ability to hold inner pain at bay through consistent pep talks with the mirror.

> *When you find yourself set free in the wilderness, the mud and the stars are yours.*

When you find yourself set free in the wilderness, the mud and the stars are yours. There is truth about today and hope for tomorrow. If you capitulate to fear of the truth, you look only at the stars. This is the way of self delusion and self indulgence. However, if you become stuck in the quagmire of clay, the fearful dysfunctions in your own life, you walk a path of self-defeat and self-destruction. Live in the tension between truth and hope.[7] It is here that God does His work of creating life in you. With God as your guard and guide, truth establishes hope; hope builds on truth.

Hold fast to *truth*: fall in love with, be engaged to, and wed truth in a holy bond. Denying the truth is a survival skill for prison inmates. As a soul set free, face your reality and shoulder your responsibility. When facing the mirror of truth, you may be tempted to play the part of a victim. You may been victimized. This is the truth; at least it is part of the truth. It is also true that dysfunction hides in your heart. Don't shrink away; get at it. It is the power and presence of God that sets you free. In prayer, alone or with a trusted soul friend or spiritual counselor, ask:

Lord, give me the courage to see what really happened. What are the facts? What attitudes and actions led to what results and consequences? What have I done? What have others done to me? Help me face it squarely.

Lord, give me the wisdom to understand what caused it to happen that way? What is beneath the facts? What perceptions, emotions, and motivations were operating below the surface? What had control over me? What did I allow to control me?

You must unearth the chains that bind so they may be broken. It is essential; it is also dangerous. Facing truth can be treacherous. Like a tsunami rising from the deep, it may overwhelm you with despair. Waves of hard truth and harsh reality pull the sea from the shore exposing all that lies beneath. The crashing wave sweeps you away in a torrid of irrational thoughts and wild emotions.

> *You must unearth the chains that bind so they may be broken.*

Oh, the temptation, the sweet temptation to avoid the truth or be carried off in despair. Each, avoidance and despair, is an escape from responsibility. Take heart. God has brought the truth to the surface. God is working, creating life in you. Choose health; press on in prayer. Pray for forgiveness and healing. In the presence of God, trace it back, talk it out, and turn it over to Him.

Trace it back. Origins are rarely singular and simple. What are the roots of dysfunctional patterns? What are the sources of poison that created your pain? What are the deep roots of hurt and fear? Can you picture it?

Talk it out. This involves a series of soul-to-soul conversations. Share your regret and rage with a wise friend or trusted counselor. Turn your soul toward God and express your anxiety and angst. Walk through the scene with Christ at your side. In faith, open your imagination to the Spirit's guidance. See the powerful love of Jesus at work in you.

Turn it loose. There is power in forgiveness. The one who has been hurt is the one who forgives. If you have hurt yourself, forgive yourself for God also forgives you. If you have been hurt by others, forgive them and be free. Ask for the forgiveness of those you harmed. If possible, make restitution and seek reconciliation.

Beyond regret and rage is forgiveness. Beyond forgiveness is healing. Beyond healing is freedom. Be courageous and wise. Pay attention. The mirror of truth will give up her hidden treasure—*hope*.

When you stop knocking on the door that was your life, when you let it go and turn away, you discover a world that is wide and open. Possibilities surround you. You may be standing knee deep in your own mud, but you are also standing under your own stars. Hope puts truth in motion. It dares to dream. It has the courage to build anew. What kind of life will you and God create? Lift your hopes in prayer:

> Lord, what dreams will we pursue? The deepest pain is a path of potential for great good. Inner passion is a promise of new life.
>
> Lord, what limitations do I need? You need physical, relational, and emotional boundaries that protect and cultivate your best.
>
> Lord, what support will we build? A support system of good people, authentic people, nurtures your true and best in Christ.

Make healthy choices by focusing your spiritual attention on the *tension* between truth and hope. At first, the truth appears so horrible that hope eludes you. Through regret and rage, forgiveness and healing, the strain between truth and hope resolves. Facing the horrible truth opens the path of true hope. Pain and passion form a single road. Forgiven failures open future doors. Set limits and boundaries as you and your Lord dream great dreams. Choose life for your soul.

VALIDATION: FRIENDS AND ENEMIES.

On the spiritual journey, you need validation. The desire to be understood, affirmed, and appreciated is genuine. How this need is met is your choice. Choose carefully. There are people who manipulate your need for validation in order to control or nullify your newly found spiritual life. Other people, true soul-friends, support and encourage your inward search for validation. Soul-friends share their inward lives so that *"we may have fellowship"* with one another, and *"our fellowship is with the Father and his Son, Jesus Christ"*

(1 John 1:3). Learning to seek and find spiritual validation is the second step in making healthy choices for your soul. It builds inner confidence and faith.

When you learn to face truth and embrace hope, you experience a new inner-dynamic. The freedom you found by facing the truth produces the energy of hope. It is exhilarating. Life begins afresh. Fresh innocence and naivety accompany your experience. You may find yourself thinking, "Everyone, or at least the people closest to me, will support my soul purpose. They will recognize my new faith and help me live true to my best." This is the longing for supportive validation, but it is not a realistic plan.

Validation is found in every walk in life. A judge validates the authenticity of a will. The politician attempts to validate the soundness of his policies. The art expert validates the genuineness of a painting. A philatelist validates the worth of a rare stamp. You also need appropriate and genuine validation on your soul's journey.

Validation can be true or false. It is sometimes difficult to distinguish the two. Legal documents, rare objects, and political policies serve conflicting agendas. For reasons of greed or glory, the genuine article is sometimes declared fake. For power or wealth, the false is presented as authentic. When you seek validation for your soul, remain vigilant and be careful. On the spiritual journey you will encounter people who, relationally, play the part of false judges, crooked politicians, and incompetent experts.

The ugly fact is that as soon as you begin your search for spiritual meaning there are people determined to invalidate you. There are enemies who want to send you back to prison, back under their control. Invalidation of your spiritual journey begins with a glance. You express your heart and receive a cruel look or a blank stare that melts your courage. Fear wells up. The old patterns of prison life re-emerge in your spiritual life.

> *The ugly fact is that as soon as you begin your search for spiritual meaning there are people determined to invalidate you.*

It is one thing to take a person out of sin and another to take the sin out of the person. Are old ways beginning to undermine your new life? Take these questions to God in prayer:

> Am I placating others because I lack courage to speak from my heart?

> Do I intimidate others in order to hide my true fears from myself?

> Do I sacrifice my identity for the approval I receive from others?

> Am I counting on my ability to succeed as proof of my inner value?

> Am I just making everyone happy at the cost of my own true joy?

Healthy choices are not convenient choices. You learn by facing and over-coming those who would overthrow your soul's purpose, the people who invalidate the spiritual life. It also means establishing and nurturing relation-ships with authentic soul friends.

People who invalidate come in two forms: those who abandon you in the wilderness and the bounty hunters who are bent on returning you to prison. You will run into people you have leaned on for support in the past who now seem to abandon you. They may never reject you outright, but they do not understand nor do they seek to understand your soul purpose. They are well meaning people whose intent is to help you, fix you, or even save you from your new self. Even though they have good intentions, they mean to help you; their purpose is to bring you back inside prison walls.

Old cell mates find it difficult to identify with those who have been set free. Something has changed. You used to swap stories, share gripe sessions, and open your secrets to each other. Now it feels superficial and empty. You have new depth in your soul and a new search for meaning. Some will not comprehend or appreciate it.

If the invalidation of some is subtle and silent, the destructive intent of others is calculated and cruel. You are now dealing with bounty hunters. At first they patronize you. Your new awareness is tolerated for awhile, politely recognized, and then subtly excused. Verbal attacks that begin as condescen-sion become ridicule. You are the brunt of a few jokes, the "touchy feely" one, the person who "can't get it together," the one on "some spiritual trip," or "the self-help guru."

Ridicule feels cruel and demeaning. That is the point, to make you feel foolish. Rejection follows. They place you on the sidelines. You are relegated to lesser positions, excluded from events, conversation, and information. Decisions are made without your counsel or consent. The issue is control; they want to control you.

Bounty hunters can be family members, friends, co-workers, or people in authority who share a single purpose, to return an inmate to prison. The goal of these tactics is to get you back in line. You can control a

> *You can control a prisoner, but it is difficult to control a heart that has been set free.*

prisoner, but it is difficult to control a heart that has been set free.

The Prodigal Son had a brother, an elder brother. When the younger "came to himself" and returned as a new person, the older sibling was not pleased. Jesus' story continues:

"The elder son was in a field, and as he drew near the house, he heard music and dancing. He called one of the servants and asked what it might be. The servant said to him—'Your brother arrived healthy and whole! Your father has killed the fatted calf in celebration.' And the elder brother was angry, and would not go in." (Luke 15:25-28).

You have to wonder: would the prodigal son have ever made it home had he run into his older brother first?[8]

You learn to make healthy choices as you overcome those who would overthrow your soul purpose. Observe carefully and learn that your prison walls were methods of control for those with greedy or evil intent. Stand firm in your freedom. Spiritual growth results from overcoming their attacks. Make your stand against bounty hunters and those who abandon you. It is essential to growth. You will develop inward poise and buoyancy. God's grace works in you. You are learning to rest in the validation of God's grace.

The need for spiritual validation is real. God works within you to meet the need. He also designed us to help each other. Indeed, God helps us as we nurture one another. We need *authentic soul-friends*. You need friends who hear your pain but do not dismiss it, excuse it, or try to fix it. You need soul friends who understand and receive inward pain as part of the journey. Join a group of faithful people who worship and pray together, who know how to wait on God and listen for His wisdom. Soul-friends seek the presence and purpose of God. They *"rejoice with those who rejoice; mourn with those who mourn"* (Romans 12:15). Seek out a small group that provides safety and freedom to be authentic. Cultivate soul-friends who validate the journey.

A journalist from The New Yorker observed a support group of bereaved parents. Like other groups of this kind, Alcoholics Anonymous, Single Parents Fellowship, or the Compassionate Friends, this was a safe place to tell your story without judgment. In such a place, a safe place, a quiet time, with special friends, you can hear your own voice and learn from your own story.

The journalist described this as "the mystery and the miracle" that is the result of "a dynamic of grace." Grace is not something that is earned, but something that is given. It is this gift of grace that soul-friends provide for one another.[9]

CONTEMPLATION: SILENCE AND WISDOM

Contemplation is the art of spiritual listening. It begins in silence and opens the soul to the voice of God's wisdom. Silencing the voices is not an act of the will but the way of the soul. It is the next lesson of exile. To review, first, it takes inner courage to pay attention to the *tension* between truth and hope. Second, finding authentic and supportive validation builds inner confidence as you turn away from bounty hunters and engage in the journey with soul-friends. Third, silencing voices in order to hear God's inner wisdom calls forth the strength of inner commitment. Learn to wait, to be still and silent. The inner voice, the voice of God in your soul, is full with wisdom. Learn to listen.

Metropolitan Anthony Bloom was bishop of the Diocese of Sourozh, the Russian Orthodox Church in Great Britain and Ireland. In a conversation about contemplation he reflected:

"Well, I think this is where contemplation begins. Sit and listen—in religious terms it may be called waiting on God—but it is plain listening or looking in order to understand. If we did that with regard to the Word of God, with regard to the prayers of the saints, with regard to the situations in which we are, to everything people say to us or what they are in life, with regard to our own selves—we would be in that position we call contemplation, which consists in pondering, thinking deeply, in waiting until one has understood in order to act. This action would be much more efficient, less hasty, and filled, probably, with some amount of Divine Wisdom."

His Eminence then cited a children's nursery rhyme as an image of contemplation:

> A wise old owl lived in an oak;
> The more he saw the less he spoke.
> The less he spoke the more he heard.
> Why can't we all be like that bird?[10]

In the classroom of the wilderness, you begin to hear the inner voice. The lesson begins in silence. Silence the voices around you. Silence the multiple and conflicting voices within you. It takes inner commitment to remain attuned to God's inner voice.

The call to be silent and still has a romantic appeal in an overstressed and busy world. "I just want a little peace and quiet." The path of silence eventually leads to peace and quiet, but it begins with conflict and noise. To be silent is to stop talking. That means giving up control. We all rely on words to manage and control others, convincing and persuading them of our needs, opinions, and plans. Inward words bounce in our heads as we evaluate, condemn, or "cut them down to size." Words keep us focused on problems and production, on gaining rewards and avoiding punishment.

> *The path of silence eventually leads to peace and quiet, but it begins with conflict and noise.*

Silence not only means setting aside outward talk; it also means quieting the many voices inside. Many voices echo inside: the voices of family, teachers, friends as well as the voice of *your* perceptions, emotions, and motivations. Each voice may speak a word of help or harm. Some voices are louder than others. The challenge is to learn to be still for a long while in order to quiet the voices inside.

What is the promise of this arduous discipline of quiet? God speaks in the quietness. Internalize and personalize the instruction of Moses to the people on the edge of the Red Sea: *"Be still and see the deliverance the Lord will bring you today"* (Exodus 14:13). This is the way of wisdom.

In Grimm's fairy tale of "The Water of Life," you find three brothers, princes all of them, of which the first two are selfish and arrogant and the third is kind and true. Their father, the king, is dying. An old man appears in the palace courtyard and declares that the water of life will save the father.

Immediately, the oldest brother sets off to get the water and thus prove his great value and supremacy. He sees a dwarf along the way, but treats him cruelly, never asking for wisdom or direction. He thinks that because he knows what he wants, he knows how to find it. The dwarf, however, sends him down a narrow ravine until he is stuck, stuck in his own arrogance and ignorance. The second brother repeats the steps, ignores the dwarf, and ends up in the same ravine. You might say that some people never learn.

The youngest brother knows that he doesn't know the way. He tells the dwarf his heart's desire and his heart's troubles. The dwarf sets him on a heroic journey where he faces many obstacles but eventually overcomes and returns with the water of life.[11]

It is wise to admit that you don't know the way. The "dwarf" in the story is the small voice within you that seeks what is best for you. The famous Chinese philosopher, Lao-Tzu offers a challenge: "Do you have the patience to wait till your mud settles and the water is clear?" Scripture instructs us. *"Be still before the Lord and wait patiently for him"* (Psalm 37:7). *"Be still and know that I am God"* (Psalm 46:10).

To hear the inner voice involves two parts: to know yourself and to concentrate on God. You must **know yourself.** If you were assigned the responsibility of making choices for another person, you would get to know that person. You would learn what he

> *It is wise to admit that you don't know the way.*

likes and dislikes, what is good for him and harmful to him. You would want to know his preferences and problems, his desires and fears, his struggles and potential.

Getting to know yourself, like getting to know any other person, takes time. It is not something done in a moment, but piece by piece. As you continue becoming your own best friend, you recognize a new voice inside you. It is new yet somehow familiar. It is the voice of your own soul directing your attention and validating your true and best in Christ.

Here is a way to begin. Take your time; don't do this in one sitting. Carry one question with you. Observe yourself. Think about it. The answer is inside you. Listen for it.

What brings out my best?

When do I feel most like myself?

What gives me a sense of purpose?

When am I most creative?

What gives my life meaning?

When am I closest to God?

This seemingly benign exercise is more problematic than first appears. When Jesus went into the desert at the beginning of His ministry, the devil followed him. In fact, the Scripture hints that the trial was part of the guidance: *"Jesus was led by the Spirit into the desert to be tempted by the devil"* (Matthew 4:1). In silence, you come to know your demons of fear, anger, greed, lust, and all their related cousins. Pay attention to both truth and hope. Find the place of grace to tell your story and hear your inner voice.

In time, the spiritual habit of silence re-orients your life map with new wisdom. It is a challenging and arduous task to re-orient your map and change your life so that it lines up with your inner compass. The compass will only point in one direction: the north star of God's perfect love. You have invested years twisting the compass to fit the map. It is time to reorient the map to fit the compass.

> You have invested years twisting the compass to fit the map. It is time to reorient the map to fit the compass.

When the devil found him in the desert, Jesus chose to **concentrate on God**. The devil tempted Jesus with imaginary ministry strategies that were less than heavenly. Jesus chose to concentrate spiritual attention on God, the Father, *"Man does not live by bread alone, but by every word that comes from the mouth of God ...Do not put the Lord your God to the test ... Worship the Lord your God, and serve him only"* (Matthew 4:1-11).

A twelfth century German philosopher and theologian, Hugh of St. Victor, aptly described the path of silence that moves from self understanding to the worship of God.

"In spiritual matters, when something is called 'highest,' it doesn't mean that it is located above the top of the heavens, but rather that it is the inmost and most intimate of all. Thus, to ascend to God is to enter into one's own self, and not only to enter into one's self, but in some unsayable manner, in the inmost parts to pass beyond one's self. He who can, as it were, enter into himself and going deeper and deeper, pass beyond himself, truly ascends to God.

"So to return from the outside to the inmost is to ascend from the lowest to the highest and to gather oneself from a state of scatteredness and confusion. Since we truly know that this world is outside us and that God is within us, when we return from the world to God ...we must pass through ourselves."[12]

INTENTION: GIFT AND GRACE.

Inner compassion is the intention of the spiritual journey. It is both our *origin and our destination*. God initiates a relationship with us and intends to lead us to His home. To live with spiritual intention is to choose to live in alignment with the love of God. This is the fourth lesson in choosing health for the soul.

The common school of thought assigns intention to human achievement rather than God's compassion. This is intention in the market place of expectation and rewards. Spiritual intention finds its source in God. God's compassion is the driving force in the universe. He intends acorns to be oaks and apple blossoms to bear fruit. Our part is to cooperate with God's intention, God's compassion. It is the theme of the ministry of Jesus.

> To the Pharisees, Jesus quoted the prophet, Hosea, *"Go and learn what this means, 'I desire **mercy**, not sacrifice'"* (Matthew 9:13).
>
> Jesus asked for the identity of a true neighbor. The expert on the law replied, *"The one who had **compassion** on him."* Jesus told him, *"Go and do likewise"* (Luke 10:37).
>
> For a man living in a graveyard, Jesus drove out his demons, set the man free, and sent him home to be a living reminder of the compassion of God, *"Tell them how much the Lord has done for you, and how he has had **compassion** on you"* (Mark 5:1-20).
>
> Jesus tells the story of a tax collector who went to the temple to pray. In his prayer, the man appealed to the compassion of God, *"God have **mercy** on me, a sinner"* (Luke 18:9-14).

God offers the *gift* of compassion as the invitation to align our lives with His intention. We are to use the gift to make healthy choices. We make choices daily: the way we greet the day, deal with colleagues at work, invest in our families, and care for body and soul. We also make choices that set direction in life.

I needed direction. I needed to hear from God. On a spring day, I went to the zoo, alone. My plan was to sit on a bench and not move until God spoke to my heart with clear direction for my life. I had tried this before in a Florida swamp when I was seeking the answer to other people's questions. Then, I heard God's question directed to me.

Now, I needed answers. It took the day. I didn't stay on the bench, but walked, opened my heart, and listened. There was an inner nudge: "What do you want to create with your life, Richard?" Again, God gave me an answer through a question.

I determined to give God an honest answer, an authentic answer, true to my best in the compassion of Christ. There were internal influences to wrestle; family, career, traditions, authority, and my own voice of defeat. By mid-afternoon, my list was complete. It had eight items on it. All were important to me, some seemed unlikely, and a few were out of reach.

That was fifteen years ago. At times I pinned the list to a cork board or taped it to the mirror. For a long time nothing developed, and in frustration, I hid the list in a drawer or at the bottom of a box of mementos. One day, several years ago, I stumbled on the list again. I read each item. To my amazement, all but one of the items had come to pass.

God's compassionate intentions are suspended in a sea of grace—He gives us what we need rather than what we deserve.

> God's compassionate intentions are suspended in a sea of **grace**—He gives us what we need rather than what we deserve.

God's gift of grace is active in all people whether they know it or not. Each person, you and I, may choose to reject it, ignore it, or cooperate with God.

The ceiling of the Sistine Chapel is Michelangelo's moving depiction of God creating humanity. God is intent, determined, stretching forth His arm and all His power, glory, and love toward Adam. This is an image of God's grace. Adam, on the other hand, is lounging on a hillside. One arm is partially lifted with only his index finger reaching toward God. It is a picture of our choosing in contrast to God's gracious compassion. Yet our choice, our cooperation, matters.

A greatly loved evangelist in the history of the church of my birth said it in a folksy way, "God voted for me. The devil voted against me. And I cast the deciding vote."[13] There is a layer of truth in his statement, but there is a deeper truth also: our ability and desire to choose, to cooperate with God, is a gift of grace.

At times we focus on our cooperation to the neglect of the active grace of God. However, we can neglect or reduce the importance of personal choice to the point of negating our responsibility to align life with Christ.

> A little child, lifted on father's shoulder, places the star on the top of
> the Christmas tree and promptly declares, "I did it myself, and
> Daddy helped."

It is our heavenly "Daddy" who makes all things possible. The mature person knows that it is our Father's gracious gift that lifts us from the mud to the stars. Finally and eternally, it is God's marvelous, infinite, matchless grace.

CHAPTER 11

A HOUSE OF PRAYER

*"You will never cease to be the most amazed person on earth at
what God has done for you on the inside."*
OSWALD CHAMBERS[1]

I t is one thing to hear about God and another to experience His presence.
Faithful attendance in church is not a substitute for full attention in the
soul. Bible knowledge is not a surrogate for intimacy with God. It is one thing
to know about God and something else to know His love in your heart. Yet
each sermon, each song, each reading from Scripture is an invitation to intimacy, an invitation to build your home in Him.

Victor Weiskopf is an astronomer and a physicist. In his book, *The Joy of
Insight,* he shares an incident that demonstrates the importance of a personal
encounter:

> Several years ago I received an invitation to give a series of lectures at
> the University of Arizona at Tucson. I was delighted to accept
> because it would give me a chance to visit the Kitts Peak Astronomi-
> cal Observatory, which had a very powerful telescope I had always

wanted to look through. I asked my hosts to arrange an evening to visit the observatory so I could look directly at some interesting objects through the telescope. I was told that this would be impossible because the telescope was constantly in use for photography and other research activities. There was no time for simply looking at objects.

"In that case," I replied, "I will not be able to come to deliver my talks." Within days I was informed that everything had been arranged according to my wishes.

We drove up the mountain on a wonderfully clear night. The stars and the Milky Way glistened intensely and seemed almost close enough to touch. I entered the cupola and told technicians who ran the computer that activated the telescope that I wanted to see Saturn and a number of the galaxies.

It was a great pleasure to observe with my own eyes and with the utmost clarity all the details I had only seen on photographs before. As I looked at all that, I realized that the room had begun to fill with people and one by one they peeked into the telescope.

I was told that these were astronomers working at the observatory. However, they had never before had the opportunity of looking directly at the objects of their investigations. I can only hope that this encounter made them realize the importance of such direct contact.[2]

Moses encountered God in a burning bush in the wilderness. God's people pitched their tents at the base of God's holy mountain. For us, contact with God is not in the desert or at the foot of Mount Sinai. God's gift of grace is Jesus Christ, the Word in human flesh. Paul penned a high and grand expression of encountering God in Christ.

"He [Jesus] is the image of the invisible God, the firstborn over all creation. For by him all things were created; things in heaven and on the earth, visible and invisible, whether thrones or powers or

*rulers or authorities; all thing were created by him and for him. He
is before all things, and in him all things hold together... For God
was pleased to have all his fullness dwell in him, and through him
to reconcile to himself all things, whether things on earth, or things
in the heaven, by making peace through his blood, shed on the cross"*
(Colossians 1:15-20).

Your Soul Has a Mate

Your soul has a mate; his name is Jesus. He knows you from the inside out.
He has put on your skin, walked in your shoes, and felt the tenderness and
terror in your heart.

He is God's Word to us. *"In the past, God spoke through prophets
and in many ways, but now he has spoken to us through his Son"*
(Hebrews 1:1).

It is not a Word shouted from the top of a mountain, but a
whisper in your soul, your human soul. *"Jesus ...being in very nature
God, did not consider equality with God something to be grasped, but
made himself nothing, taking on the very nature of a servant, being
made in human likeness"* (Philippians 2:5-7).

He comes to pitch his tent with us. *"And the Word became flesh
and made his dwelling among us"* (John 1:14).

His invitation is to live in Him. *"As the Father has loved me, so
have I loved you. Now remain in my love"* (John 15:9).

He is your soul mate, for He is able to *"sympathize with our
weaknesses ...we have one who has been tempted in every way, even as
we are—yet without sin."* (Hebrews 4:15)

He comes to dwell with us; we are to remain in Him. In your most inner
place, your heart of hearts, the deepest chamber of your soul, Jesus wants to
pitch His tent, and He asks you to remain with Him and in Him. It is an
imaginary house, a spiritual house where you meet with Jesus.

What is a spiritual house; what does that mean? We are attempting to describe something that is deeply personal and private. It is also beyond the reach of our measuring tools and accounting systems. We are talking about spiritual intimacy with God, the unseen meeting place of the soul and the Holy Spirit. Across the centuries, God's people have searched the Scriptures and found wonderful images of the inward meeting place, the inward place of prayer.

In Psalms, we read and imagine the inner sanctuary. *"I have seen you in the sanctuary and beheld your power and your glory"* (Psalm 63:1-3).

In Song of Solomon, the bridal chamber is a picture of the inward place: *"Your lips drop sweetness as the honeycomb, my bride! Milk and honey are under your tongue"* (Song of Solomon 4:10-12)

The Holy of Holies is the spiritual room where we meet Jesus. *"...we have confidence to enter the Most Holy Place by the blood of Jesus"* (Hebrews 10:19).

It is a hiding place. *"You are my hiding place; you will protect me from trouble and surround me with songs of deliverance"* (Psalm 32:5).

Moses saw the glory of God from a shelter in the Rock. *"When my glory passes by, I will put you in a cleft in the rock and cover you with my hand until I have passed by"* (Exodus 33:22).

The inner place can also be imagined as the wing of the Almighty, His shield, or a strong tower. *"He will cover you with his feathers, and under his wings you will find refuge; his faithfulness will be your shield and rampart"* (Psalm 91:4).

AT HOME WITH JESUS

Jesus called the inward place of prayer a "room." *"When you pray, go into you room, close the door and pray to your Father who is unseen"* (Matthew 6:6). What is this "room" like? The only way to see it is in your imagination. One insightful and inspirational image or picture is the home of the sisters, Mary and Martha, and their brother Lazarus. The Gospel of John recalls the moment Jesus visited their home just before the crucifixion. In this meeting, in this home, I see a picture of the inner room or home, the secret place of prayer.

> *"Six days before the Passover, Jesus arrived at Bethany, where Lazarus lived, whom Jesus had raised from the dead. Here a dinner was given in Jesus' honor. Martha served while Lazarus was among those reclining at the table with him. Then Mary took a pint of pure nard, an expensive perfume; she poured it on Jesus' feet and wiped his feet with her hair. And the house was filled with the fragrance of the perfume"* (John 12:1-3).

This is a picture of the inner home, the heart, given over to Jesus. Martha serves the Lord. Lazarus talks with Him. Mary worships Him. The sweet fragrance fills the house. In your inner room, you are at one time Martha, Lazarus, and Mary. The inner house of prayer is a place of service, conversation, and worship. This is a high and holy picture of an inner life of prayer. This is a picture of direct contact.

Jesus came to earth as a human being; you encounter Him in all his humanity. God gave you His heart in Jesus. The only way to God's heart is through your own. It is a divine-human engagement. This is God's covenant or promise:

> *"The time is coming, declares the Lord, when I will make a new covenant ...I will put my laws in their minds and write it on their hearts. I will be their God, and they will be my people"* (Jeremiah 31:33 and Hebrews 8:10; 10:16).

On the night before his death, Jesus announced that the blood that flows through His heart is the promise fulfilled: *"This cup is the new covenant in my blood, which is poured out for you"* (1 Corinthians 11:25).

God promises to write His word on your heart. This is a wonderful promise fulfilled in Jesus. It is also a great inconvenience. It means that to read God's word, you must look into your own heart. Oh, how we wish the words were only written in the Book; then we could look with our intellect and at a distance. To read the handwriting on the wall of your heart is a personal and intimate calling. It is here the Living Word of Jesus brings the written Scriptures to life.

> *To read the handwriting on the wall of your heart is a personal and intimate calling.*

GOD'S HOME IN YOUR SOUL

In the third and fourth centuries of the Christian era, as the Roman Empire was decaying, thousands of young men and women left the clamor and confusion of the cities and moved to the desert. They did not go to escape, but to seek understanding and to reconnect with what gives life meaning and significance. Out of this spiritual movement the wisdom of the desert fathers and mothers was born.

Anselm Gruen, O.S.B., is a Benedictine monk and Cellarer of the abbey of Muensterschwarzachy in Germany. He regularly offers workshops for European executives and professionals about the wisdom of the desert fathers and mothers. His approach is to help leaders resist the temptation to climb the heights of idealism. Rather, he teaches the way of the desert where one enters spirituality or soul life from below:

> The desert fathers teach us spirituality from below. They show us that we have to begin with ourselves and our passions. The way to God, for the desert fathers, always passes through self-knowledge. Evagrius Ponticus puts it this way: "If you want to know God, learn to know yourself first."
>
> Without self-knowledge we are always in danger of having our ideas of God turn into mere projections. There are pious individuals who take flight from their own reality into religion. They aren't

transformed by their prayer and piety; they simply use it to lift themselves over others, to confirm their own infallibility.

In the desert fathers we meet an entirely different form of piety. The goals here are, above all, sincerity and authenticity.[3]

Your inner home in Jesus is a place to be still and get reacquainted with your soul. Jesus writes the wisdom and way of God on the walls of your heart. Many of the young men and women who left the crumbling empire of Rome to seek a spiritual life in the desert of North Africa received a wise word from one of the desert fathers: "Go to your hut and sit down. The hut will teach you everything."[4]

In this instance, the "hut" is a metaphor or image of the inward home. It is the place where the soul meets with God. You must come home to yourself. In doing so, you will meet God.

There are practical steps for building an inner home in your soul. *First*, establish your house of prayer. *Then*, turn your house of prayer into a spiritual home. *Finally*, in your spiritual home, your inner sanctuary, empower your life of prayer.

ESTABLISH YOUR INNER HOUSE OF PRAYER

You need a physical place and time to open your soul to God. You need a quiet place to think, write, reflect, and pray. Externally, it may be a walking trail, a coffee shop, or a comfortable chair. Internally, it is a time and place to engage Jesus in your soul. Make this an appointment and keep it as a priority.

Perhaps some brief construction plans are in order. Simple is better. Make an appointment with your soul and keep it. Choose a place and time that works for you. Listen to music or read a small portion of a book that warms your heart and opens your mind. Read from the Bible, particularly the Gospels and the Psalms. Imagine yourself in the gospel scene; identify with the experience of the psalm writer.

You may find that the discipline of writing is helpful. Writing focuses attention, requires reflection, and slows the pace. What should you write?

Anything you like. It can be a journal, a prayer, a story or just a collection of disjointed thoughts. Let your thoughts flow freely; fill two or three pages.[5] Some days your writing will be meaningful, and other days it may seem quite dull. It is a simple way to open your soul.

If writing doesn't work for you, try listening to music. The point is that you are establishing a pattern that slows your pace, turns your attention inward, and opens your mind, heart, and soul to the wisdom of God. Think of it as the time when you leave the outer world and go home to your soul.

Be as consistent as is reasonable. If you miss a day or two, don't fret. The soul does not seek an apology, but simply anticipates your next soul-to-soul meeting. You are establishing a pattern: a time, a place, a routine where you return from the world around you and come back home to yourself.

Once you establish a pattern, you launch an inner conversation. It is a conversation that, at first, you may feel you are having with yourself. However, in time you will discover that God is at the table. He leads you all along the path, even if you do not realize it. He makes a promise, *"I will entice you into the desert and there I will speak to you in the depths of your heart"* (Hosea 2:14).

The conversation centers on your hopes and fears. The discussion deals with two questions: 1) Lord, who am I in you; and 2) Lord, what kind of life do You want to create with me?

Lord, who am I in you? Sydney Harris wrote, "Most of us go almost all the way through life as complete strangers to ourselves." Getting reacquainted with yourself is not an easy thing to do, especially if it has been a while. You'll be tempted to avoid yourself: time pressures, work demands, family expectations, or just about anything that keeps you from going home to your soul. John W. Gardner, Secretary of Education during the Civil Rights Movement and exceptional writer on the practical and inward life, describes the temptation to avoid ourselves.

> *Getting reacquainted with yourself is not an easy thing to do, especially if it has been a while.*

Human beings have always employed an enormous variety of clever devices for running away from themselves, and the modern world is particularly rich with such stratagems. We keep ourselves so busy, fill our lives with so many distractions, stuff our heads with so many people, and cover so much ground that we never have time to probe the fearful and wonderful world within. More often than not, we don't want to know ourselves, don't want to depend on ourselves, and don't want to live with ourselves. By middle life, most of us are accomplished fugitives from ourselves.[6]

I found it true for me; at mid-life I had become almost a stranger to myself. As such, the admonition to "get to know yourself" was not only frightening, but also seemed impossible. I told myself it could not be done. I was too old, and it was too late. This is another trick of avoidance; because it is frightening, we want to believe it is impossible and, thus, we get out of the soul work of dealing with ourselves.

Avoid the tragedy described by Beryl Markham, "You can live a life time, and, at the end of it, know more about other people than you know about yourself."[7] The greater tragedy is that if you do not know yourself, you cannot know the wonders of God. God writes on the walls of your mind and heart; you must enter your inner life to hear from God.

Lord, what kind of life do You want to create? The second question is the natural result of the first. To know who you are is to get at the truth. To create life is to aim for your best. What kind of person do you want to be? Jesus has come to make all things new; that includes you. He makes you new from the inside out.

A great minister of another generation, Harry Emerson Fosdick, declared, "One must have the adventurous daring to accept one's self as a bundle of possibilities and undertake the most interesting challenge in the world—making the most of one's best."[8]

In many motivational seminars and self-help workshops, similar language can be heard: "Make something of yourself! Be the person you want to be! Live up to your potential!" The exhortations are inspiring and disheartening. It is a lonely challenge; a challenge to create your own life by yourself. Another piece of information is needed at this precise point: You are not the creator, God is. God creates life, life in you. Talk to Him in the inner chamber of your heart.

Lord, what do You want to create *in* my life? What are the core
beliefs, personal attitudes, character traits, and significant relationships you want to create in me? The question for discussion in the
soul is, "Are you living true to your inner best or hiding behind a
mask?"

Lord, what do You want to create *with* my life? Think about the
people you love, the people you serve, the greater good, and your
lasting legacy. The inner dialogue asks, "Are you fulfilling your life's
purpose or avoiding a challenge you don't want to face?"

Lord, what do You want to create *for* my life? Now, consider the
practical issues, your standard of living, financial security, personal
experiences, lasting accomplishments, and the life style you want to
create. Invite God into this conversation. His inner wisdom probes,
"Are you choosing out of your inner life or meeting unreasonable or
irresponsible expectations; pleasing others, proving your own inde-
pendence or do you want to serve with Me?"

The house of prayer is a place where you and God meet. In my growing
years, the emphasis was on meeting God. There was little discussion of dealing with personal identity. However, through my own failings and my faith, I
found that to encounter God is to discover myself and surrender to Him.

> All this is the self which has to be surrendered as we slowly and
> dimly discover our identity with God,
> > discover the me within me
> > which is a greater than me
> > and also authentically me.
> In the end we find ourselves stripped of everything except that
> dull, dim, rather remote awareness that we are an articulation of
> God's own Being,
> > a limb of his body, to use St. Paul's phrase,
> > or to use St. John's, a branch of the vine which is himself.
> > > H. A. WILLIAMS[9]

TURN YOUR HOUSE OF PRAYER INTO A SPIRITUAL HOME

Once the *house of prayer* is established, the deeper work of surrender and cleansing begins. The inner house becomes a spiritual home, a time and place to be genuine and authentic.

The Gospel of Mark opens with Jesus under considerable strain. The world of demons, Pharisees, and even the demands of His own followers crush against Him. Christ models His spiritual life for us: *"Early in the morning while it was still dark, Jesus got up, left the house and went off to a solitary place where he prayed"* (Mark 1:35).

It didn't take long for all the anxieties and expectations to come looking for Jesus. *"Simon and his companions went to look for him, and when they found him, they exclaimed, 'Everyone is looking for you'"* (Mark 1:36–37).

Jesus did not acquiesce to the demand, but responded with a renewed sense of purpose and identity. In prayer, He clarified His purpose: *"Let us go somewhere else—to the nearby villages—so I can preach there also."* In prayer, identity was solidified, *"This is why I have come"* (Mark 1:38). Jesus understands the need and grace of an inward "room."

Your spiritual home is a place to encounter God. Your relationship with God is to be filled with love and desire. A house becomes a home when it is filled with love; you love being there, love the people there, and when you have been away, you love to return. When you have a soul-to-soul encounter with God, the *inward house* becomes your house of prayer. Your house of prayer becomes your spiritual home when it is filled with love.

> *Your house of prayer becomes your spiritual home when it is filled with love.*

Another way to describe the change in your relationship with God is the difference between a menu and a meal. A person who is full sees the presentation of a meal on a plate and compliments the way it looks. A person who is starving sees the taste of the food, its nourishment, and its potential to satisfy. The blessing of a full relationship with God is for *"those who hunger and thirst…* *"for they will be filled"* (Matthew 5:6).

> The highest prayer is to the goodness of God, which comes down to
> us in the lowliest part of our need. God's goodness created our soul
> and keeps it alive and makes it grow in grace and in virtue. The soul
> is nearest in nature to God and most ready for God's grace. For it is
> the same grace that the soul seeks and ever shall, till we truly know
> our God, who has enclosed us all in himself.
>
> DAME JULIAN OF NORWISH[10]

Your spiritual home is a quest for truth. When you encounter God, you encounter yourself. But how do you actually do this? In His presence, you conduct a dialogue with your emotions and thoughts. Here is an example from my own life. I was haunted by an old and familiar thought: "Richard, you are such a disappointment." That night, the thought robbed me of sleep and turned my inner life into a downward spiral of discouragement, headed for defeat. How do you pray through on such a bad night?

> First, consider the consequences of the thought; what is it doing to
> your true and best in Christ?
> Next, unearth the story beneath it; what caused the thought to
> settle in on you just now?
> Ask for God's truth; ask Him to bring His truth to your mind
> and heart, the word of truth you need.
> Speak the truth against the lie; rage against the lie; it will create
> the strength of liberation, you will be victorious in the spiritual battle.

"You are such a disappointment" rumbled through my mind like an endless train. I wanted to hide under the covers, but I knew I needed to get out of bed and face it. I thought. I prayed. I asked God for a word from heaven and in that moment His truth burst on my mind like the sunrise: "You are my son in whom I am pleased." That night, my God and I won the battle.

Empower Your Prayer Life

How does one begin to pray? How does one begin to breathe? Once birthed from the womb, the baby breathes in order to live. Once you escape from your prison into your wilderness exile, prayer is your spiritual breath. Begin as you wish, but begin.

> *Once you escape from your prison into your wilderness exile, prayer is your spiritual breath.*

Let me suggest three ways to empower your life of prayer. First, *try different ways of praying.* I will share a list I developed many years ago for a group of lay pastors who led small groups in the church where I served as senior minister. Each Wednesday evening I met with the group as they shared ministry reports and I provided tools and training. One evening the team was quiet, unusual for this group. I asked, "What's happening?"

"The members of our groups love meeting together. They especially appreciate the open discussion and Bible study, but they are not comfortable praying together," reported one lay pastor on behalf of the others.

I inquired, "What do you think is causing this?"

The discussion that followed was rich, insightful, and personal. A member of the team summed it up: "We have all been told to pray, but no one has ever taught us to pray."

We discussed ways and means of helping each other learn to pray. I took all the suggestions, worked on them, and developed this short list of different ways to pray. I suggested to the group that each one should "Start where you are comfortable and, when you are ready, stretch to the next step."

Repeat a phrase: repeat a short phrase such as "have mercy on me" or "be still and know God" or "my life is in your hands" or "I am created, loved, and kept by God." This type of prayer can go with you throughout the day; repeat the phrase often, silently and sincerely.

Read prayers: there are many excellent collections of prayers. Read a prayer as your own. Look over several prayers, and choose one that relates to your situation. Intentionally connect what you are reading in your mind with what you feel in your heart.

Write your prayer: writing forces you to slow down and think more deeply. Write your prayer in common language. Your soul and God's Spirit are not concerned with grammar, but sincerity. It is not a work of art, but an expression of sincerity.

Pray from your heart: speak from your heart as you would to a friend, a true soul-friend. Tell God about your day and your concerns. Express your love, gratitude, and praise, as well as your frustration, disappointments, and fear. Try speaking aloud. It is good to hear your own words with your own ears.

In recent years I have returned to this list for the care of my own soul. Across my life I have prayed countless prayers in public and private. However, I am continuing to discover that these four simple means of prayer are doors of intimacy with my Lord.

You cannot begin too poorly, just begin. Prayer is breath to your soul. In the language of the Old Testament, the word "breathe" and "spirit" are the same word. Every time you need a breath of air, it is a reminder you need the Spirit of God. The thing is not *how* to begin to pray, but to begin.

Let me share a second way to empower your life of prayer. Learn to **think before you pray.** Christians often want to pray for each other and with each other. However, we often pray for each other without inquiring how best to pray. Someone might ask you to pray for a family situation, a medical problem, financial issue, or any of a hundred categories of human need.

In seminars, retreats, congregations, and university classes, I have taught people to think through their prayers by asking questions. It is a wonderful thing to pray with a friend at just the moment she asks for your prayers. You will find the prayer to be more meaningful and powerful if you talk about the prayer first. How does your friend need to picture or imagine God? What are the specifics of her situation? What does she want God to do for her? If you discuss these simple questions, you can pray directly and personally for your friend.

I have also used this method of asking questions to help individuals learn to pray. The advantage of this procedure is that it pushes you to think through your prayer. Yes, think about what you want to say to God. It will empower your prayer life.

Think through each question below. In fact, jot down a note or brief answer to each question. Then, with your heart open, speak your prayer from your soul into the soul of heaven.

What will you call God? You may refer to God as Father, Friend, or Savior. The term you use opens your imagination. Do you need to see God as your Rock, Fortress, or Open Door? You can call God your Champion, Creator, or Guide. For the situation you are facing, how do you need God to come to you? Call Him, and call Him by a name that describes the quality of God's character you need right now. Prayer comes *"out of the depths"* (Psalm 130:1), the depths of your need, your soul.

What will you tell God? You have a specific situation to present to the Lord. Tell God the facts and the feelings that accompany the facts. What are your attitudes, your emotions, and your desires? Your statement might include praise, thanks, complaints, or explanations. Sometimes your message to God is simply the question, "Why?" God does not measure the length of your praying, but the genuineness of your heart. You do not gain God's attention with *"many words"* (Matthew 6:7). Telling God about your situation is focusing your attention on God's presence and power in your situation.

What will you ask God? Will you ask God for aid, forgiveness, hope, love, guidance, or joy? Remember, *"Your Father knows what you need before you ask"* (Matthew 6:8). The process of asking is not to inform God, but to reform us. Laying the request from the depth of your heart in the hands of God is faith. *"I wait for the Lord, my soul waits, and in his word I put my trust"* (Psalm 130:5)

A third way to deepen your prayer life is to *pray the Psalms.* The *Psalms* are tiny containers of soul-to-soul communication with God. The *Psalms* provide an instruction manual on prayer. It is a powerful experience to model your own prayers after the *Psalms.* I have taught pastors, lay leaders, and Christians at every stage of growth how to pray the psalms. Select a psalm that speaks to your soul and your situation. It may be the whole psalm, part of a psalm or pieces from several *Psalms.* Read the Psalm slowly and aloud a couple of times. Think about it. How is your experience the same or different? Write the psalm as your own. Use your own words. If possible and appropriate, courageously read your prayer aloud to a soul-friend. Here is an example based on Psalm 43.

> O Lord, please make things right for me. I am struggling. I am tired. It feels like you have rejected me, like you are not listening to me.
>
> Lord, please show me the way; show me your truth. I confess that, like a child, I need to be led.
>
> Pull me to you, O Lord. Bring me close so I can feel you near me, so I can bow down to you, so I can learn to depend upon you for my joy and for my happiness, and O how I will praise you, God.
>
> But maybe, I should be praising you now, putting my hope in you now because you are my God and you will keep your promises. You will hold me securely in the palm of your hands for you have promised me that new life is possible with you.

For almost a decade I have helped people learn to express their prayers based on the Psalms. I once produced a small collection of them titled *When Pastors Pray.* They are not Sunday Morning prayers, but private, intimate prayers of anger, joy, and gratitude. Here are examples that, I hope, will give you courage to create your own private psalms.

A Prayer of Anger
   O God, the whole thing crumbled and slipped through my fingers. Is this what You had in mind?

I don't care about their criticisms or accusations—They acted
like twits. So did I. But to crumble, fall apart, is this what You had
in mind?

Can't You see Satan's glee as the world mocks—They mock me
not; they mock You! Is this what You had in mind?

Come now, Lord, strengthen me now. Pick up the pieces. Come
now, Lord, build on them. Is this what You had in mind?

O my God, You are a mystery to me; You called me out of
1000 better choices, out of 10,000 better choices, You, O God, my
God called me! When I thought You were mistaken, You lifted me.
You protected me and supported me, and now somehow I sense
You were right all along.

A Prayer of Joy

O God, You are awesome. You are my everything. You are my
sufficiency. You have been faithful to me when I have not been faithful to You. You have been good to me when I have not been good to
others. You have been patient with me when I have not been patient
with myself. You continue to bring about Your purposes for my life.
You continue to provide grace. My life continues to be in Your
hands. For all of this and so much more, You are to be praised.

A Prayer of Gratitude

I thank you for my husband who has become my best friend in
these dark and lonely hours. I know and am assured that You will
use our strengths to help us encourage one another as a team. With
You, Lord, on our side, we cannot fail.

The soul finds strength, safety, and spiritual life for the journey through
healthy choices and the vitality of prayer. This is the practical response to
God's call to live in Him, a call to choose well and live *"out of the depths"*
(Psalm 130:1). Yet the spiritual journey is more than a solo flight. The spiritual journey involves more than personal choices and a hidden life of prayer.

We need each other. We need the help and healing of holy listening. In the final chapter, we turn to the privilege and discipline of listening together for the presence and purpose of God.

CHAPTER 12

HOLY LISTENING

*"Where two or three gather together in my name,
I will be in the midst of them."*
JESUS OF NAZARETH

I sat at a square of tables in a small class room at the original Quaker House in Philadelphia. It was an academic meeting and we were having a "break-out session." I had come to expect these sessions to be of little value, just superficial conversations yielding negligible results. However, this time I was wrong. There was a moment of authenticity that silenced all of us. It was a moment that reminded and renewed my calling in Christ.

A young woman who did not understand the perfunctory nature of these events took the conversation quite seriously and chose to unburden her soul. Her situation and difficulties were professional, yet deeply personal. It took the group by surprise. The easiest response was to give advice. And advice was fired back and forth around the table. The young woman listened but did not find help in the debate about her problem. We soon ran out of theoretical opinions.

An uncomfortable silence blanketed the group. People avoided eye contact. Some looked away from the table. There was one person who knew what to do. She was an older woman with a great academic mind. However, it was her spiritual wisdom that came to the surface. She turned to the young woman, took her hand, and spoke to her as if they were the only two in the room. She said, "There are several faithful solutions to your problems. I don't know which one is best for you, but I will help you listen for it."[1]

The spiritual journey was not designed as a solo sport. We need each other. There is a private challenge: build a spiritual home, a sanctuary, where you meet with God. However, there is also a relational dynamic; we need friends to share the journey.

> The spiritual journey was not designed as a solo sport.

Jeremy Taylor understood the value of a spiritual friendship. He was a clergyman in the Church of England during the difficult years of the middle 1600's. At one time he was chaplain to the king. Later, he was imprisoned by the Puritan Parliament. From personal experience, he explains:

Friendship will alleviate our sorrows, ease our pain, discharge our opposition, be a sanctuary in our calamity, a counsel in times of doubt, bring clarity to our minds, help us discover our true thoughts, and challenge and empower our dedication.[2]

In moments of holy listening with true soul-friends we are exposed and embraced, challenged and comforted, admonished and validated. It is a sanctuary of protection in the painful process of healing and the hard work of hope.

Holy listening is embedded in a spiritual conversation to 1) *explore* what is going on in the inner life right now, 2) *listen* for the guidance of God, and 3) *submit* the inner life to the love of God. Holy listening requires faithful attentiveness to the presence of Christ and authentic commitment to the purpose of Christ.

Those who are accustomed to the modern church know that we gather in large crowds as we experience the pageantry, the music and inspiration of congregational worship. In this setting, God works in the soul. God also moves intimately and privately in our inner house of prayer. Our love for him grows and the house of prayer becomes a home in the wilderness.

> *In moments of holy listening*
> *with true soul-friends we*
> *are exposed and embraced,*
> *challenged and comforted,*
> *admonished and validated.*

However, there is a third way in which we experience the presence of God: when two or three spiritual friends come together in order to discover the presence and purpose of Jesus in a specific situation. The Holy Spirit works in our spiritual conversations and holy listening in ways that are unique and essential for our spiritual journey. It is unlike the meeting of larger groups in worship or the intimacy of the private inner room.

In moments of holy listening, we may not bow our heads or close our eyes. However, holy listening is prayer; it is praying together. Together, we lift our souls to heaven, open our inner lives to each other and earnestly seek to know the will, the way, and the wisdom of God for a specific problem or issue. It is spiritual dialogue in which we connect with ourselves, with God, and one another.

WHEN WE LISTEN TOGETHER

On a snowy Sunday evening when the congregation was exceptionally small, the minister languished in a half hearted manner, "Well, at least we know that where two or three gather …" His voice trailed off as a forced smile appeared. In a church that limits success to numbers, the significance of two or three gathering together is not fully appreciated.

Yet in small and meaningful conversations we often experience spiritual breakthroughs, the soul's release, the power of forgiveness, or the light of hope in darkness. We meet together to deal with a specific issue, problem, or situation. It may be the challenges of daily expectations and demands, inner confusion and chaos, or harmful and poisonous relationships. The specifics may involve family, friends, church, work, or tragedy. With one or two spiritual friends, we meet together to lay it out openly, forthrightly, in the hope and faith that we, together, will hear from heaven.

It is a wonderful thing, a holy thing, when you sit with a true soul-friend who listens. Your conversation begins cordially. The discussion may take many directions. Then, your dialogue finds focus. A perplexing issue becomes clear. Your spiritual attention and authenticity come to life. You unburden yourself, confess your need, say things that astonish you, and you are able to say things with such clarity that you come to a new awareness of your inner life and God's purpose and presence.

> It is a wonderful thing, a holy thing, when you sit with a true soul-friend who listens.

In such a moment of holy listening, you and your friend realize without a word that God is here. He is active in your conversation. You hear, trust and follow the wisdom of God. Such a conversation is prayer. Heaven and earth are joined; God is at work; Jesus is near. The confusion or calamity either clears with specific answers or fades into perspective in the presence of heaven's compassion. It is the promise of Scripture:

> "I tell you the truth, whatever you bind on earth will be bound in heaven and whatever you loose on earth will be loosed in heaven. Again, I tell you that if two or three of you on earth agree about anything you ask for, it will be done for you by my Father in heaven. For where two or three come together in my name, there am I with them" (Matthew 18:18–20).

We discover the presence of the living Jesus in holy listening. The Gospel of Matthew presents the risen Lord amidst the miracles and wonders of earthquakes, open graves, and the epiphany of angels. In Mark, rather than a parade of evidence, the living Lord never appears; the individual is left to trust and obey, to go to Galilee and wait for him. It is in the gospel of Luke that we find a third way to encounter the resurrected Jesus. Rather than the grandeur of what is happening around us or the private commitment to follow, it is where two, walking together, discover the living Jesus in holy conversation.

Two disciples were traveling together. It is a picture of the soul's journey. They walked the seven miles from Jerusalem to Emmaus on that first Easter afternoon, the day Jesus rose from the dead. Yet they did not know with certainty that Jesus was alive. Their conversation centered on all that had happened, especially the death of Jesus.

The two disciples opened their inner lives. With the death of Jesus, their hope had been sorely wounded. Faith was put to the test. They were discouraged, almost to the point of despair. Yet they had heard stories of an empty tomb and their imagination was stirred. They did not know what to think or believe.

Jesus joined the conversation. The Lord was present. He was with them physically, but they did not recognize Him. Through their open hearts, He entered their souls and explained the purpose of God. Mile after mile they walked and talked. Jesus was there all the time, joining in. Yet they did not realize it was Jesus. They thought He was a stranger who was accompanying them.

Their hearts burned within them. They invited the stranger, Jesus, to join them in their home and at their table. When the Lord took bread, blessed it, broke it, and gave it to them, their eyes were opened. They realized it was the risen Lord. Reflecting on the event, they said, *"Did not our hearts burn within us while he talked with us on the road and opened the Scriptures to us"* (Luke 24:32).

The story contains an odd phrase, *"they were kept from recognizing him" (Luke 24:16).* Did God prevent them from recognizing Jesus? Was His resurrected body unrecognizable to the disciples? Were they so convinced Jesus was dead, they could not accept what was before their eyes? I don't know why the disciples could not recognize Jesus; I do understand why we struggle to recognize His presence. It is fear, busyness, stress, and a thousand other distractions

that dim our inner eye to the presence of Christ's Spirit. In holy listening, we
help one another see again.

Practical Matters

The first lesson is the most difficult: *to engage in holy listening, you must stop
talking*. It is a certain type of talk that must stop: common conversation. We
engage in common conversation each day. We must and should. Yet holy listening requires a different kind of dialogue. There are four practices we must
set aside. In common conversation, we talk from our *internal critic*. We tend
to critique what others say rather than simply accepting them as they are. We
must evaluate what we hear in the normal course of daily life. However, the
critique will stamp out holy listening. We must seek to understand rather than
appraise. It takes a bit of intention and focus, but we can turn off our internal critic.

In common conversation we also consult with the *internal advisor*. We
respond with advice; we have an obsessive need to fix other people's problems.
This practice will deafen our spiritual ears. It is
better for us to attend to what others say, feel,
and mean rather than tell them what to do
and be. A third source of common conversation is the *internal defender*. Someone touches
a sore point, and we automatically protect,
guard, or shield. In holy listening, we need to pay attention to what is behind
the barricade.

> It takes a bit of intention
> and focus, but we
> can turn off our
> internal critic.

A final source of common conversation is *storytelling*. Your friend tells her
story which reminds you of a story to tell. A barrage of story swapping will
harm holy listening. When a friend opens her soul and shares her story, blan-
keting it with your story will quite likely muffle the wisdom from heaven.
Rather than tell your story so quickly, help your friend tell hers; you may also
learn something about yourself in the process.

Holy listening is not common conversation ladled with religious ideas.
Rather than judge, advise, defend, or tell another story, seek to understand.

When spiritual friends help each other explore the inner life, seek Christ, and submit to His compassion, we invite God's presence and purpose.

Holy listening is grounded in spiritual openness rather than moral superiority. Acceptance, compassion, and forgiveness are the foundation stones of holy listening. Start with what is rather than what ought to be. The conversation cannot begin until pride, superiority, and accusation are set aside. There must be a safe zone free from ridicule, the danger of betrayal, or the supremacy of one over the other. The conversation begins in authenticity and not with a hierarchy of authority.

Holy listening engages our perceptions, emotions, and motivations. The process of holy listening requires an investigation of the inner life. Ask yourself and each other the following questions:

> ➤ How do I/you understand what is happening, why it is happening, and the meaning of it?
> ➤ How do I/you feel at this moment, what is the root of that feeling, and what is the lesson in the emotion?
> ➤ What is moving me/you to think, feel, and act this way?

It is when we look into each other's souls that we see God looking back at us. Woody Allen jokes, "I flunked out of metaphysics class because I cheated on the test. I looked into my neighbor's soul."[3] If you look only at the soul struggles of others, you will flunk the course. You must reveal your own soul. These conversations are dialogues of prayer in which we open our hearts to one another.

The intention of holy listening is to submit to the presence and purpose of God. Submit the emotions you are feeling at the moment; confess the motivation you experience now; turn loose of your present understanding of the situation. Give it to God. To recognize an emotion does not mean you must act on it. To discover a hidden motivation is the way to be free from it. When you confess your perceptions, you can question them. Submit your inner life to God.

Authentic submission opens the way for spiritual attention. God reveals His purpose. It may come as God's will, way, or wisdom.

God's will: God may reveal a specific will for the situation. It may come
as a flash, an inner nudge, or through the words of your soul friend.

God's way: the way or path of God is revealed in Scripture. You understand a biblical story, verse, or phrase in context, yet it is personal
and applicable to your situation.

God's wisdom: the wisdom of God is guidance as you make personal
decisions. God's wisdom often includes what you learn from your
experience and the experience of others.

Holy listening is essential to the spiritual journey. It is especially applicable in three areas: *first,* overcoming daily challenges that distract us from our
spiritual authenticity and attention; *second,* inner turmoil expressed in anger,
sadness or restlessness; and, *third,* dealing with difficult people. We will
explore each of these.

HOLY LISTENING AND DAILY CHALLENGES

The "how" questions jealously consume our attention and energy. Accompanied with worries, cares, fantasies, contingencies, strategies, and tactics, we
must deal with the "how to" question every day.

How will I get to work since the car is in the shop?
How will I survive this latest round of office politics?
How will I get the kids through college?
How will I make the mortgage payment this month?
How will I get everything done when I am overwhelmed?
How will I approach my spouse about the money problem?
How will I position myself for the new job opening?
How will I lose weight?
How will I manage an unexpected child?
How will I tell my employee I am letting her go?
How will I manage my aging parents?
How will I increase production at work?
How will I deal with the family this Christmas?

The quiet, inner voice that echos in the soul is drowned out by the pounding beat of "how to" questions. The soul's considerations and reflections—"Who am I? What kind of life do I want to create?"—appear time consuming, frivolous, and without practical benefit. It makes more sense to get things done first and then, if there is opportunity, reflect on such metaphysical issues.

"How" is the daily, necessary, practical yet *menacing* question. The danger is a double-sided ambush where the trail is narrow and difficult. *First*, under stress, you obsess over "how" questions until you forget who you are and neglect the life you want to create. Life degenerates into a series of problems to be solved, dangers to be avoided and empty experiences to dull the pain for a while.

The *second* attack of the "how" question is the subtle re-negotiating of an unsatisfactory compromise. Compromise is the survival skill in the "how to" world; meet in the middle, concede, give in, cobble together what works, at least temporarily. But you cannot strike a bargain with your soul. The soul will not compromise on authenticity. It is an evil entity, the devil himself, who tries to negotiate a contract with your soul. Barter with iniquity and you unwittingly redefine who you are and the life you are creating.

The challenge is to manage the questions of practical living while upholding integrity to the soul's intent, your true and best in Christ. It is accurate that you *"do not live by bread alone, but by every word that comes from the mouth of the Lord"* (Deuteronomy 8:3). Yet it is *also* true that you cannot live without bread. The tangible questions compete with the spiritual foundations of life. The "how" questions are loud and pushy. Give them too much and they will supersede your soul-life.

> You cannot strike a bargain with your soul. The soul will not compromise on authenticity.

HOLY LISTENING BRINGS US HOME

Everything clamors for your attention. They are important things, needful things, and demanding things: get the car washed, have lunch with a friend, deal with my angry teenager, go to the movies, manage an unexpected expense, play a round of golf, meet my sales quota, have a date night with my spouse, or turn in next year's budget. You cannot abandon these pleasures and obligations. That would be a life of ascetic retreat or irresponsible self-indulgence.

Listening to each other helps us turn away from the challenges, the duties, the obligation and demands, in order to refocus on our journey in Christ. A true friend who listens, really hears our confusion and conflict, helps break the spell of the demands and expectations. Holy listening helps us realign our spiritual and practical life with who we are in Christ.

We focus attention on our inner life in order to bring our true and best in Christ to the task of dealing with our outer lives. To focus inwardly means, first, to slow down, to sit, to breathe. Holy listening helps us come home to our souls. It helps us come home to the life God is creating in us.

> *To focus inwardly means, first, to slow down, to sit, to breathe.*

Through holy listening we experience the presence of Christ. We touch what keeps us alive in Him.

This kind of listening is based on principles that open the soul to the presence and purpose of God. They are:

> ➤ *To explore* motives, emotions, and perceptions, *not to justify* beliefs, opinions and judgments.
> ➤ *To reveal* the need to change and grow, *not to debate* an issue, a cause, or a stand.
> ➤ *To understand* another person's perspective, *not to convince* others of my perspective.
> ➤ *To be open* to God's great love, *not to argue* for my point and against your point.
> ➤ *To surrender* my inner life to the love of God, *not to defend* my inner life from exploration and transformation.
> ➤ *To grow* in life in God, *not to prove* that I have been in the right all along.

On the road to Emmaus Jesus participated in holy listening, but this was not the only time. The Gospels of Matthew, Mark, and Luke also provide snapshots of conversations, summaries of in-depth dialogue with Jesus. These conversations often surround His miracles, moments with His disciples or with people who sought out Jesus. Yet it is in the Gospel of John we find more complete recordings of spiritual conversations.

> *Jesus and a religious leader* (John 3:1–10): Nicodemus, a deeply religious man, came to Jesus at night in order to engage him in a discussion of the spiritual life. *"Rabbi, we know you are a teacher who has come from God. For no one could perform the miraculous signs you are doing if God were not with him"* (John 3:2). Jesus startled the man by telling him, *"…no one can enter the kingdom of God unless he is …born again"* (John 3:5–7). Nicodemus could see the miraculous signs, but he could not see God's kingdom in Christ. Spiritual vision requires a new identity and a new purpose in life: to be spiritually born again.

The distraction and demands of life seduce us away from our spiritual heritage. In conversation with a friend, we come home to our true identity and intention. Holy listening enlivens the moment of new birth; this is who I am in Christ, and this is the life God is creating.

> *Jesus and a broken woman* (John 4:1–26): Samaria, in the time of Christ, was a place of outcasts and forgotten people. Jesus chose to journey through Samaria and while there, He also chose to engage in conversation an emotionally and spiritually wounded woman who was drawing water from a well. *"Jesus said to her, 'Will you give me a drink?'"* (John 4:7). The fact that He would talk with her was a surprise. The conversation moved from water to living water to eternal life. Her soul was open, *"Sir, give me this water"* (John 4:15). Jesus then moved from the depths of life in God to the deep wounds in her life: a series of broken marriages resulting in a relationship of convenience and comfort without commitment or covenant. She faced the questions: Who am I and what kind of life am I creating?

Holy listening helps us face ourselves. But there is more; the answer is the presence and purpose of Christ. For us, truth is a person, Jesus (John 14:6). The conversation turned on Jesus' statement, *"I who speak to you am he" (John 4:26)*. Holy listening does its work when we experience afresh the identity and intention of Christ in the world and in our lives.

HOLY LISTENING AND INNER TURMOIL

A second application of holy listening on the spiritual journey is to still the storm of inner turmoil. Jesus knew the challenge of inner turmoil; He faced His temptations in the desert immediately following His baptism. He moved from the high point of spiritual validation to personal and private uproar. The devil tempted Him to use His power to meet His own needs by turning stones to bread, to impress the crowds by leaping off the temple, or to take the easy road to success by bowing down before the devil. Jesus knows the inner struggles of the soul.

Yet these struggles were experienced in private[4] over a forty-day period of isolation. Here is a question to consider: How did the story of this spiritual battle find its way into the pages of the gospels? Only Jesus knew about it. The disciples were not there; in fact, at that time of the temptations, Jesus had not even chosen His disciples. There is only one answer; Jesus told the story to His followers. Imagine the conversation that took place when Jesus disclosed His spiritual battle with His closest friends. Jesus wants to enter the conversation concerning your spiritual battle. When two or three gather to discuss in openness and honesty their spiritual struggles, Jesus is there.

There are three classic struggles of the inner life that are discussed by the desert fathers and spiritual leaders of the third and fourth centuries: sadness, anger, and restlessness.[5] These are signals that the soul needs to talk. These inner emotions are not wrong; they just are. They signal that something is happening within; lingering negative emotions distort perceptions and twist motivations. The soul needs to sort it out,

> *If we ignore the signs or cover the issues, sadness, anger, and restlessness will harm the inner life.*

place it before God, and make a healthy choice. If we ignore the signs or cover the issues, sadness, anger, and restlessness will harm the inner life, life with God.

Sadness drains the soul. It often lingers not only because there is loss but also because there is a loss within the loss. I know lost my marriage, but there was a loss within the loss. At another level I lost my self-respect. Self-pity is the passive response to unfulfilled wishes, "I want my old life back." Grief is the spiritual response to sadness and loss. Grief is the way the heart prepares to let go, say good-by, and press forward in the hope that a meaningful life will continue. Holy listening moves from self-pity to authentic grief to inner healing.

Anger eats away at the soul. Its lasting form, resentment, is acid sloshing in the chamber of your inner life. This is the active response to unfulfilled wishes. The spiritual response to resentment is holy rage: rage against the evil that has been done to you, including what you have done to yourself; rage to reestablish your boundaries and be assertive enough to protect them; rage in order to choose; choose health, choose forgiveness, and choose freedom from resentment. Your hope is to be authentic, not defensive or aggressive. In prayer, you complain and confess. In holy listening, you rage in safety, release your resentment, and rest in freedom.

Restlessness tears the soul apart. Nothing satisfies. You hitchhike on either side of the road because you have no direction. What will you do? Who will you be? Restlessness is a denial of unfulfilled wishes. It is the opening for the demon of despair. The soul knows what to do; it listens for God's inner voice, God's purpose for you.

HOLY LISTENING HELPS US OVERCOME

Sadness, anger, and restlessness are experiences in life common to all people and all followers of Christ. How do we deal with them? This is certainly a private struggle in the soul. That struggle can be greatly assisted with the support and compassion of true spiritual friends. First, being attentive to each other helps us **pay attention to what is happening in the inner life.** God speaks His word in our hearts; we must listen. We must look at what is happening in ourselves to hear the word of God for us.

> Norman Maclean's 1976 novella, A River Runs Through It, was made into a Robert Redford film fifteen years later. A Presbyterian minister and father of two boys teaches them about life and fly fishing. Looking over their fly fishing river, he explains that under the ripples are the stones and under the stones are the words of God. God speaks in and under the turmoil.[6]

This kind of listening certainly requires that we pay attention to what we are hearing from each other. But there is more: it is paying attention to what the words mean to the person who utters them. When we engage in holy listening, questions of clarification are better than providing a prescription for relief. To listen for the holy words of God in a conversation is to listen at still a deeper level. What is the meaning under the meaning?

> I spoke with a young man who said he wanted to give up on his engagement. He had had enough and couldn't take anymore. The words are plain, but what does he mean? Does he mean that he is afraid of marriage and feels he is not ready? Does he mean that the relationship with his fiancé is wounded and he has no hope for healing? Perhaps he is responding to pressure from some other source: parents, friends, or some person in authority. Only a listener who is careful, patient, and persistent will ever know.
>
> In time the young man began to talk about his own expectations as a husband: the struggle to provide, the fear of failure, and the lack of confidence he had in his own ability to fulfill his vision of a good husband. Truthfully, he loved his bride to be with all his heart. Underneath was his inner life, which was hidden to him. Holy listening goes beneath the ripples of the surface, the rattle of loose stone, and listens for the meaning under the meaning.

A further way holy listening helps overcome inner turmoil is by *enlivening our spiritual imagination.* Imagination is a powerful tool of the soul. It is a blessed moment to look out on the pain and perplexity of life and see in the eye of the soul the wonder of God's power and love at work. Soul-friends are used of God to help guide our spiritual imagination through prayer and Scripture.

The evil one will do all he can to fill the mind with harmful imaginings. He seeks to have us ruminate on our anger, sadness, and restlessness. Pictures of continued resentment, melancholy, and impatience flood our minds. When in the desert of turmoil, the devil placed harmful imaginings in the mind of Jesus: bread made of stones, floating off the temple heights, seeing all the kingdoms of the world. Jesus countered these images with pictures from Scripture: bread from the words of God, withstanding rebellion, serving the Lord of all.

God-guided imagination produces pictures in the mind and emotions in the heart. It enlightens and empowers faith. Perspective changes; motivation is cleansed. We are tempted to stamp down the emotion, hold it in, or seal it away. The power of imagination brings the experience to life within the workshop of the soul.

A woman in middle life lost her husband in a tragic fall. His death broke her heart, shattered her children, damaged their standard of living, and plunged the family into a struggle to survive. She knew she could be quagmired in the loss or do the hard work of grief, the soul's work of healing. In private and in the company of soul-friends, she poured out her feelings: sadness, rage, fear, emptiness. Images empowered holy listening, images from poetry, daily life, and Scripture.

I remember an image she shared with me. She was standing on a bridge with Jesus, weeping, filling a tissue with her tears and sadness. When all the tears and sadness had been emptied from her soul, she turned to her Lord. Jesus held her in His arms as she made the choice to release the tissue. It fell from her trembling hands into the water below. In her mind's eye she watched as her grief was carried down the stream and out to sea as she rested in the secure arms of her Savior.

We can also help each other *listen for ways to cooperate with God* as we battle inner turmoil. You will make discoveries in your holy listening that may be disturbing. You will find a habit you wish to overcome, a memory that continues to harm you, or patterns of behavior that are not true to your best. There are few things more difficult than to stop negative thinking.

The temptation is to leap on the quick fix, repress what is negative, or deny the significance of the issue. The quick fix is characterized by intellectualizing, justifying, and denying. Picture again the Nazi prisoners at Dachau who were set free, stepped out into the sunlight, blinked, and then returned to their dark prison cells.

> *The temptation is to leap on the quick fix, repress what is negative, or deny the significance of the issue.*

You are not on your own. God is within. Cooperate with Him. *"Work out your own salvation; for it is God who is at work in you"* (Philippians 2:12–13). With the guidance of spiritual friends, use your imagination to see God at work. Ask God for strength. Be humble enough to accept that His strength will often include spiritually supportive friends. Indeed, we strengthen each other as together we work out our salvation. God's help moves in you and me, in us, to bring to life our true and best in Christ.

I remember an old tree on the street where I grew up. In the fall, it would fill the yard with hours of work. I was often enlisted to help with the raking. It would take more than one Saturday morning. The early leaves would fall. Then, after an autumn storm, another batch would float onto the grass. A few stubborn leaves required the first freeze before they let go.

One year there was one leaf high on the tree that would not turn loose. It held to a bare limb all winter. Wind, rain, snow, and ice could not dislodge it. However, it did fall in the spring. The sun had warmed the earth. New life was flowing from the roots up through the trunk and into the limbs. When the bud of a new leaf pushed through just at the place where the old leaf was hanging on, it happened. The old leaf fell as new life took over.

Listen for God's movement within your soul: in your memories, your imagination, and in your intentions. You can work out your spiritual struggle, for God is working in you to bring to life your true and best in Christ.

HOLY LISTENING AND DIFFICULT PEOPLE

Of course, not all listening is holy. There are weapons drawn and wounds inflicted by unholy listening. There are toxic relationships that harm us. Like you, I can also recall wounding moments: being ignored when expressing my heart, the soul's secrets are used to control and manipulate, misplaced trust ends in betrayal.

> *Not all listening is holy. There are weapons drawn and wounds inflicted by unholy listening.*

These poisonous people come from all walks of life; family, work, school, church, clubs or civic duties. Some people have an uncanny ability to push the wrong button, upset our day, land a stinging blow, or pour salt in an open wound. They upset us. Then, as good people, we are upset with the fact that we allowed them to upset us. Why could we not take the blow and just go about our day? Why do we linger and languish over it?

There are also deeper wounds. We are victimized by lies and gossip, and then tried in the court of public opinion. There are people who will protect their own image, power, and prestige by trashing a caricature of our souls. They weave a tapestry of innuendo and deceit and spread it over the phone lines, email, and in cynical conversations. There is no way to plead your case, set the record straight, or correct the hearsay.

There are also the wounds inflicted on the people we love. We watch helplessly as an organization harms someone we cherish, destroying their dreams, career, relationships, and the quest for a happy life. The pain is particularly acute when it happens in the family. It may be played out in the family business or simply the business of being a family; holiday rituals are lost, rumors fly, and the family is divided. Particularly in the family, when money changes hands, personalities change.

We all deal with people who are self-serving. They use others for gain and greed. Perhaps more than at any other point, we need each other and the discipline of holy listening to deal with difficult people. Indeed, in the Scripture, the context of the verse, *"where two or three gather in my name,"* (Matthew 18:20) is set in a rogues' gallery of scoundrels and evil doers.

The One Who Causes Others to Sin (Matthew 18:6–9): You are enraged when someone seduces a good person into bad behavior, especially if it involves one of your children: the person who first gave your child drugs on the school playground; the group of teen girls who brought a harmful influence into your daughter's life; the business owner who gave your son a job, but now expects him to cut corners in order to advance in the business. How do you approach your child? How do you manage your anger toward the one who is harming your child?

The Lost Sheep (Matthew 18:10–14): How do you deal with someone who has lost their way, their marriage, or their moral compass? In biblical terms, they have left the flock. Some folks who are safe within the fold coldly criticize, "let them go," "they made their bed," "it is not your problem." But your heart is with the lost one. With Jesus, you search for them in your fears, your broken heart, and your loss of sleep. You want to straighten them out; you want them to know you love them unconditionally. What should you say? What should you do?

The brother who sins against you (Matthew 18:15–17): It is one thing when a stranger harms you, when you are cheated in a business deal, or when some faceless organization wreaks havoc in your life. It hurts, and hurts deeply. Yet it is another kind of pain when you are betrayed by a friend, a soul-friend, a brother in faith. Relationships may be destroyed, churches divided, and a generation lost.

You go to them privately, but to no avail. You find the courage to talk to them again with a mutual friend; but the problem increases. Should you involve the friends you trust, people of faith? Will they gossip? What kind of justice is possible?

It is at this point in Scripture, at the point of dealing with the scoundrels, evil doers, and difficult people that the promise is given: *"For where two or three come together in my name, there am I with them (Matthew 18:18–20).* Especially when dealing with relationships, we need the support, the insights, and the power of soul-friends engaged in holy listening.

HOLY LISTENING AND GOD'S EAR

Relational complexities and pain put us under great stress. Our thinking is clouded. It is almost impossible to sort it out alone. We need the help, the holy listening of dear and trusted friends. The painful conversations usually dance around three concerns; wisdom, justice, and peace.

> *The painful conversations usually dance around three concerns; wisdom, justice, and peace.*

Wisdom: What should I do about my
children, marriage, job, or church? How do I make sense of the complexities and chaos? What should I say? Who should I trust? How should I deal with the mistakes I have already made?
Justice: How do I seek justice? When do I seek it? When does the quest for justice become a pursuit of vengeance? When is justice too costly, unwise, or out of reach? How do I leave it in God's hands?
Peace: How can I find rest in my soul? How do I restore harmony in the family? What should I do to bring back calm to the workplace or serenity to the church? I am so tired; I just need peace and quiet.

We listen because we care. We listen because we want to help. How can we listen in ways that are faithful to what is true and best in Christ? We must listen to the story, the injustice, and the pain. Also, we must listen for what is underneath, in the inner life, in the call of Christ. Underneath is an issue, a calling, indeed, a command, *"love your enemies, pray for those who persecute you that you may be sons of your Father in heaven"* (Matthew 5:44–45).

> To forgive an enemy is to remind the world of the grace of Christ.

It is a hard command and it is only possible through forgiveness. Alexander Pope's phrase has been reduced to a truism, "...to forgive is divine." Yet forgiveness and love of enemies is the family business for the children of God. To forgive an enemy is to remind the world of the grace of Christ.

> "Let the beauty of Jesus be seen in me
> All His wonderful passion and purity!
> O Thou Spirit divine,
> All my nature refine
> Till the beauty of Jesus is seen in me."
> ALBERT ORSBORN[7]

However, when we have been hurt, wounded deeply, our passions are not pure and our nature is to be resentful or depressed. The command to forgive and love our enemies is a harsh command. It cannot be done with an easy decision in the mind. It takes a change of heart and a transaction in the soul.

Peter understood the difficulty of forgiving enemies. Immediately following the rogues gallery of scoundrels, just as Jesus promised to be with *"two or three who gather together in my name* (Matthew 18:20), Peter asked in astonishment, *"Lord, how many times shall I forgive my brother when he sins against me? Up to seven times?"* (Matthew 18:21).

The command to forgive seems impossible, at least unreasonable when we have been hurt. To complicate matters all the more, the enemy will probably not even request forgiveness from you. It seems like a callous and cruel command, but there is a reason. You forgive your enemy so you do not become like your enemy. You forgive in order to be free from the tyranny of your enemy. You forgive to be true to your best in Christ, to live as an offspring of your Heavenly Father.

Something wonderful happens in moments of forgiveness. You find wisdom, a clearer understanding of what to do. You see the path of justice, what is possible in this life and what must be left in the hands of God. And you experience peace in your heart and life.

However, you cannot turn on forgiveness like a lamp in a dark room. Forgiveness is not an intellectual decision; it is an experience in the soul. It is not a moment, but a series of moments. In the deepest pain and injustice, forgiveness is like layers of the onion: you forgive and then forgive again. It is possible that the same person has hurt you seven times; it is also possible that one wound can be so deep that it requires seven layers of forgiveness. Jesus answered Peter, *"I tell you, not seven times, but seventy-seven times"* (Matthew 18:22). Some wounds are so evil and personal that it calls for seventy times seven moments of forgiveness.

> *In the deepest pain and injustice, forgiveness is like layers of the onion: you forgive and then forgive again.*

TO HELP EACH OTHER

How can we help each other forgive? How can we listen in the spirit of holiness in order to lead each other into the presence and purpose of perfect love? In my own journey, deep-level forgiveness was essential to living true to my best in Christ. I needed to experience forgiveness in my soul and, from my soul, forgive others. Moments of worship were moving. I also benefited and grew from private times of sincerity and solace in the Spirit of Christ as well as with small group gatherings and conversations. Additionally, I was honored to experience the wonder of holy listening on multiple occasions. I recall one time especially.

Sarah Rowan was an older woman of great maturity and spiritual insight. She lived across the street from the university. Her home was old and beautiful, a museum of lovely things and gracious memories. Her quiet agenda was to use her home as a place of healing.

On occasion, I spoke in the worship services at the school. Sarah heard me speak and truly believed in me when I had such a small amount of confidence.

She also heard the pain and struggle within that I was not ready to recognize. I was invited for tea at her kitchen table.

We chatted for a while when Sarah began telling me a heartbreaking story of the death of her infant grandchild. I took on the role of listener. Her frankness, candor, and the depth of her emotions, the brilliance of her faith, and her gift of authenticity moved me. In a matter of three-quarters of an hour, my soul recognized the deep feelings and conflicts in me. I had lost family, friends, and a planned future. I was hurt and angry.

Our roles reversed; she became my holy listener. There were few words, and the silence was safe in the deep spirituality of the moment. She seemed to read the look on my face, the ache, tenderness, and trouble. Gentle tears welled in my eyes; I made no attempt to wipe them away. Sarah heard, really heard my soul. In that instant, I sensed another Person in the room.

I knew, knew in the depths of my inner life, another Listener was with us. It was the same One who listened to the soul of Jacob, Moses, and Paul. This was the same God in flesh, Jesus Christ, who spoke out of the depths of humanity. It was the same Spirit of God who *"helps us in our weakness. We do not know what we ought to pray for, but the Spirit himself intercedes for us with groans that words cannot express. And he who searches our hearts knows the mind of the Spirit, because the Spirit intercedes for the saints in accordance with God's will"* (Romans 8:26–27).

I was face-to-face, soul-to-soul, with God. Through spiritual intuition and maturity, Sarah stepped out of the role of listening to me and took on the task of prompting me, helping me, and encouraging me to take the deep truth and hope of my heart, form words, and lay them out before my Lord.

I was with God. In this place, all things are possible: healing from hurt, release from anger, and freedom from resentment. In the presence of God, inner turmoil gives way to peace. An old hymn came out of my heart, a hymn based on Psalm 139:

> *Search me, O God, and know my heart today,*
> *Try me, O Savior, know my thoughts, I pray;*
> *See if there be some wicked way in me;*
> *Cleanse me from every sin, and set me free.*

I praise Thee, Lord, for cleansing me from sin;
Fulfill Thy word and make me pure within;
Fill me with fire, where once I burned with shame;
Grant my desire to magnify Thy name.

Lord, take my life, and make it wholly Thine;
Fill my poor heart with Thy great love divine;
Take all my will, my passion, self and pride;
I now surrender, Lord, in me abide.

J. EDWIN ORR[8]

A PERSONAL POSTSCRIPT

It has been more than fifteen years and a long spiritual journey from a day in a swamp in Florida when God clearly asked, "Richard, what is your question?" Today, I know the questions: Lord, who am I in Christ and what kind of life do you want to create with me? I also know the answer: to become and live true to my best in Christ.

In the intervening years of healing and new hope, God has provided a beautiful new marriage; our children, all grown, are wonderful, and happiness abounds in our family. I am an Associate Professor of Education at Trevecca Nazarene University and minister in churches, faith-based organizations, and businesses through preaching, teaching, seminars, and retreats. I want to *"Give thanks to the Lord, for he is good; his love endures forever...*

> *Some wandered in desert wastelands, finding no way to a city where they could settle.*
> **He led them to a city where they could settle.**
> *Some sat in darkness and the deepest gloom, prisoners suffering in iron chains.*
> **He brought them out... and broke their chains.**
> *Some became fools through their rebellious ways and suffered affliction because of their iniquities,*
> **He sent forth his word and healed them.**
> *Others when out on the sea in ships...a tempest... lifted high the waves... they were at their wits ends.*
> **He stilled the storm and He guided them...**
> *Let them give thanks to the Lord for his unfailing love and his wonderful deeds for men. Let them exalt him in the assembly of the people and praise him in the council of the elders.* (Psalm 107:1–32)

APPRECIATION

I want to share some words of appreciation. This book is the result of a long, inward, personal and spiritual journey. Along the way, wonderful soul-friends made the book possible.

First, I want to thank Mark Maish for his consistent support, encouragement, and wise counsel. Rod and Cindy Bushy became family to me at my darkest and most need-filled time. They believed in me and for me when I had such little hope.

Also, my pastor, Dr. Gary Henecke, the pastoral staff and lay leadership of Nashville First Church of the Nazarene believed in the book and invested in the ministry of *Soul Purpose*.

My Sunday School class as well as a faithful group of people that attended a Wednesday evening series openly and willingly received and applied these lessons. Their heartfelt questions and positive response helped shape the final manuscript.

There are also a number of individuals who have left their fingerprints on this project. I want to express my thanks to Dr. Dee Freeborn, Dr. Esther Swink, Dr. Toby Williams, Dr. Millard Reed, and Carla Hendershot. And I thank Dr. Donna Gray for her skill and care as editor and proofreader.

Finally, my wife, Shirley, supported, encouraged and assisted me at each stage of the writing process. Her loving prayers and persistent faith are embedded on each page of this book.

NOTES

1. **C. S. Lewis** (1898–1963). The quote on the title page is from *Mere Christianity*, by C. S. Lewis. The book is an adaptation of a 1943 series of radio lectures while Lewis was at Oxford. The book is a classic work in Christian apologetics.

2. **Thomas Raymond Kelly** (1893–1941). The quote is from *A Testament of Devotion*. Kelly was an American Quaker missionary and educator. He taught and wrote on the subject of spirituality. He was born in 1893 in Ohio to a family that belonged to the Religious Society of Friends (Quaker). The Quakers in Ohio are influenced particularly by the Holiness tradition.

   Kelly graduated from Wilmington College with a major in chemistry and continued his education at Haverford College in Philadelphia, Pennsylvania. At Haverford he explored the more traditional and mystical vein of the Religious Society of Friends. Kelly went on to Hartford Theological Seminary to be trained as a missionary.

   During World War I, he followed the Quaker Peace Testimony and signed up to do civilian non-combatant service in Europe. In England he worked first with the YMCA and then with German prisoners of war. Following the war, he earned two doctorates, the first at Hartford Seminary and the second at Harvard. The dissertation for his second doctorate was published in 1937, but he failed in the oral defense due to a memory lapse. This failure resulted in a period of deep grief. Out of this experience of grief, Kelly had a profound spiritual awakening.

   In 1938 Kelly went to Germany to encourage Friends living under Hitler's regime. To his great joy, he received word on January 17, 1941, that the publishing company of Harper and Brothers was willing to meet with him to discuss the publication of a devotional book. He died of a heart attack later that same day. Three months later Kelly's colleague, Douglas Steere, submitted five of Kelly's devotional essays to the publisher along with a biographical sketch of Kelly. The book was published under the title *A Testament of Devotion*.

3. **Douglas Steere** (1901–1995). The quote is from *Gleanings*. Steere was educated at Michigan State, Harvard, and Oxford in the early 1900's. He was a Rhodes Scholar,

brilliant thinker, and skilled author of many devotional books. He spent most of his
life teaching philosophy at Haverford College in Pennsylvania and was a Quaker.
He was one of a few American authors who, in the past century, combined academic
integrity with spiritual authenticity. He found authentic spirituality in the delicate
balance between contemplation (the inner life) and action (the outer life).

Chapter 1: What's Your Question

1. **Martin Buber** (1878–1965) was an Austrian-Israeli-Jewish philosopher and educator. His writing evokes vivid images and is often poetic. He retold Hasidic tales,
   wrote Biblical commentaries and metaphysical dialogue. His influence extends
   across the humanities, particularly in the fields of social psychology, social philosophy, and religious existentialism.

2. *"The essence of your humanity and the hope of eternity resides in your soul."* In the
   opening chapter of the Bible, God said, *"Let us make man in our image, in our likeness…" (Genesis 1:26).* "The Lord God formed the man from the dust of the
   ground and breathed into his nostrils the breath of life, and the man became a
   living being," (Genesis 2:7)

3. *The baby's …beckoning eyes …*Robert Kegan, professor of Adult Learning and Professional Development, and Chair of the Institute for the Management of Lifelong
   Education, is author of *The Evolving Self: Problems and Process in Human Development.* I have built on his observation that our survival and development as infants is
   dependent "on our capacity to recruit the vested attention of others to us. Nature is
   nowhere more graceful than in the way she endows each newborn infant with
   seductive abilities…. none is more powerful than his (the infant's) eyes" (p. 17).

4. **Simone Weil** (1909–1943) was a Christian mystic, social activist, and French
   philosopher. While in Assisi, she had a religious experience in the same church as
   St. Francis, which led her to pray for the first time. She was attracted to the Roman
   Catholic Church but refused baptism. She explained her refusal in "Waiting for
   God."

5. **Carlo Carretto** was born on April 2, 1910, in northern Italy. He studied to become
   a teacher, but political difficulties under the fascists altered the direction of his
   career. Instead he immersed himself in the dynamic youth movement of Catholic
   Action, which sought to mobilize the laity in advancing the religious and social

message of the church. He spent nearly twenty years immersed in a blur of meetings, conferences, and public organizing.

All of this came to an abrupt halt in 1954 when he surprised his friends by resigning from Catholic Action and announcing his intention to join the Little Brothers of Jesus, the community of desert contemplatives inspired by the spirituality of Charles de Foucauld. In explaining his decision, Carretto said only that he felt summoned by a call from God: "Leave everything and come with me into the desert. It is not your acts and deeds that I want, but faith and your prayer, your love."

6. **Evelyn Underhill**, (1875–1941) is well known for her works on religious experience, practice, and mysticism. Her book *Mysticism* was the most widely read of its type in the first half of the 20ᵀᴴ century. *The Spiritual Life* was published in 1936 and again in 1999.

7. **Confucius** (551–479 BCE), according to Chinese tradition, was a thinker, political figure, and educator. The image of the archer is quoted by his grandson Tzu-ssu in *The Central Harmony*, traditionally ascribed to him as author. Confucius' influence in Chinese history was like that of Socrates in the West.

8. *an endless sea* ...John Dominic Crossan, co-founder of the *Jesus Seminar*, describes the contemporary spiritual condition in these words: "There is no lighthouse keeper. There is no lighthouse. There is no dry land. There are only people living on rafts made from their own imaginations. And, there is the sea."

9. **Howard Thurman** (1900–1981) was an author, philosopher, theologian, educator, and civil rights leader. In 1923, Howard Thurman graduated from Morehouse College as valedictorian. After completing his study at the Colgate Rochester Theological Seminary (now Colgate Rochester Crozer Divinity School), he was ordained a Baptist minister in 1925. He then decided to pursue further study as special student of philosophy in residence at Haverford College with Rufus Jones, a noted Quaker philosopher and mystic. Rufus Jones was a mentor to Thomas Kelley and influence in the life of Douglas Steere. The quotation cannot be found in written form: Professor Thurman shared the thought with his students who in turn shared it with others.

10. **Eric Liddell** (1902–1941) was an Olympic champion of the 1924 games held in Paris. He then served as a missionary to China. His story was captured in the film *Chariots of Fire* (1981).

11. **Douglas Steere**. From *Together in Solitude*, 1982.

Chapter 2—Soul Purpose

1. **Wystan Hugh Auden** (1907–1973), was an English-American poet, regarded by many as one of the greatest writers of the 20th century. He dealt with moral and political issues. The central themes of his poetry are personal love, politics and citizenship, religion and morals, and the relationship between unique human beings and the anonymous, impersonal world.

2. **Albert Edward Day** (1884–1973) was a Methodist minister, author, and founder of the Disciplined Order of Christ. The quote is from his book *The Captivating Presence*.

3. *"…between what happens to you and how you respond"* is a concept built on the observation of **Robert Kegan.** In his book, *The Evolving Self,* he recalls Ernest Hemingway's story "Indian Camp" in which an assortment of diverse individuals deal with the screams of agony from an Indian woman who suffers in childbirth. The men of the tribe leave as does an uncle who goes off to get drunk. The doctor saves the woman and child, yet the father, bed ridden in the bunk above his suffering wife, takes his own life in response to her pain. Kegan suggests that the story directs us "to the most human of 'regions' *between* an event and a reaction to it— the place where the event is privately composed, made sense of, the place where it actually *becomes* an event for that person" (page 2).

4. *"…day by day."* The original prayer was authored by **Richard Chichester** (1197–1253). Born the son of a prosperous farmer, Richard was orphaned at a young age and an incompetent guardian lost the family fortune. Richard worked hard to restore the fortune, gave it to his brother and went to study at Oxford. He knew poverty and wealth, acceptance and rejection. He was Chancellor of Canterbury, also walked barefoot among the people preaching to farmers and fisherman.

5. **Beowulf** is an Old English heroic epic poem of anonymous authorship. This work of Anglo-Saxon literature dates to between the 8th and the 11th century, the only surviving manuscript dating to circa 1010. At 3183 lines, it is notable for its length. It has risen to national epic status in England.

   A wonderful telling of Beowulf is found in David Whyte's, *The Heart Aroused: Poetry and the Preservation of the Soul in Corporate America* (Doubleday, 1994), chapter 2. The classic discussion of myths as means of expressing the soul's life is found in Joseph Campbell's *The Hero with a Thousand Faces* (1949).

6. *Faith, Hope and Love* is a well known expression of the Apostle Paul found in his first letter to the Corinthians, chapter 13, where he writes, "Now remains faith, hope and love, but the greatest of these is love." The trio of spiritual virtues is also found in 1 Thessalonians 1:2-3, 2 Thessalonians 1:3-4, Colossians 1:3-4, Ephesians 1:15-18, 1 Timothy 1:5, 1 Peter 20-22. For an analysis of faith, hope, and love, see Gene A. Getz, sharpening the Focus of the Church, pages 51-61. The book is published by Moody Press, 1974.

7. **Archibald McLeish** (1892–1982) was an American poet, writer and the Librarian of Congress. In 1959 his play *J.B.* won the Pulitzer Prize for Drama.

8. **Brother Lawrence**, (1614–1691). The quote is from the fourth conversation in *The Practice of the Presence of God.* At the age of 18, Brother Lawrence had a spiritual awakening. He became a lay brother in a monastery and spent most of his life working in the kitchen. His character and love of Christ attracted many to him. His letters and conversations were published in a small book that has lifted the hearts of millions. John Wesley and A.W. Tozer recommended it.

9. *"…as if there is some static and fully formed person inside you."* This thought builds on the work of **John Powell** in his book *Why Am I Afraid to Tell You Who I Am* (1969). He writes, "There is no fixed, true and real person inside of you or me, precisely because *being a person* necessarily implies *becoming a person, being in process."* In an era of deep unrest, Father Powell's simple and clear writing on the inner life and the quest for authenticity received a wide reading. He is reported to be the second most widely read Christian author in history.

10. **Ray Bradbury** (1920—) is an American writer of science fiction, fantasy, horror, and mystery. His best known works are *Fahrenheit 451* and *The Martian Chronicles.*

11. *Book Burning.* On April 6, 1933, the German Student Association declared an "Action against the Un-German Spirit." On the night of May 10TH, right-wing students marched in torchlight parades. They threw the "un-German" books into bonfires with great ceremony, singing, and incantations.

Chapter 3—Spiritual Meaning

1. **Howard Thurman**, (1899–1981). The quote is from his book *The Inward Journey.* Thurman served as dean of Rankin Chapel at Howard University from 1932–1944. He later became the first Black dean of Marsh Chapel at Boston at University (1953–1965).

Thurman traveled broadly, heading Christian missions and meeting with world figures like Mahatma Gandhi. When Thurman asked Gandhi what message he should take back to America, Gandhi said he regretted not having made nonviolence more visible worldwide and suggested some American Black men would succeed where he had failed.

Thurman was, in fact, a classmate and friend of Martin Luther King Sr. at Morehouse College. Martin Luther King, Jr. visited Thurman while he attended Boston University and Thurman in turn mentored his former classmate's son and his friends.

Ebony magazine named Thurman one of the 50 most important figures in African American history, and Life magazine rated him among the 12 best preachers in the nation. Thurman was the author of 20 books of ethical and cultural criticism. The most famous of his works is *Jesus and the Disinherited*, published in 1949.

2. **Evelyn Underhill,** *The Spiritual Life*, published in 1936 and again in 1999.

3. **Albert Einstein** (1879–1955). In 1999 Einstein was named *Time* magazine's "Person of the Century," and a poll of prominent physicists named him the greatest physicist of all time. The quote "Not everything that can be counted counts, and not everything that counts can be counted," is attributed to him.

4. **Francisco de Osuna** (1492–1540). The reference to Osuna is found in **Evelyn Underhill's** *The Spiritual Life*. Osuna's most widely read book is *The Spiritual Alphabet*.

5. **Mark Twain** (1835–1910). The quote is found is several forms and all are attributed to Mark Twain.

6. *Watch-maker* …Philosophers of the Enlightenment used the new vision of technology and the scientific method to envision God. Some saw God as a "watch-maker." God wound up the universe and then let it go. The thought was made famous by William Paley (1748–1805). The analogy has been revived in the intelligent design movement.

7. *Here be dragons* (Latin, *hic sunt dracones*) is a phrase used by ancient cartographers to denote dangerous or unexplored territories. The only known use of this phrase on a medieval map was the Lenox Globe from 1503-07. Today, software programmers sometimes use the term to indicate especially difficult or obscure sections of code in a program so that others do not tamper with them.

8. **James Stewart**. The quote is from *River of Life*, page 134, published by Abingdon in 1972.

Chapter 4—Eternal Value

1. **Kentucky mountain woman**–quoted by Carl R. Woodward in the *Wonderful World of Books*, edited by Alfred Steffefrud, 1953.

2. *Trust and Obey* was written by John Sammis (1846–1919). The music was composed by Daniel Tower (1850–1919). It was Daniel Tower who heard the testimony, jotted down the phrase, and gave it to John Sammis.

3. *Lamb of God* is a biblical phrase found in particularly in the Gospel of John and the Book of Revelation. John the Baptist declares that Jesus is *"The Lamb of God"* (John 1:36) while John the Revelator sees the *"Lamb upon the throne"* of heaven (Revelation 5:6).

4. **Charlotte Elliot** (1789–1871) is the author of *Just As I Am* (1835). The song is, perhaps, the most famous hymn of invitation in use. J. Vernon McGee in his commentary on James 2:13, tells the story of the hymn's origin:

   A story is told that took place in London when a great preacher, a very fine young man, by the name of Caesar Milan was invited one evening to a very large and prominent home where a choice musical was to be presented.

   On the program was a young lady who thrilled the audience with her singing and playing. When she finished, this young preacher threaded his way through the crowd which was gathered around her. When he finally came to her and had her attention, he said, "Young lady, when you were singing, I sat there and thought how tremendously the cause of Christ would be benefited if you would dedicate yourself and your talents to the Lord. But," he added, "you are just as much a sinner as the worst drunkard in the street, or any harlot on Scarlet Street. But I am glad to tell you that the blood of Jesus Christ, God's Son, will cleanse you from all sin if you will come to Him."

   In a very haughty manner, she turned her head aside and said to him, "You are very insulting, sir." And she started to walk away. He said, "Lady, I did not mean any offense, but I pray that the Spirit of God will convict you."

   Well, they all went home, and that night this young woman could not sleep. At two o'clock in the morning she knelt at the side of her bed and took Christ as her Savior. And then she, Charlotte Elliott, sat down and wrote the words of a favorite hymn, "Just As I Am."

5. *Love, Acceptance, and Forgiveness*, is a title of a book by Jerry Cook and Stanley Baldwin, Regal Books, Ventura California, 1979

6. *Zombie* …A **zombie** is a reanimated human corpse. Stories of zombies originated in the spiritual belief system of Voodoo, which told pf people controlled as workers by a powerful sorcerer. Zombies became popular in modern horror fiction because of the success of George A. Romero's 1968 film, *Night of the Living Dead*.

7. **T. S. Eliot** (1888–1965) was a poet, dramatist, and literary critic. Born in St. Louis, he became a British citizen in 1927. His drama *Murder in the Cathedral* was published in 1935.

8. *"Jesus is patient, Jesus is kind"* is an adaptation of I Corinthians 13. I first heard this adaptation of the Scripture in a sermon delivered by Dr. Reuben Welch at Eastern Nazarene College in 1972.

9. *"Adam knew Eve … "* The phrase comes from Genesis 4:1; however, the meaning of physical intimacy is expressed in Genesis 2:24; *"For this reason a man will leave his father and mother and be united to his wife, and they will become one flesh."* The word "know" indicates deep, physical and emotional intimacy.

10. **Dame Julian of Norwich** (1342–1416) was the earliest woman writer in English and the most open hearted of Christian authors. Her revelations took place in 1373, and she recorded them in *Revelations of Divine Love*. She tells of seeing a hazelnut in the palm of her hand. She thought about how the single seed continues in the life of the tree. She writes, "And I answered in my understanding: 'It lasts, and ever shall last, for God loves it; and even so everything has its being, by the love of God.'

    "In this little thing I saw three properties. The first is that God made it, the second that God loves it, the third that God keeps it. And what did I see in this? Truly, the Maker, the Lover, and the Keeper."

11. *"…in remembrance of me."* The words of Jesus are found in Luke 22:17-20, Matthew 26:26-29; Mark 14: 22-25; 1 Corinthians 11:23-25. The cultural meaning of the word "remember" at the time of Jesus was not simply to recall facts, but to re-experience. Jesus is not asking us simply to recall historical facts or theological propositions. Jesus calls us to experience anew and afresh the gift of his love.

12. **David Steindl-Rast;** the quote is found in *Gratefulness, the Heart of Prayer*, published in 1984.

13. *"...beside still waters ...valley of the shadow ... "* The phrase is from the 23RD Psalm.

14. *"Praise God from whom all blessings flow... "* is the first line of what is commonly called "The Doxology." It was written by Thomas Ken, a priest in the Church of England, in 1674. The words are:

> *Praise God, from Whom all blessings flow;*
> *Praise Him, all creatures here below;*
> *Praise Him above, ye Heavenly Host;*
> *Praise Father, Son, and Holy Ghost. Amen.*

Chapter 5—Personal Uniqueness

1. *Tract Houses*—The tract house was a new suburban vision that began in a 1,500-acre Long Island potato farm bought out by William J. Levitt in 1949. The concept was to apply the systems of mass-producing automobiles to home construction. See William Manchester, *The Glory and the Dream, A Narrative History of America, 1932-1972* (New York: Bantam Books, 1980), page 432.

2. *What kind of life do you want to create?* The question is inspired by the work of Robert E. Quinn, especially in his book *Building the Bridge As You Walk On It: A Guide for Leading Change* (2004). He opens the first chapter of the book with the question, "How do we create extraordinarily positive organizations? This is the central question that integrates the research of my colleagues at the Center for Positive Organizational Scholarship" (page 3). It was my privilege to participate in a seminar on *Leading Deep Change* under the scholarship of Dr. Quinn at the University of Michigan.

3. **Thomas Merton** (1915–1968) was a Trappist Monk who wrote more than 60 books. The quote is from *The Seeds of Contemplation*, published in 1961 by the monastery where he lived and served, The Abbey of Gethsemani in the state of Kentucky. He was one of the most influential Catholic authors of the 20TH century. Merton was an acclaimed Catholic spiritual writer, poet, author, and social activist. His autobiography, *The Seven Story Mountain*, has sold over one million copies and has been translated into over fifteen languages.

4. **Stephen D. Bryant** is the editor and publisher of Upper Room Ministries. The

quote is from his editorial in *Weavings*, May/June, 1989.

5. **He will be our God, and we will be His People;** I am especially indebted to conversations with Dale Stoffer, academic dean of Ashland Theological Seminary. He has done expansive work on what he terms, "the people formula."

6. *never forget how you made them feel;* Maya Angelou, (1928–) is the author of numerous books including Letter to *My Daughter, I know Why the Caged Bird Sings,* and *The Heart of a Woman.*

7. *fearful and wonderful* is found in Psalm 139:13-14; *"For you created my inmost being; you knit me together in my mother's womb, I praise you because I am fearfully and wonderfully made; your words are wonderful, I know that full well."* The Psalm expresses the angst of a man who cannot escape an encounter with God.

Chapter 6—Soul Crisis

1. **Meister Eckhart** (1260–1328). Eckhart von Hochheim was a German theologian, philosopher, and mystic. Meister is German for "Master," a reference to the Master of Theology he obtained in Paris. The essence of his preaching was the presence of God in the soul of the individual and the dignity of the soul of a just man. He summarized his preaching: "When I preach, I usually speak of detachment and say that a man should be empty of self and all things; and secondly, that he should be reconstructed in the simple good that God is; and thirdly, that he should consider the great aristocracy which God has set up in the soul, such that by means of it man may wonderfully attain to God; and fourthly, of the purity of the divine nature."

2. *Softly and Tenderly* was written by an Ohio poet-composer, Will L. Thompson, in 1880. It is reported that when the world renowned lay preacher Dwight L. Moody lay on his death bed in his Northfield, Massachusetts, home Will Thompson came to visit him. Moody's doctor refused to admit him to the sickroom. Moody heard them talking and recognized Thompson's voice and called him to his bedside. Taking the composer by the hand, D. L. Moody said, "Will, I would rather have written 'Softly and Tenderly Jesus is Calling' than anything I have been able to do in my whole life."

3. *Ashland Theological Seminary* is an evangelical seminary with 800 students. Ashland Seminary defines its core values as commitment to Scripture, academic excellence, spiritual formation, and community. Seventy different denominations are represented in the student body. The school is accredited by the Association of

Theological Schools and the North Central Association of Colleges and Schools.

4. *Lose the Battle to win the war.* This is a principle of Chanakya. Some scholars consider Chanakya to be the "the Indian Machiavelli." *Choose the right moment* is also Hindu in origin.

5. *Your interest rate and service charges may change without notice.* Type the previous statement into a search engine and you will produce a list of thousands of banks and credit cards.

6. *Executives… are turning inside for answers.* Fortune Magazine, September 19, 1994.

7. **Isaac Pennington** (1617–1679) was an early Quaker and the son of the Lord Mayor of London. He was imprisoned six times for his beliefs. His writings, especially his letters, have been read continually for their spiritual counsel.

8. **Augustine** (354–433 CE) was a philosopher, theologian, and one of the most influential Christian leaders and teachers.

9. *My prayer …* The quote is from *The Saviors of God: Spiritual Exercises*, by Nikos Kazantzakis (1883–1957).

Chapter 7—A Lost Soul

1. **Carole King** (1942–) is an American singer, songwriter, and pianist. She was most active as a singer during the first half of the 1970s, though she was a successful songwriter for considerably longer both before and after this period. In 1971, she wrote the number one hit "You've Got a Friend."

2. *Bread and belonging…* is a phrase used by John C. Harris in *Stress, Power, and Ministry.* It is an expression that captures our practical and relational needs. The book was published by Alban Institute in 1977.

3. *The pressure on those in the public arena …* is a thought built on the work of **James M. Kouzes and Barry Z. Posner**, authors of *The Leadership Challenge*, one of the best books on leadership ever written. They write, "Leaders must learn how to balance their personal desire to achieve important ends with the constituents' need to believe that the leader has others' best interests at heart…. Leaders have to learn to thrive on the tensions between their own calling and the voice of the people" (page 16).

4. *The frog in the boiling water …* is a widespread anecdote that is thought to have come from the work of a German physiologist, Fredrick Goltz (1834–1902), who is said to have physically demonstrated the phenomenon. It was told during the

time of the cold war as a warning against sympathy toward the Soviets. Dr. James Dobson, the creator of *Focus on the Family* used the story as a warning against a deteriorating culture. Again the story appeared in the 1990's as a metaphor of climate change.

5. *Angry psalms...* for a discussion of the psalms of vengeance, see *Praying the Psalms* by Walter Breuggerman, St. Mary's Press, 1986.

6. *Sharpen the saw*.. Habit number seven in **Steve Covey's** *The 7 Habits of Highly Effective People* is called "sharpen the saw"; Covey uses the common analogy of a woodcutter who is sawing for several days straight and is becoming less and less productive. The process of cutting dulls the blade. The solution is to sharpen the saw periodically.

7. *Little altars ...Little Altars Everywhere* by Rebecca Wells is the first book in the Ya-Ya Sisterhood series. It chronicles the adventures of the Ya-Ya Sisterhood—four eccentric women—and their children.

8. **Rufus Jones** (1863–1948) was one of the most influential Quakers of the 20TH century. He was a writer, historian, theologian, and college professor. The quotation is from his book, *The Double Search* (1906, available in Digital Quaker Collection).

9. **Martin Luther** (1483—1546) is credited with opening the protestant reformation and being one of the key leaders of the movement. His vision and movement changed the course of Western Civilization. He is best known for the doctrine of justification by faith alone. He explains:

The first and chief article is this: Jesus Christ, our God and Lord, died for our sins and was raised again for our justification (Romans 3:24–25). He alone is the Lamb of God who takes away the sins of the world (John 1:29), and God has laid on Him the iniquity of us all (Isaiah 53:6). All have sinned and are justified freely, without their own works and merits, by His grace, through the redemption that is in Christ Jesus, in His blood (Romans 3:23–25). This is necessary to believe. This cannot be otherwise acquired or grasped by any work, law or merit. Therefore, it is clear and certain that this faith alone justifies us .... Nothing of this article can be yielded or surrendered, even though heaven and earth and everything else falls (Mark 13:31).

10. *Dysfunctional and addictive ...*The common roots of addiction and dysfunction are discussed by A. Comerford in the *Journal of Substance Abuse Treatment*, Volume 16, Issue 3, Pages 247-253.

11. **John Newton** (1725–1807), was raised in a religious home, but upon the death of his mother (when he was seven) and the retirement of his father ten years later, the young man entered his wandering years in which he reports that he lost all sense of religion. After serving time on the crew of a slave ships, he was converted in March of 1748. He celebrated the day every year for the rest of his life. It took some time before he realized the evil of the slave trade. In 1788, 34 years after he had retired from the slave trade, Newton broke a long silence on the subject when he published *"Thoughts Upon the Slave Trade,"* in which he described the horrific conditions of the slave boats. He apologized for "a confession, which…comes too late…. It will always be a subject of humiliating reflection to me, that I was once an active instrument in a business at which my heart now shudders."

Chapter 8—Finding God

1. **Augustine** (354–433 CE) wrote of his personal spiritual struggle and journey in his *Confessions.* The quote is from this autobiographical work written in 397-398 CE.

2. *Bootstraps* …The quotation is from the Madison City Express, February 2, 1843. Originally, the phrase "lift yourself by your bootstraps" depicted a fool attempting to do the impossible. It was only in the 20TH century that the phrase acquired a positive meaning.

3. *At the heart of the Christian faith* …This beautiful quotation is from *The Lord of the Journey: A Reader in Christian Spirituality* by Roger Pooley and Philip Seddon, London: Collins, 1986.

4. **John Bunyan** (1628–1688) was an English writer and preacher. His book, *Pilgrim's Progress*, is, arguably, the most famous book ever published with the exception of the Bible. The quotation is from his testimony of conversion.

5. **Blasé Pascal** (1623–1662) was a mathematician of the first order. He wrote a defense of the scientific method and, through his correspondence with Pierre de Fermat on probability theory, greatly influenced the modern understanding of economics and social science. He recorded his religious vision and kept it close to him at all times. He wrote, ""Fire. God of Abraham, God of Isaac, God of Jacob, not of the philosophers and the scholars …" and concluded by quoting Psalm 119:16: *"I will not forget thy word. Amen."* He seems to have carefully sewn this document into his coat and always transferred it when he changed clothes; a

servant discovered it only by chance after his death.

6. **John Calvin** (1509—1564) was a *French Protestant reformer; generally regarded as second in importance only to Martin Luther as a key figure in the Protestant Reformation. He broke with the Roman Catholic Church at the age of 21. Due to persecution, he fled to Switzerland and there wrote his most famous work,* Institutes of the Christian Religion. *The quotation is the opening paragraph of the first chapter of the* Institutes.

7. **Parker Palmer**. The quote is from *Let Your Life Speak*, published by Jossey-Bass in 2000.

8. **Parker Palmer**, *Let Your Life Speak*

Chapter 9—Soul Journey

1. **Dante** (1265—1321) was an Italian power from Florence. His greatest work, *The Divine Comedy*, is considered the greatest literary work composed in the Italian language and a world masterpiece in literature. In Italy he is known as "the Supreme Poet" (*il Sommo Poeta*). As *translated by Henry Wadsworth Longfellow*, the opening lines read:

   Midway upon the journey of our life
   I found myself within a forest dark
   For the straightforward pathway had been lost.
   Ah me! how hard a thing it is to say
   What was this forest savage, rough, and stern,
   Which in the very thought renews the fear.

2. *Robinson Crusoe, Alice in Wonderland, and the Wizard of Oz* are familiar stories of exile. Crusoe lost civilization. Alive was exiled from rational thought. Dorothy just wanted to go home to Auntie Em. *Exile* means to be away from home, either by having no permission to return or by threat of punishment. The Old Testament describes the exile of the Hebrew people who were deported by Nebuchadnezzar the Second of Babylon in 597 BC. The 14TH Dalai Lama was exiled to India from Tibet in 1959. Dante describes the pain of exile in *The Divine Comedy*:

   "…You will leave everything you love most:
   this is the arrow that the bow of exile
   shoots first. You will know how salty

another's bread tastes and how hard it

is to ascend and descend

another's stairs …"

(Paradiso XVII: 55-60).

3. **John Simpson**. The quotation is from Simpson's *The Oxford Book of Exile*, published by Oxford University Press in 1995.

4. *What ifs* is the title of a wonderful children's poem by Shel Silversten in his book, *Where the Sidewalk Ends*, published in 1973.

5. **Clara Scott** (1841–1897) was a prolific hymn writer and composer. Her *Royal Anthem Book* is said to be the first book of anthems edited by a woman. Almost all her work has disappeared except for this hymn that is still loved by so many, "Open My Eyes."

Chapter 10—Healthy Choices

1. **Charles Wesley** (1707–1788) was a leader in the Methodist movement along with older brother, John Wesley. Charles wrote many hymns including, *"And Can It Be."* The quotation is from the following verse:

Long my imprisoned sprit lay,

Fast bound in sin and nature's night;

Thine eye diffused a quickening ray;

I woke, the dungeon flamed with light;

My chains fell off, my heart was free,

I rose, went forth, and followed thee.

My chains fell off, my heart was free,

I rose, went forth, and followed thee.

2. **Oswald Smith** (1889–1986) was an enthusiastic supporter of missions. He traveled throughout the world and used his radio broadcast to evangelize and promote mission awareness.

3. **Exodus 15:21** …Matthew Henry's commentary states, "This song is the most ancient we know of. It is a holy song, to the honour of God, to exalt his name, and celebrate his praise, and his only, not in the least to magnify any man. Holiness to the Lord is in every part of it."

4. **Victor Frankl** (1905–1997) was an Austrian neurologist, psychiatrist, and a

Holocaust survivor. His book *Man's Search for Meaning* (first published in 1946) tells of his experiences in the concentration camp. A significant moment came while marching to work on the railroad tracks: Other prisoners talked about the fate of their wives. Frankl began to think about his own wife and realized that she was present within him: "The salvation of man is through love and in love. I understood how a man who has nothing left in this world still may know bliss, be it only for a brief moment, in the contemplation of his beloved" (p. 59).

5. *Two men look through prison bars* ... The quote is often rendered as anonymous, but on occasion it is credited to James Allen (1864–1912). He was a philosophical writer of British nationality, known for his inspirational books and poetry. Allen's most famous book *As a Man Thinketh* was published in 1902. It is now considered a classic self-help book. Its underlying premise is that noble thoughts make a noble person, while lowly thoughts make a miserable person. In short, you are what you think.

6. *The Odyssey. The Odyssey* is one of two ancient Greek epic poems attributed to Homer. The poem is commonly dated 700 BC. The poem is, in part, a sequel to Homer's *Iliad* and mainly centers on the Greek hero Odysseus and his long journey home to Ithaca, following the fall of Troy.

   It takes Odysseus ten years to reach Ithaca after the ten-year Trojan War. During his trip home he has many trials and challenges. Odysseus is cunning. In the incident with the Cyclops, he tells the monsters that his name is "Nobody", then escapes after blinding the beast. When other monsters ask why the Cyclops is screaming, he replies that "Nobody" is hurting him. It sounds as if "Nobody" is hurting him.

7. *...the tension between truth and hope.* Spiritual transformation is found in the tension. In his Letter from the Birmingham Jail, Martin Luther King writes: "Just as Socrates felt that it was necessary to create a tension in the mind, so that individuals could rise from the bondage of myths and half-truths ...so must we ...create the kind of tension in society that will help men rise from the dark depths of prejudice and racism."

8. *The Elder Brother.* In the famous painting of the return of the prodigal son, Rembrant shows the merciful father of the parable pardoning the Prodigal Son, while the Elder Brother is represented with a knife, conspiring a murder. The

painting is housed in the Ermitage in St. Petersburg, Russia. I want to credit Lloyd
Ogilvie for the questions, "What would have happened to the prodigal had he run
into his elder brother first?' It is found in his book, *An Autobiography of God*, Regal
Books, 1979.

9. *A dynamic of grace*, *The New Yorker*, April 23, 1990, page 31.

10. **Anthony Bloom** (1914–2003) was founder and for many years bishop, archbishop,
    and metropolitan of the Russian Orthodox diocese for Great Britain and Ireland.
    He spent his early childhood in Russia and Persia. During the Russian Revolution
    the family had to leave Persia, and in 1923 they settled in Paris. By his own words,
    he met Christ when he was a teenager: "I met Christ as a Person at a moment when
    I needed him in order to live, and at a moment when I was not in search of him. I
    was found; I did not find him."

    The conversation reported in the text is found in Maxie Dunnam's *Alive in Christ*.

11. *The Water of Life*. The Grimm Brother's story of "The Water of Life" ends with the
    third son telling all to the father: "And the old king was very angry, and wanted to
    punish his wicked sons; but they made their escape, and got into a ship and sailed
    away over the wide sea, and where they went to nobody knew and nobody cared.
    And now the old king gathered together his court, and asked all his kingdom to
    come and celebrate the wedding of his good son and the princess. And young and
    old, noble and squire, gentle and simple, came at once on the summons; and
    among the rest came the friendly dwarf, with the sugarloaf hat, and a new scarlet
    cloak."

12. **Hugh of St. Victor** (1078–1141) was a mystic philosopher, born in Saxony,
    entered the Abbey of St. Victor in Marseille and later the Abbey of St Victor in
    Paris where he became the canon in 1125.

    He regarded knowledge not as an end in itself, but as the vestibule of the mystic
    life. Reason was but an aid to the understanding of the truths which faith reveals.
    The ascent towards God and the functions of the three-fold eye of the soul *cogitatio*,
    meditation, and *contemplatio* were minutely taught by him in language which is at
    once precise and symbolic.

13. *God voted for me. The Devil voted against me* ...The quote is attributed to
    Reuben (Uncle Bud) Robinson (1860–1942). Born in a log cabin in the primitive
    mountain region of Tennessee, he moved to Texas with his mother after the death

of his father. In August of 1880, during a camp meeting under the reaching of a Methodist circuit rider, he received Christ as his Savior. That same night while lying under the wagon he felt the Lord call him to preach. He stuttered and stammered his folksy and inspirational message for 62 years. More than 100,000 people came to salvation through his preaching. My grandfather served as a driver for Uncle Bud when he held a series of meetings in Indiana.

Chapter 11—A House of Prayer

1. **Oswald Chambers** (1874–1917) was a Scottish minister and teacher. Although Oswald Chambers wrote only one book, Baffled to Fight Better, more than thirty titles bear his name. With this one exception, published works were compiled by Mrs. Chambers, a court stenographer, from her verbatim shorthand notes of his messages taken during their seven years of marriage. For half a century following her husband's death, she labored to give his words to the world.

   My Utmost For His Highest, his best known book, has been continuously in print in the United States since 1935 and remains in the top ten titles of the religious book bestseller list with millions of copies in print. It has become a Christian classic.

2. **Victor Weiskopf,** (1908–2002) was an internationally known physicist. Born in Vienna, in 1937, just before the Nazis took over Austria, he came to the United States to the University of Rochester, where he served as instructor and then assistant professor.

   In 1943 he joined the Manhattan Project at Los Alamos, N.M., where he worked on the atom bomb project as a group leader and associate head of the theory division on the exploitation of nuclear energy.

   In 1944 he was one of many physicists who participated in the founding of the Federation of Atomic Scientists. Its purpose was twofold: to warn the public of the consequences of atomic war—thus hoping for the creation of an international agreement against the use of atomic weapons—and to support the peaceful use of atomic energy.

   In 1945 he was appointed associate professor of physics at MIT and became a full professor a year later. Together with John M. Blatt, he wrote a textbook, "Theoretical Nuclear Physics," probably the most-used book in that subject. In 1949 he became a member of the Emergency Committee of Scientists whose president was Albert Einstein. This committee fought for control of atomic weapons and for an understanding between the countries of the East and West concerning atomic armaments.

In 1991, he wrote *The Joy of Insight*, a personal memoir published by Basic Books

3. **Anselm Gruen** has a Ph.D. in theology as well as advanced studies in business. He has written more than 200 books that have sold more than 14 million copies. The quotation is from *Heaven Begins Within You*, published in 1999.

4. *"Go to your hut and sit down. The hut will teach you everything."* The thought is from Evagrius Pointicus (345–399 CE), who was a Christian monk, a keen thinker, and a polished speaker and gifted writer. The quote is found in Gruen's *Heaven Begins Within You*, 1999.

5. *Fill two or three pages with writing.* Spiritual journaling is a time honored tradition. The journals of John Wesley and John Woolman are read for inspiration and insight. There are many books on journaling. On the web you can find posted journals.

All this can be a bit intimidating. I suggest the simple instructions provided by Julia Cameron in her work *The Artist's Way* (1992). She writes, "In order to retrieve your creativity, you need to find it. I ask you to do this by an apparently pointless process I call the morning pages.... Put simply, the morning pages are three pages of longhand writing, strictly stream-of-consciousness ..." (pages 9–10).

6. **Sydney Harris** (1917–1986) was an American journalist for the Chicago Daily News and later the Chicago Sun Times. His column, "Strictly Personal," was syndicated in many newspapers throughout the United States and Canada.

7. **John W. Gardner** (1912–2002) was secretary of Health, Education and Welfare under Lyndon Johnson. He received the Presidential Medal of Freedom in 1964, the same year his book *Self Renewal* was published. The quotation is from *Self Renewal*, page 13.

8. **Beryl Markham** (1902–1986) was a British born Kenyan author, pilot, horse trainer, and adventurer. She is best known for her memoir *West with the Night*, first published in 1942, which became an international bestseller upon its republication in 1982. Beryl made aviation history in 1936, when she became the first person to fly solo across the Atlantic Ocean from East to West.

9. **Harry Emerson Fosdick** (1878–1963) was an American clergyman who became a central figure in the conflict between fundamentalist and liberal forces within Amer-

ican Protestantism in the 1920s and 1930s. He presented the Bible as a record of the unfolding of God's will. He saw the history of Christianity as one of development, progress, and gradual change.

10. **H. A. Williams** (1919–2006) was Fellow and Dean of Trinity College, Cambridge, until 1969 when he joined the Anglican Community of the Resurrection at Mirfield, West Yorkshire. He is the author of *The Joy of God, The True Wilderness,* and *True Resurrection.*

11. **Dame Julian of Norwich** (1342–1416) is considered to be one of the greatest English mystics. Little is known of her life aside from her writings. At the age of thirty, suffering from a severe illness and believing she was on her deathbed, Julian had a series of intense visions. They are the source of her major work, called Sixteen Revelations of Divine Love (circa 1393).

Although she lived in a time of turmoil, Julian's theology was optimistic, speaking of God's love in terms of joy and compassion as opposed to law and duty. For Julian, suffering was not a punishment that God inflicted, as was the common understanding. Julian's ground-breaking theology was that God loved and saved us all. Her most famous saying is "…all shall be well, and all shall be well, and all manner of things shall be well."

Chapter 12—Holy Listening

1. *Quaker House in Philadelphia* is a room with no pulpit, stained-glass windows, religious icons, or shrines. Instead, you step into a great, square room filled with row after row of wooden pews, from all sides facing the center. A balcony supported by Doric columns spans three sides of the room. The windows and shutters are plain, and the floors are unvarnished wood. It is a place for being together in silence. The Quakers are known for the practice of holy listening, a term used by Douglas Steere in a lecture given in 1955 at the British Yearly Meeting of the Religious Society of Friends. The Lecture was later included in *Gleanings, A Random Harvest,* published by The Upper Room in 1986.

2. **Jeremy Taylor,** (1613–1667) was a clergyman in the Church of England who achieved fame as an author during the time of Oliver Cromwell. He is sometimes known as the "Shakespeare of Divines" for his poetic style of writing. Among his many books on theological, moral, and devotional subjects, the best known are *The*

Rule and Exercises of Holy Living (1650) and The Rule and Exercises of Holy Dying
(1651). A century later, Charles Wesley reported finding these books to be of great
spiritual benefit.

3. **Woody Allen**. The joke is reported in several forms. The one that seems to be closest to the original, "I was thrown out of NYU (New York University) for cheating
on my Metaphysics final. I looked within the soul of the boy sitting next to me."

4. *These struggles were experienced in private* ...Jesus shared His spiritual battle in the
wilderness. I first ran across this insight in *The Life and Teachings of Jesus Christ*, by
James Stewart, an excellent introduction to the message and meaning of Christ. The
book is published by Abingdon Press, 1957.

5. *Sadness, Anger, Restlessness* ...A fuller discussion is found in Gruen's *Heaven Begins
Within You.*

6. *A River Runs Through It* was written by Norman MacLean in 1976. The quote
from the book is "Eventually, all things merge into one, and a river runs through it.
The river was cut by the world's great flood and runs over rocks from the basement
of time. On some of the rocks are timeless raindrops. Under the rocks are the
words, and some of the words are theirs." The film version added "the words of
God."

7. *Let The Beauty of Jesus Be Seen In Me*. The text of the first stanza was written by
Albert W. T. Orsborn (1886–1967). No other information is available except that
it is dated around 1916. Orsborn is identified as an early Salvation Army leader.
The music was composed by Tom Jones (1891–1978).

8. *Search Me O God* was written by J. Edward Orr in 1936 and set to the Maori
Melody.